The Business of Winning

The Business of Winning

Insights in transformation from
F1 to the boardroom

SECOND EDITION

Mark Gallagher

KoganPage

First published in Great Britain and the United States in 2014 by Kogan Page Limited
Second edition published in 2021

2nd Floor, 45 Gee Street
London
EC1V 3RS
United Kingdom
www.koganpage.com

122 W 27th St, 10th Floor
New York, NY 10001
USA

4737/23 Ansari Road
Daryaganj
New Delhi 110002
India

Kogan Page books are printed on paper from sustainable forests.

ISBNs
Hardback   978 1 3986 0272 4
Paperback   978 1 3986 0270 0
Ebook   978 1 3986 0271 7

British Library Cataloguing-in-Publication Data

A CIP record for this book is available from the British Library.

Library of Congress Control Number

2021943152

Typeset by Hong Kong FIVE Workshop, Hong Kong
Print production managed by Jellyfish
Printed and bound by CPI Group (UK) Ltd, Croydon CR0 4YY

Contents

Foreword

It has been almost a decade since Mark told me he was writing a book about Formula One with the goal of providing insights to a general business audience. From working together at corporate events, we know only too well how the sport triggers the interest and curiosity of business people, so it was great to see the success of that first edition.

We also know how dynamic an environment Formula One is, thanks to the speed with which technology is evolving and the world around us changing. So when Mark explained that a second edition of *The Business of Winning* was under development, and that it would focus on business transformation, I was only too happy to contribute.

When I wrote the Foreword for the first edition Red Bull Racing had dominated Formula One for four consecutive seasons and we were looking forward to a new set of technical regulations in 2014. Since then, Mercedes-Benz has won every World Championship, and Lewis Hamilton has equalled Michael Schumacher's record of winning seven Drivers' titles and is set to exceed 100 Grand Prix victories.

Our industry has never witnessed such sustained domination by one team. The temptation may be to think that Formula One has somehow stagnated during this time, and yet the reverse is true. We are witnessing profound change across almost every aspect of its business and operations.

The sport is thriving. Much of that is to do with dramatic changes that have occurred in recent years, changes that promise to make the next decade one of the most exciting in Formula One's history. In 2022 a completely new set of regulations will arrive, and there has seldom been a greater opportunity for more teams to compete to win in our sport.

The end of Bernie Ecclestone's 40-year reign has been followed by a new era for the sport under Liberty Media, former CEO Chase Carey overseeing a successful renegotiation of the sport's commercial model with its teams and the introduction of a budget cap. Newly arrived CEO Stefano Dominical is passionate about Formula One and determined to continue growing the sport, irrespective of the challenges ahead.

We are in a decade during which the automotive industry is going through major changes as regards the electrification of cars. The sport has itself set ambitious targets in response to help limit the impact of man-made climate change, including the World Championship producing net zero carbon emissions by 2030.

My own experience of the transformation taking place within the sport has been significant. This includes the way in which the world of media is evolving, the growth of esports and the long-overdue push for greater diversity and inclusion in our sport.

Over the last decade I have been able to apply some of the lessons I have learned from Formula One in growing my media company, The Whisper Group, employing talented people from diverse backgrounds in creating best-in-class media content. It has been an exciting journey, reminding me why we place so much importance on cultivating the right values and behaviours in a Formula One team. Whatever the sector, all successful businesses rely on great teams of people.

As a former Formula One driver I never quite imagined myself as a computer gamer, but the growth of esports has been one of the most intriguing developments in our industry. Together with the growth in the sport's social media engagement since 2017, we are seeing younger audiences being attracted to Formula One as a result, and it is opening up significant new opportunities for teams and their commercial partners.

As non-executive chairman of the all-women W Series championship I am hopeful that the increased gender diversity we are witnessing across our industry will ultimately result in a woman Formula One driver competing in races for the first time in over forty years. Ideally, we wish to see that become a permanent feature of Formula One. With the W Series becoming a supporting event to Formula One in 2021 we are seeing real progress towards that goal, while the sport's significant investment in diversity and inclusion is genuinely encouraging.

I know that the changes we are seeing within Formula One reflect the challenges and opportunities being encountered by many businesses. In writing this latest edition Mark was keen once again to focus on topics and themes that the business reader can relate to, whether an avid Formula One fan or not.

Recognizing that there is a desire to learn how successful Formula One teams unlock high levels of performance through teamwork, innovation and their relentless focus on winning, I know that Mark has developed a range of relevant insights. We often present at events and I know just how well the storytelling from Formula One translates to business, so I hope you will enjoy reading a little of what our sport has to offer.

David Coulthard
Monaco, May 2021

Preface

One of the most appealing aspects of Formula One is the relentless quest for performance against a backdrop of constant changes in technology, regulation and business environment. When I wrote the first edition of *The Business of Winning* the sport was about to go through a major change following the decision to introduce hybrid engines in 2014.

It was an expensive exercise, which for many observers diluted the spectacle of Formula One thanks to much-reduced noise levels. A question mark also hung over the International Automobile Federation's (FIA) push towards making Grand Prix motor racing more sustainable, reducing fuel consumption, extending engine life and developing technologies aimed at keeping Formula One somehow road relevant.

Eight years later and no one is arguing about that decision, for not only has Formula One achieved and then surpassed the energy efficiency targets of those regulations, but the sport is soon to end its addiction to fossil fuels. In 2025 we are likely to see Formula One cars powered by a synthetic fuel, possibly created from the very carbon dioxide with which humankind has polluted the atmosphere. Meanwhile the entire FIA Formula One World Championship is aiming to achieve net zero carbon emissions by 2030, every team fully committed to playing its role in combating climate change.

We have witnessed seismic events that have served to remind us that change is not only ever-present but accelerating in this increasingly interconnected world. Under normal circumstances the change in leadership as a result of CVC Capital selling Formula One to Liberty Media in 2017 would have been a major talking point. Instead, our industry has had to deal with its first driver fatality in over 20 years, an acceptance that it has far to travel in relation to diversity and inclusion, and learned to cope with the devastating effects of a global pandemic.

The loss of Jules Bianchi as the result of an accident in the 2014 Japanese Grand Prix reminded us that safety can never be assured. Formula One has become extremely good at managing risk, but Bianchi's death reminds us that complacency is our greatest enemy.

Lewis Hamilton's domination of the sport has illustrated a machine-like ability to sustain an extraordinary level of performance. He won his first Grand Prix in Canada in 2007 aged 22 and is still winning in 2021 at the age of 36. Whilst his talents as a racing driver have long been appreciated, the dialogue around the fact that he is the sport's first black driver has been much less obvious, until now.

The death of George Floyd in 2020 led to Formula One rethinking its approach to diversity, Lewis Hamilton using his profile to support the Black Lives Matter movement and forcing a discussion about topics some found uncomfortable. A sport that the all-women W Series CEO Catherine Bond Muir has rightly described as 'male and pale' was forced to make a stand for diversity and inclusion, evidenced by a range of initiatives launched by Formula One and the FIA.

In a world wracked by COVID-19, Formula One has played to its strengths, displaying resilience and adaptability. During the initial stages of the global pandemic Formula One's teams joined together, using their innovation mindset and rapid-prototyping capability to develop ventilators, breathing aids and healthcare equipment in a matter of days and weeks.

Unable to stage real racing between March and June 2020, Formula One pivoted online to provide virtual racing. Esports has become an even more important pillar of the business, attracting new and younger audiences in the process. Meanwhile the sport's owners, together with the teams and regulator, somehow managed to stage a 17-race World Championship. This was made possible by reconfiguring the sport's global logistics and introducing a robust Covid-testing regime. Thankfully Formula One was able to provide entertainment to its fan base at a time when many sports struggled to continue.

In writing this second edition I have drawn upon my experiences of speaking alongside Formula One drivers at corporate events, which, in 2020, included Lewis Hamilton, Mika Häkkinen, Mark Webber and long-time associate David Coulthard. I have also enjoyed interviewing subjects while producing my podcast, and through my work as columnist and features writer for *GP Racing* magazine. I would like to thank everyone who has contributed their time and energy.

Finally, I would like to thank my publisher, Kogan Page, for their patience and support in making this book possible.

CHAPTER ONE

Formula One – a global business

At the wheel of his ornately decorated Proton, bounding its way along one of Kuala Lumpur's wide, undulating motorways, the Malaysian taxi driver was worrying me. His eyes were fixed on the rear-view mirror instead of the road ahead.

For several minutes we'd been engaging in conversation starting with the form shown by Manchester United. We had since moved on to discussing the weather in England and the flying time to KL.

What made the conversation intriguing was that neither of us spoke each other's language. What was impossible to achieve using words was more than substituted by gesticulation combined with sharing names we both recognized.

His car was a shrine to Manchester United. Everything was red. A United scarf covered the dashboard, causing the team's name and crest to reflect alarmingly in the windscreen. Every surface was covered with team and player stickers, photos of tackles and goal celebrations. A figurine of goal-keeper Peter Schmeichel hung, gallows style, from the mirror.

I was impressed, not least since we were 6,500 miles from Old Trafford. Among the things I least expected to learn about on my trip to the inaugural Malaysia Formula One Grand Prix in October 1999 was the skill and prowess of Teddy Sheringham and Eric Cantona.

It was when we progressed to discussing the weather in England, summoned by frantic hand gestures simulating wind and rain, that we got as far as him asking why I was in Malaysia.

'Formula One', I replied, simply.

'Eff one?' he shouted, looking at me intently in the rear-view mirror, then weaving the taxi from side to side to show me that he knew exactly how to keep the tyres on a Formula One car up to temperature whilst running behind the safety car.

'Schumacher!' he shouted and then, loudly, 'Häkkinen!' More weaving, this time more violently than before.

'Go, go, go!' he added, delighted with his knowledge of the latest sport to arrive on Malaysia's shores.

I'd already been impressed by his knowledge of an English Premiership football team, his awareness of two of Formula One's major superstars and his ability to keep his car's tyres up to temperature whilst in traffic. This was nothing compared to my shock on realizing that his only English was thanks to famed Formula One commentator Murray Walker.

If ever I needed an education in the power and reach of television, and the fact that by 1999 Formula One really was beginning to 'go global', this was it. Malaysia's addition to the F1 calendar had surprised many. The sport was of little interest to the local population, and ticket prices were likely to make attendance well beyond the means of the average Malaysian household income of £500 per month for city dwellers, half that figure for those living in rural areas.

Any question over the wisdom of adding this event to the calendar was soon dispelled. Formula One was changing, reflecting the desire of its owner for expansion and tapping into the opportunities afforded by a rapidly shrinking world.

Racing in Malaysia was a new development in the sport's business model. One in which a country's sovereign government had taken a hard look at Formula One and decided that it represented an unrivalled opportunity to promote their nation's interests.

Malaysia recognized that a worldwide televised sport could be used to demonstrate a country's confidence in itself as a global player, and attracted international media attention for a full week to 10 days each year. It ensured that 'Malaysia' as a brand reached hundreds of millions of households and billions of eyeballs.

'Malaysia, Truly Asia' was the tourist board's campaign at the time, broadcast in key western markets. Formula One offered a way to sell it as a destination.

Bernie Ecclestone, then CEO of Formula One, had realized that while the four-yearly Olympic Games and Football World Cup could offer countries a prestigious tournament for a month, Grand Prix motor racing could offer something better – a multi-year commitment and an easier way to secure it. Unlike the Olympics or the World Cup, governments would not have to tender for it against competing nations.

Ecclestone's proposition was quite straightforward. Build a circuit, commit to paying an annual promoter's fee to Formula One, and we will come. For year after year.

The world was Formula One's stage and, more than 20 years later, we can reflect on how the inaugural Malaysian Grand Prix heralded the beginning of a transformation that continues to this day.

Globalization is nothing new. The modern definition combines the notion of global trade with the breaking down of physical and commercial barriers. The speed and ease of communication across continents has accelerated in recent years, so too the ability to build global brands with a commonality of look, feel and purpose.

What is extraordinary is how recently the transformation in Formula One has taken place, half a century after it made its first steps towards becoming a fully professional sport.

The commercialization of sport was a feature of the post-war world, and the arrival of television grew audiences along with the fame of top sportsmen and women. With his slicked-back hair cricketer Denis Compton became advertising's original 'Brylcreem Boy'. Before long brand endorsements developed into full-blown sponsorships during the 1960s.

A key moment came when a Cleveland-based Yale law graduate by the name of Mark McCormack decided to suspend his personal golfing ambitions in favour of managing a young Arnold Palmer. He soon added both Gary Player and Jack Nicklaus to his roster. In negotiating his first deal – a US $5,000 endorsement by Palmer of Wilson sporting goods – I doubt even McCormack and his fledgling International Management Group (IMG) could have imagined the transformation that would overtake the world of sport in the decades ahead. Ultimately IMG would manage Formula One stars including Alain Prost, Ayrton Senna and Michael Schumacher.

McCormack was a decade ahead of the man who would buy a Formula One team and subsequently set about transforming a semi-professional motor-racing championship into one of the world's most successful sports businesses.

For over 40 years Bernie Ecclestone was the pivotal figure, the man rightly credited with creating the Formula One business we know today. Whilst there are countless other highly professional team sports, it can be argued that none possesses the combination of ingredients served up by Grand Prix motor racing.

This is due to the requirement for all its entrants to be technology companies, producing a complex product that just happens to be a Formula One racing car. Before a team can even contemplate the challenge of beating the opposition, merely participating requires world-class engineering capability.

The uniqueness of the sport continues with the range of challenges it creates for the competing teams and drivers. These are compounded by the immovable timescales and deadlines determined by the World Championship calendar. This means competing at events on fixed dates, around the world, at all times under the scrutiny of a global media and viewing public from March through to December.

While public companies concern themselves with meeting quarterly targets, Formula One teams see their results published every other Sunday in front of the media, fans, customers, staff and suppliers. For these high-tech teams there is no room to hide. Other sports offer the same results-based scrutiny, but few involve the multifaceted challenges faced by Formula One teams.

To be successful, each Formula One team has to become a world-class engineering business, working to aerospace standards with a low-volume, prototype-manufacturing capability. The end product is produced by integrating technologies from sectors including automotive, aerospace and information technology. A Formula One car is effectively part jet fighter and part supercar, built and operating using digital technologies.

Each new car, the result of a collaboration between people and companies spanning many months, has to be fully compliant with the strict rules and regulations enforced by the sport's governing body, the FIA. Yet despite this compliance, teams must also innovate and differentiate in order to gain competitive advantage.

The high-technology Formula One car, designed to meet new regulations each season, will incorporate developments that in some cases have taken years. It must then compete directly against the opposition in a truly hostile environment involving extremes of heat, vibration, noise and speed. Not to mention wheel-to-wheel combat.

The driver, as end user, demands high performance and competitive advantage. These requirements can make for uneasy bedfellows considering that the technology must also be strong, safe and reliable.

Formula One teams face the same challenges of any business operating in high-technology manufacturing, but with timeframes compressed to meet rigid, non-negotiable deadlines. To design, develop and bring to market a Formula One car requires high levels of teamwork within the business, but also seamless collaboration with key suppliers and technical partners.

In the last 25 years Formula One teams have been through both extremes of the supply model, from running very small teams heavily reliant on suppliers through to larger organizations that bring most functions in-house. Today a team such as Haas F1 can employ little more than 250 full-time staff, contracting out to companies such as Dallara and Ferrari. Meanwhile, Mercedes' Formula One operation employs close to 2,000 staff at its UK facilities in Brackley and Brixworth.

In my own experience the fact that Jordan, a small, independent, 'challenger' team, became a winner whilst Toyota, with a team six times the size, failed to do so is a story to which we shall return. Two very different approaches to the same industry, one reliant on agility, the other on strength in depth.

The demands placed upon teams has changed over time and will continue to do so. Formula One is more than 70 years old. In the 1950s and 1960s teams focused on automotive technologies, learning how to build cars that would extract performance from the chassis, suspension, engine, gearbox and tyres.

The 1970s saw the focus shift towards aerodynamics, closely followed by the use of aerospace materials in the 1980s. The 1990s saw digital transformation move from infancy to rapid growth, giving teams the opportunity to improve every aspect of their operations and unlock new capabilities. No matter what aspect of Formula One is considered today, the data-driven environment has created a revolution.

From effective risk management to optimizing performance, driving efficiency and ensuring reliability, digital tools have given Formula One's engineers and scientists the ability to generate outcomes that may have seemed impossible only a few years ago. Perhaps the most significant change brought about by digital transformation has been in relation to safety. The detailed analysis of data from past events has improved future outcomes, saving countless lives.

While engineers have never given up on their quest for improved performance, their work has also ensured that the cars fully protect the driver irrespective of what happens during a Grand Prix. This means being able to routinely sustain up to 5g in corners, and many times that in the event of an accident. Romain Grosjean's apparently miraculous escape from a 67g impact at the 2020 Bahrain Grand Prix illustrated just how capable today's designs are, thanks to the lessons learned from previous accidents.

As a result, the research and development (R&D), design and manufacturing operations in Formula One are just as focused on ensuring the safety and integrity of the product as they are on outright performance. The push–pull between safety and performance, lightness and strength, efficiency and outright capability means that Formula One's designers and engineers are often faced with apparently conflicting goals.

Yet by 2020 not only were Formula One's cars the safest they have ever been, they were also the fastest, the most energy efficient and – as Lewis Hamilton's Mercedes has demonstrated – almost completely reliable. In four years of racing from 2017 to 2020 his car suffered just one technical failure.

If the technical outcomes have been transformed, so too has the stage on which Formula One operates, thanks to Ecclestone's vision. When I started working in Formula One in the mid-1980s the championship consisted of 14 races, of which 10 were staged in Europe and four at 'long-haul' destinations. Its 'world' status was bestowed upon it by virtue of having races in Australia, Japan, Brazil and Canada. The United States figured at times, but until recently the US love affair with Formula One has involved a series of desperate flings rather than anything enduring. Only with the 2012 opening of the purpose-built Circuit of the Americas in Austin, Texas, does Formula One have a permanent presence in the United States.

As a Eurocentric business, Formula One's nod towards the rest of the world meant that for 48 weeks of the year the sport, and the business, was almost entirely focused on a single continent. Then as now, the teams were European, while the predominance of the European press corps underlined the parochial nature of the sport.

Prior to changes driven by the Covid-19 pandemic and its impact on global travel, the draft 2021 Formula One calendar featured 23 events,

13 of which were outside Europe. In a little more than the two decades since my Kuala Lumpur taxi journey, Formula One has become a globalized sports business. Ecclestone's decision to sell events to publicity-hungry countries and cities, governments and international event promoters, has borne fruit. In their desire to promote nationhood, tourism, business and global prestige, officials from Russia to China, Saudi Arabia to Mexico and Azerbaijan to Singapore have demonstrated their appetite for Formula One.

The growth will not end here. The African continent beckons and the United States will move towards staging a second Grand Prix each season. The world's largest market has long held an appeal, but it is only as a result of new ownership that the sport seems likely to realize its potential.

Having changed hands several times, whilst always remaining under the Ecclestone leadership, Formula One moved into a new era in 2017. In January of that year US media giant Liberty Media Corporation concluded its US $4.6 billion purchase of Formula One, ousting Ecclestone and bringing in a homegrown CEO in the form of media executive Chase Carey.

That deal brought about a positive outcome for CVC Capital, the private equity group that had taken a controlling interest in Formula One in 2006. Their tenure was marked by growth and profitability under Ecclestone's leadership. However, it was also marred by a bribery scandal in Germany relating to a previous change in ownership, plus a growing view that Ecclestone had blind spots when it came to new media, particularly as regards the rising importance of social media and changing viewing habits among younger audiences.

Formula One's core business model needed to evolve, and in selling to a company like Liberty, CVC and Ecclestone placed it in the hands of a company that better understood the fast-changing media landscape. The absence of a succession plan had long been a concern. A new regime was required to take the sport onto the next level, developing the product for the 21st century.

While the revenues generated from television, race promoters' fees, trackside advertising and corporate hospitality had been pushed ever higher, unlike Ecclestone, Liberty had the appetite and expertise to explore new avenues. Their ambition was clear: 14 races had already become 16, then 18, so why not 23 or 25? Although placing an enormous human and logistical burden on the teams, this opportunity for growth drives the sport into new markets, attracting new audiences, accelerating the presence of Formula One around the world.

The sport's commercial partners have also been demanding more events, new markets and fresh audiences. It is a commercial ecosystem that has to work for all stakeholders.

When Ecclestone first kick-started the expansion back in 1999, Asia was a natural place to start. Japan had been on the calendar since 1973, while the presence of the Australian Grand Prix since 1985 meant that logistically Formula One was already geared towards visiting the eastern hemisphere up to twice a season. Malaysia in 1999 was followed by Bahrain and China, both of which joined the World Championship in 2004.

The inaugural Chinese Grand Prix in Shanghai was sanctioned by the government, in part to demonstrate China's ability to run world-class sporting events in the run-up to the 2008 Beijing Olympic Games. Meanwhile the palatial facilities in Sepang, Shanghai at Bahrain's International Circuit made the traditional European venues in Silverstone, Monza and Spa-Francorchamps appear outdated.

Wealthy governments could see the benefit in generating a fortnight of global sports coverage, so it was inevitable that this would lead to the Gulf. The addition of Bahrain Grand Prix in 2004 was followed by Abu Dhabi in 2008, while Saudi Arabia has elected to make a decade-long commitment starting in 2021.

Singapore famously joined the fray with a downtown street circuit in 2008, its innovation being to introduce night racing. This has become a glittering spectacle, sometimes referred to as 'The Monaco of the East'. The Singapore Grand Prix has become one of Formula One's most prestigious events, giving a strong return on the estimated US $400 million that the circuit construction and initial five-year deal cost.

Admittedly not every new event has worked. The addition of Korea in 2010–13 and India in 2011–13 was followed by disappointment. The poorly attended Korean events were limited by the circuit's remote location in Yeongam, while the Indian Grand Prix ground to a halt due to financial challenges combined with a tax dispute with the government of Uttar Pradesh.

Turkey joined the Formula One circus in 2005, but elected not to renew its deal after 2011, citing costs. It has, however, re-emerged as a venue during the course of the Covid-19 pandemic.

Russia hosted its first Grand Prix at Sochi in 2014, two years after the United States had rejoined the schedule, while Mexico rejoined in 2015 and Azerbaijan hosted its first event in Baku in 2017.

Not every new event is breaking new ground, however, as some traditional events have returned in Formula One's European heartlands. Under the ownership of Red Bull, Austria's Spielberg circuit returned to Formula One in 2014 after dropping off the schedule in 2003. Meanwhile the Netherlands is also set to return, thanks in no small part to the interest generated by national superstar Max Verstappen.

The need to reschedule Formula One's calendar during the course of the Covid-19 pandemic saw events staged at venues old and new across Europe. Grands Prix in Imola, Istanbul Park and Nürburgring reminded fans that these circuits used to be part of the fabric of the Formula One season, while the races in Portugal's Autodromo Algarve and Italy's Mugello demonstrated that the sport has no shortage of high-quality venues.

Others keen to join Formula One's tour include Vietnam, raising the prospect of a World Championship that may in the future extend to half the weekends in the year. More events mean increased revenues, and ultimately allow the teams to stiffen their sponsorship rate card as the championship visits additional key markets.

Each new territory brings with it multiple benefits: new audiences, more media, and potential new sponsors from among the domestic, regional and global brands. The role of commercial sponsors in helping to promote Formula One has been a key feature of the sport for the last 40 years. However, the nature of those sponsorships has changed significantly. The transformation in the world of business and technology is reflected in the companies and brands now investing in the sport.

The 10 teams had no fewer than 241 commercial sponsors, technology partners and official suppliers at the start of the 2021 Formula One season. These came from more than 20 different business sectors, the largest number by far from the world of information technology, whether hardware, software or the solutions associated with a connected world fuelled by data.

In a little over 15 years, the types of customer most attracted by the platform provided by Formula One has changed dramatically. For some time the accepted wisdom has been that the first commercial sponsorship in Formula One was undertaken by Imperial Tobacco in 1968. Through its Gold Leaf brand Imperial commenced support for Team Lotus with drivers Jim Clark and Graham Hill. However, the South African journalist Dieter Rencken has pointed out that Imperial were beaten to it, and by a rival tobacco company.

On 1 January 1968 a Brabham sponsored by Gunston cigarettes, privately entered for Rhodesian (now Zimbabwe) John Love, competed in the South African Grand Prix. In doing so they beat Gold Leaf and Lotus to their debut by five months.

Although tobacco sponsorship marked the start of Formula One's commercial awakening, the financial and trade support provided by oil giants including Castrol, tyre suppliers Dunlop or automotive brands such as Ferrari, Honda and Ford predated that. What made the Gold Leaf deal different is that it marked a pivotal change, a non-automotive brand tapping into the sport's popularity.

Today the ability of Formula One's teams to adapt their commercial model to the fast-moving economic realities of the modern world is impressive, even if it has not been easy. The last 20 years has witnessed unprecedented disruption, whether it be the 2005 ban on tobacco sponsorship, the effects of the 2008 global financial crisis or the need for the sport to address concerns over environmental sustainability. The types of customer and their requirements, geographical markets and industry sectors have therefore changed remarkably.

It was appropriate that the Gold Leaf deal became viewed as the trigger point of commercial sponsorship in the manner we know today. Tobacco's relationship with the sport accelerated from that point on, with Gold Leaf itself soon replaced at Team Lotus by the iconic black-and-gold livery of John Player Special. Even 40 years later, research showed that JPS Lotus had strong brand recognition among motorsport audiences.

JPS was joined by Marlboro, Philip Morris's marketing prowess initiating a sponsorship relationship with Formula One that, against the odds, continues to this day with Ferrari's 'Mission Winnow' deal. The Mission Winnow project is Philip Morris International's 'unconventional' communications tool aimed at tracking, sharing and promoting dialogue around its evolution as a business.

Marlboro started with the Iso Marlboro team in 1972 and migrated to McLaren in 1978, developing the Marlboro World Championship Team programme that supported multiple teams. The red-and-white chevron became synonymous with the sport as Marlboro's brand managers developed a hugely effective sports marketing template that has been copied by many since.

When Marlboro was credited with being the world's most recognized brand in the late 1980s, their CEO gave a speech at the Monaco Grand Prix outlining the reasons behind their success. He gave two reasons: the success of the Formula One sponsorship and the company's iconic 'Marlboro Man' advertising campaigns.

The success of Philip Morris's Marlboro sponsorships caused rivals to follow suit during the 1980s and 1990s; Camel, JPS, Barclay, Gauloises, Gitanes, Mild Seven, West, Rothmans, Winfield, Benson & Hedges, Sobranie, 555 and Lucky Strike. By 2000 the sport had become addicted to tobacco.

When, in late 2002, it was announced that the European Union's proposed directive banning tobacco advertising and sponsorship would be enforced at the end of July 2005, the sport faced a seismic shift. To some in the industry it felt like an existential crisis. It certainly marked the start of a period during which sponsorship would be harder to find and budgets reduced.

Teams began looking for other rich seams to mine: automotive, oil and gas, beverages, financial services, IT, telecommunications. In the late 1990s we had seen a flurry of US technology companies arrive, only to depart following the crash of spring 2000.

Mobile phone companies joined the fray with brands including Orange, Virgin Mobile and Vodafone, while IT firms also lined up. HP had invested in the early 1990s and would be joined by Compaq, Acer, Dell, Toshiba, Intel, EMC and Sun Microsystems. Tobacco was giving way to tech, hardware predominating.

The 2000s saw banking sponsorship flourish, then disappear almost entirely as a result of the effects of the 2008 global financial crisis. HSBC, Credit Suisse, ING, The Royal Bank of Scotland, UBS and Santander enjoyed the global reach of the sport, and the opportunity to entertain business leaders in five-star hospitality. The financial crisis led to a rethink about the optics of bankers being seen to splash out on Formula One. A new approach to corporate governance, added to regulations such as the UK's Bribery Act, helped stifle enthusiasm for corporate junkets.

Formula One's high-end Paddock Club hospitality business, originally founded by Paddy McNally and operated through his Geneva-based Allsport Management business, suddenly took a dive. Even at the time of this book's first edition, in 2014, the industry was still suffering the after-effects of the financial crisis.

Of the four new teams invited to enter Formula One in 2010, none survived. Each in its own way was a journey of hope against a harsh commercial reality. To compete demands significant resources, and post-financial-crisis funding was harder than ever to find.

Even teams such as McLaren were still looking for the big-ticket title sponsors to replace tobacco, their pain initially eased by Vodafone, a deal which ended in 2013. Increasingly many teams became reliant on Formula One's central prize fund to provide the cornerstone of their budget.

The ability to adapt quickly remains one of Formula One's greatest strengths, however. At its heart is a sports entertainment business rooted in technology. Its leadership teams have come to learn the importance of playing to core strengths and capabilities.

Several key factors have helped transform Formula One's business in less than a decade. The teams have learned the importance of diversification, selling technology goods and services to industries far beyond Formula One. McLaren's Applied division takes its capability in areas such as data analytics and provides it to clients including Heathrow Airport and Singapore's transit system. Williams Advanced Engineering successfully tackled projects as varied as creating portable baby incubators and energy efficiency solutions for supermarkets. Mercedes Formula One's business now works with Ineos in America's Cup racing and cycling, while Red Bull Advanced Technologies developed Aston Martin's Valkyrie hypercar and is now developing a hydrogen-powered sports car for the Le Mans 24 Hours.

The sport has tackled environmental issues head on, starting with the need to focus on energy efficiency. The 2014 rule change that saw the adoption of small, highly sophisticated hybrid engines led Formula One teams to develop the most efficient internal combustion engines of all time. When combined with the sport's target to end the use of fossil fuels by the middle of this decade, and for Formula One to become fully carbon neutral by 2030, the external optics have changed. Companies want to be associated with a sport that can effect radical change in a short term.

Commercially, teams have come to realize that although the days of tobacco-level title sponsors are over, spreading risk by attracting a large portfolio of smaller deals is more effective and desirable. McLaren, which had lost many of its longstanding sponsors by the end of 2016, has seen a resurgence under the leadership of CEO Zak Brown, with 42 organizations supporting the team in 2021 – numerically the most extensive line-up of commercial partners. In a world where every customer is demanding more for less, teams are delivering much more tailored partnership programmes.

The end of the Ecclestone era and arrival of Liberty Media as Formula One's owners has led to major changes in the sport's governance, promotion and business models. A more transparent style of management, driven in part by the scrutiny to which publicly listed US companies are subject, has created a more collegiate, less combative relationship between Formula One, the FIA and the teams. A new Concorde Agreement, the commercial deal between the teams and Formula One, was agreed in the summer of 2020. It ensures that the sport's prize fund is more equitably distributed among the teams.

In addition, for the first time in the sport's history, a budget cap has been agreed, commencing in 2021. Each team is limited to spending US $145 million on car development and performance, dropping to $140 million in 2022 and $135 million in 2023. Although the cap does not include sums such as driver salaries or marketing, these figures represent a substantial adjustment downwards for the leading teams, and a realistic objective for everyone else. In 2019 Mercedes spent US $442 million on its Formula One programme, and although the cap's exemptions will allow for a spend well above the $145 million technical budget, the adjustment is significant.[1] Ultimately the budget cap promises to create an environment in which more teams will have the opportunity to succeed.

Parallel to shoring up the governance of Formula One and creating a more equitably distributed prize fund, Liberty Media's management has invested heavily in order to build the sport's audiences.

In 2021 Formula One has a complex network of terrestrial, satellite and cable television deals providing live and delayed broadcasts. These involve 87 channels in 49 individual countries, while deals with major regional broadcast networks such as Fox Sports and SuperSport cover large areas of Asia, Latin America and Africa.

In 2019, pre-Covid, a cumulative audience of 1.922 billion watched the World Championship, averaging 91.5 million per event.[2]

Meanwhile F1 has also operated its own direct streaming channel, F1TV, since 2018. This is an OTT (over the top – straight to consumer) product, a three-tier subscription service enabling fans to access video content online in up to 118 territories.

A groundbreaking deal with Netflix in 2018 saw the launch of the *Formula 1: Drive to Survive* series, documenting the people, personalities and dramas behind the scenes. Highly successful, the series has captured the attention of both diehard fans and casual observers, introducing the sport to a new generation of fans. This was most notable in the United States where, in March 2021, the series had three times the average demand for docuseries. It is yet another pillar of Formula One business re-engineered to meet the changing demands of consumers.

Formula One's pre-Covid financial results showed an overall income of US $2.022 billion, with a small profit of $17 million. The teams' prize fund totalled $1.012 million, effectively half of Formula One's central revenues from the sale of broadcasting rights, race hosting fees, licensing and sponsorships.[3]

Naturally the 2020 and early 2021 figures were hit by the cancellation of some events, and the fact that spectators were unable to attend races. What is interesting to note is how Formula One's online presence has strengthened the sport, even in a time of crisis.

Since 2017 the sport has opened up to social media, showing clips and highlights across global platforms including Facebook, Twitter and YouTube in addition to regional platforms such as China's Weibo, WeChat and Toutiao. Ecclestone's view was that social media companies could not add value unless they paid a rights fee, whereas Liberty recognized that this had become a key channel through which to engage and grow audiences.

In 2020 that translated into 810 million engagements, a 99 per cent increase on 2019. Meanwhile, video views across Formula One's digital platforms and social media accounts were up 46 per cent to 4.9 billion. The success of Formula One's esports competitions resulted in 11.4 million live stream views of its Esports Series 2020, the final triggering 1.7 million social media engagements.[4]

From computer gaming to social media, video content delivered live, delayed or streamed, and new audiences able to delve inside the sport on Netflix, Formula One has been transformed.

With a decade of unprecedented change and disruption ahead the industry will continue to adapt quickly. The last 20 years have already provided many of the lessons. Through playing to its core strengths and listening to customers, the Formula One business seems set to thrive.

Notes

1 Baldwin, A (2020) Motor Racing – Mercedes F1 Spent $442 Million in 2019 But Still Made Money, *Euro Sport*, https://www.eurosport.co.uk/formula-1/motor-racing-mercedes-f1-spent-442-million-in-2019-but-still-made-money_sto7870722/story.shtml (archived at https://perma.cc/F93S-RAQ9)

2   Dixon, D (2020) Revenues Pass US$2bn as Motorsport Series Posts US$17m Profit for 2019, *Sports Pro Media*, https://www.sportspromedia.com/news/f1-finances-revenue-profit-2019-liberty-media (archived at https://perma.cc/4RK9-XDGY)

3   Dixon, D (2020) Revenues Pass US$2bn as Motorsport Series Posts US$17m Profit for 2019, *Sports Pro Media*, https://www.sportspromedia.com/news/f1-finances-revenue-profit-2019-liberty-media (archived at https://perma.cc/4RK9-XDGY)

4   Bassam, T (2021) F1 Sees Social Engagements Grow 99% In 2020, *Blackbook Motor Sport*, https://www.blackbookmotorsport.com/news/f1-social-media-growth-data-2020-tv-ratings-audience-global (archived at https://perma.cc/34JC-EJPV)

CHAPTER TWO

Insights on leadership

As Formula One has evolved, so too has the style of leadership best suited to achieving success. During the sport's seven-decade history we have witnessed periods of domination by individual teams. When we ask for examples of great leadership, this invariably provokes a list of successful team bosses – Enzo Ferrari, Lotus founder Colin Chapman, or Sir Frank Williams whose eponymous team won no fewer than 16 World Championship titles between 1980 and 1997.

In Formula One success is primarily measured by on-track results. Everything flows from that because winning races and championships leads to increased prize money, more sponsorship and a healthier bottom line.

As David Coulthard succinctly put it, a Formula One team's results are posted at about 4 pm on every Sunday afternoon immediately following a Grand Prix. Everyone can see how you are performing against the competition. It is clear, measurable and very public.

Since 2010 Formula One has been dominated by two teams, Mercedes-Benz and Red Bull Racing (RBR). No other team has won either the Formula One World Championship for Constructors or Drivers for the last 11 years. In 2021 the early indications are that this domination will continue.

There are a number of reasons for this level of domination. One is that these teams have developed technical innovations that have provided a competitive advantage within a specific set of regulations. They have then sustained that advantage through a relentless focus on continuous improvement and development. Both teams have also benefitted from leadership stability during this period, with Toto Wolff as CEO and Team Principal of Mercedes, Christian Horner his counterpart and rival at RBR.

Meanwhile the sport's most famous and longest standing team, Ferrari, has had four Team Principals in that time, during which it finished second in the World Championship for Constructors on five occasions. In 2020 the team failed to win a single Grand Prix, enduring its worst season in 40 years, primarily due to a regulatory issue relating to the engine technology it had deployed the previous season.

Leadership stability has clearly helped Mercedes and RBR, and not only at the CEO level. Both Wolff and Horner have benefitted from having extremely capable lieutenants – or perhaps more accurately leadership colleagues – at their side.

Horner's appointment of Adrian Newey in the role of Technical Director in 2006 was an inspired decision, and one influenced in part by driver David Coulthard. He had worked with Newey at Williams and McLaren, and when he joined RBR one of his tasks was to help the team develop a winning structure.

'When I first sat down with Dietrich Mateschitz [owner of Red Bull] I realized they were serious about doing what was necessary to win, and part of that was to identify and bring on board the best people', recalls Coulthard. 'I was brought in mainly because of my experience of working with championship-winning teams such as McLaren and Williams, so part of my job was to identify some of the strengths and weaknesses. They had a core of very good people, but we also had to make some changes and bring in fresh talent, including recruiting Adrian.'

Newey had first come to prominence when designing Formula One cars for the March team between 1988 and 1991. With a degree in aerodynamics and astronautics, Newey subsequently was snapped up by Williams, his designs winning 59 of the 114 Grand Prix that took place between 1991 and 1996, after which he joined McLaren. In his book *How To Build a Car* it is clear that Newey did not enjoy the command-and-control style of leadership under McLaren CEO Ron Dennis, attempting to move to Jaguar Racing in 2001 and finally being announced as RBR's Technical Director at the end of 2005.[1]

At RBR Newey was given increased freedom and the support necessary to build winning cars. Mateschitz's determination to disrupt Formula One was matched by Newey's ability to create innovative designs.

Together Horner and Newey forged a partnership that worked, and continues to this day. In simple terms Newey's focus has been on the technical side, while Horner's role has been everything else. In this respect they are not that dissimilar from some of the very successful partnerships we have seen in the past, including that of Frank Williams and Patrick Head at Williams, and Ron Dennis and John Barnard at McLaren.

What is very different is that today's Formula One leaders have much greater levels of complexity to manage. At Mercedes-Benz the team employed an average of 1,016 staff during 2019, with 872 working in roles across design, manufacturing and engineering, supported by 144 colleagues in administrative positions. The company turned over £363 million leading to a profit of £14.7 million.[2] Based in Brackley, at the epicentre of the UK's 'motorsport valley', it is a substantial business, However, this only tells half the story.

Twenty-seven miles away in Brixworth lies the Mercedes AMG High Performance Powertrain (HPP) division. This business, a Daimler subsidiary, is responsible for design and manufacturing the complex hybrid engines used by Mercedes and its customer teams, Aston Martin, McLaren and Williams. In 2019 it employed 742 staff, which is why seven-times world champion Lewis Hamilton often refers to the almost 2,000 teammates who lie behind his success.

While Wolff runs the F1 team, HPP is structured quite differently, a four-man leadership team reporting to non-executive chairman Markus Schäfer, the member of the Daimler board responsible for Group Research and Chief Operating Officer of Mercedes-Benz Cars.

Wolff joined Mercedes' Formula One team in 2013, on the eve of the introduction of the hybrid engine formula that was introduced the following year. The Austrian businessman had always had a passion for motor racing, and was himself a very competent driver, but it was his success in finance and venture capital that provided him with the funds to invest in the sport.

Having purchased 49 per cent of the shares in the HWA motorsport business in Germany in 2006, Wolff would later acquire a shareholding in Williams before being presented with the opportunity to take a stake in Mercedes Formula One. This move tells a story in itself, because while it was clear to many that Wolff was the ideal candidate to lead Williams into the future, succession planning at the family-owned business clearly did not allow for that. Williams's loss would be Mercedes gain.

At Mercedes, Wolff joined forces with three-times world champion Niki Lauda, a fellow Austrian whose leadership on the race track had successfully converted into success in the aviation industry with companies including Lauda Air and Laudamotion. Some initial friction gave way to a strong partnership between these straight-talking businessmen and racing enthusiasts, and Lauda's death in May 2019 was a clear loss to Wolff and the business they led.

In his role as non-executive chairman of Mercedes F1 Lauda played a key role in attracting Lewis Hamilton to the team. In the years that followed he acted as an adviser, sounding board and close ally to Wolff.

Wolff, meanwhile, set about the development of the Mercedes team, which would subsequently dominate the sport. He has recalled sitting in the reception of the team's headquarters, noting the old coffee cups and magazines dotted around, and feeling this was unrepresentative of what a Mercedes-Benz Formula One team should look like.

Wolff's first year at Mercedes witnessed some significant changes, including the departure of former team boss Ross Brawn and technical director Bob Bell. This was not unrelated to the arrival of Paddy Lowe from McLaren, Wolff creating an exceptionally strong technical leadership team that also included former Ferrari technical director Aldo Costa and experienced British design engineer Geoff Willis.

As with Horner's first year at RBR, Wolff's initial moves were to ensure that he had appointed a strong technical team capable of developing a winning product. It was also vital that the structure worked, with clear roles and responsibilities underpinned by the trust that is such an important ingredient in any successful team.

Ross Brawn is one of Formula One's most successful leaders, having been the technical mastermind behind Michael Schumacher's seven titles at Benetton and Ferrari before staging a management buyout of Honda's F1 team to create Brawn Grand Prix and win both World Championships in 2009. It was this team that Mercedes-Benz purchased.

That Brawn and Wolff did not forge a long-term partnership puzzled some observers, yet the demands of Formula One are such that strong individual leadership is important. A team cannot have two leaders.

What is interesting about both Horner and Wolff is that although both had experience in owning and operating motor-racing businesses prior to Formula One, neither had run an enterprise of the size or complexity of a contemporary Grand Prix team – a technology business that must produce a new, high-end product each year and battle against long-established teams.

As Team Principals both Horner and Wolff have a wide range of responsibilities, including stakeholder engagement. This includes dealing with shareholders, customers, key suppliers and employees, as well as the regulator at the FIA, the Formula One Group and the international media that follows the sport so closely. The political side of Formula One has always been intense, and the CEOs of teams often find themselves sitting in meetings with bitter rivals. This can include trying to find common ground when it comes to the overall direction of the sport, whilst also recognizing that the person sitting beside you is almost entirely focused on beating you.

Leading styles vary, of course, but there are common traits between Horner and Wolff as well as significant differences. Both are highly articulate communicators, well versed in giving a voice to their businesses, and that confidence clearly serves them well, whether communicating internally or externally. They enjoy good relationships with key media, recognizing how important that can be in influencing the messaging about their businesses, but each has shown an edge to interviews that reflects a steeliness to their ambitions. Always affable, you are never left with anything other than the impression that they live and breathe their teams' performance every day.

These two industry leaders operate within quite different structures, however. Horner does not own the company he leads, whereas Wolff owns one-third of the Mercedes F1 team, the balance shared equally between Daimler and Ineos, the global chemicals business owned by British entrepreneur Sir Jim Ratcliffe.

The structure at RBR means that Horner and Newey liaise with the parent company via Red Bull's motorsport boss Dr Helmut Marko, while the energy drinks' co-founder Dietrich Mateschitz becomes involved in key strategic decisions. For example, the 2021 move for RBR to create its own engine division, following the withdrawal of Honda, involved all four.

For a CEO whose team has dominated Formula One in recent years it is surprising that Wolff admits to learning on the job, firstly at Williams, then at Mercedes. Yet his experience in venture capital, in providing the funding for start-ups to flourish and achieve their potential, provides a clue as to his 'people first' approach in leading Mercedes to record-breaking success.

A sport that is known for its technology, complexity and big-business reminds us, every season, that it is people working in teams who achieve success. The way in which they are led, given clear targets, strong support and the opportunity to be the very best versions of themselves. Most of all a team culture that creates a safe environment within which people want to excel and have no fear of failure.

A contrast to the recent success achieved by Mercedes and RBR can be seen in the inability of four of the world's major car companies to achieve significant sporting or commercial success in Formula One during the 2000s. These failures ultimately led to their withdrawal, unable to compete as the more agile, entrepreneurial teams flourished and came to dominate the industry just as they did during its growth phase of the 1980s and 1990s.

Ford, Honda, Toyota and BMW each created their own teams, operating them as subsidiaries of their parent company, and yet failed to achieve their objectives within the sport. Considering that the goal of a large, well-funded Formula One team is to win, each of these failed.

BMW and Honda each won a race during the 2000s, but those individual victories underlined an inability to discover the formula for achieving sustained success. Neither Jaguar nor Toyota were able to break through to the winners' circle. Four companies, spending billions of dollars, were unable to crack the code to achieve and sustain success in the Formula One business.

In two cases the decision to withdraw from Formula One was followed by a fire sale, only for the new owners to take hold of the very same teams and become world champions. In Ford's case, an embarrassing foray into the sport as Jaguar Racing became an abject lesson in poor leadership and top-heavy management structure. Sold to Austrian energy drinks company Red Bull in November 2004, within five years the world's leading energy drinks company had a Formula One car capable of winning. Based at the same headquarters facilities as Jaguar Racing, with the majority of the staff retained, Red Bull Racing went on to win four consecutive World Championship titles.

The difference was the day-to-day leadership of Horner and Newey, underpinned by the support of Mateschitz and Marko.

Mirroring that achievement, Honda's withdrawal from the sport in December 2008 was followed by Ross Brawn taking over the business in a management buyout and promptly winning the very next year's World Championship in a Mercedes-Benz-powered Brawn. Quite what Honda's management will have made of this, one can only imagine. An estimated US $2 billion spend had failed to achieve the success required by a company in whose DNA racing could be found. From the outset, Soichiro Honda's vision of powered bicycles had grown into a legendary success story, a post-war Japanese business famed for its efficient, reliable cars and motorcycles that were often promoted by the company's successful motorsport programmes.

In the white heat of contemporary Formula One, however, Honda was unable to find the winning formula. Yet under Ross Brawn's leadership the same team, with technology created whilst still owned by Honda, took the World Championship by storm and would be snapped up by Mercedes at a relatively knock-down price one year later.

All too often when discussing the reasons for Ford, BMW, Toyota or Honda's difficulties, the answer from senior management would come back that the issue was 'Tokyo', 'Munich' or 'Detroit'. The point was clear: the F1 teams were answerable to head office, to an extent that meant there was a layer of management bureaucracy that did not lend itself easily to the fast-paced business of Grand Prix motor racing. The agility needed to run a fast-paced Formula One team was held back by unwieldy management structures and a lack of empowerment.

David Coulthard relates that when he joined Red Bull Racing shortly after their takeover of Jaguar he found a culture where 'doing reports' was more important than planning a winning strategy. It was as though the financial reporting demanded by Ford had infected the entire business, becoming more important than delivering successful outcomes.

'In Formula One we don't drive by looking in our mirrors, we look at the road ahead', says Coulthard. 'Similarly in business we can learn from past mistakes, but we need to plan for what's coming up and keep our focus on future performance.'

Constantly looking for the opportunity to improve, to win, is what infects the successful leaders within the sector.

Eddie Jordan was fascinating to work for, and remains underestimated as regards his leadership qualities. I came to recognize Eddie's strength in that regard as our small, independent team achieved significant sporting and business success under his leadership.

At the time, some people used to say Eddie was only interested in money, better known for his parties than his podiums. He was certainly unorthodox, and his approach sometimes jarred in the increasing corporate environment of Formula One, but this acted as a differentiator and there was no doubting the calibre of his team.

Eddie created something out of nothing, an old-school entrepreneur who climbed the motorsport ladder the hard way. Ultimately, he built a highly profitable Formula One team that he successfully sold to a private equity company, winning races and almost a World Championship in 1999. He achieved more, in other words, than four major car manufacturers.

It was an offhand comment to none other than Dietrich Mateschitz, co-founder of Red Bull, that prompted me to reconsider Eddie's achievements and leadership of Jordan Grand Prix. I made a light-hearted comment about Eddie's sometimes unorthodox means of doing business, to which Mateschitz reacted by pointing out his admiration of 'EJ'.

I first came across Eddie Jordan in the paddock of a Formula Atlantic race in Kirkistown, Northern Ireland, in 1978. I asked him for his autograph; he gave a rather rude reply as he was in the midst of a pre-race crisis. I was a 16-year-old, he was 30 and driving for Marlboro Team Ireland. It was an unexpected response.

The next time was in the Lisboa Hotel in Macau in 1987 when I was reporting on the Macau F3 Grand Prix. I was also supporting my friend Martin Donnelly who would win the event, enormously boosting his ambition to reach Formula One. One of my public relations contracts involved providing editorial services support to Marlboro, at that time the largest sponsor in motor racing. EJ knew that my race reports were influential given that the Marlboro management were constantly evaluating teams as part of their driver development programme.

'Gallagher, I need to see you', was EJ's greeting on seeing me. He explained that he was vying with rival F3 team West Surrey Racing to secure the services of a young Northern Irish driver by the name of Eddie Irvine, backed by Marlboro. His proposition was that I should put in a glowing report about his team in return for a fee, an inducement I had to decline.

It was an insight into his ambition, and his understanding that money lubricates motor racing. His forte was deal making, an approach that helped to build a successful race team and driver management company.

There are many easier ways of making money than running a professional motor-racing team. It is a harsh and unforgiving industry. While Eddie's commitment to making money was sometimes criticized he understood that, in the dog-eat-dog world of international motor racing, deal making is crucially important. As an entrepreneur he was as passionate about building a profitable business as he was about winning races. Ultimately he knew the pinnacle was Formula One and that if he worked hard it would be enough in building a successful, well-funded team.

After a failed attempt to buy Team Lotus, EJ opted to take his own team into F1 in 1991. So it was that at the 1990 Italian Grand Prix I found myself typing out a one-page press statement announcing Jordan Grand Prix's plans to enter the top flight.

Two months later we launched the Jordan Ford 911, the car given its shakedown test by five-times Grand Prix winner John Watson. The press conference was attended by around 20 media. It prompted the leading French journalist Jabby Crombac to wonder why we were bothering. Failure seemed inevitable.

Little did Jabby realize it but his words helped to motivate Eddie even more, and one of his leadership qualities was to treat adversity as a spur to achievement. The more he was told what he and the team could not do, the more determined he became to achieve his goals. That was a determination and focus that he instilled in all of us. It was infectious.

Eddie liked to remind us that it was his name that hung over the door to the business. As a result, the buck stopped with him, and he made it clear that he would have the ultimate say in key decisions.

His tiny Irish-registered team based at Silverstone entered F1 with a spectacular green livery thanks to top-quality sponsors from 7UP, Fujifilm and Marlboro. It also had a neat, quick car designed by a three-man team headed by Gary Anderson. In its first season Jordan would finish fifth in the Formula One World Championship for Constructors, out of 18 entrants. It would score multiple points finishes, embarrass the factory Ford-based Benetton team and launch the career of a relatively unknown German driver by the name of Michael Schumacher. Ever the deal-maker, Eddie ensured that Schumacher's backers at Mercedes-Benz paid for the privilege.

Add to that the fan-friendly enthusiasm that the Jordan team brought to F1, including Eddie's manic sense of fun, and the stage was set for a decade and a half of highs and lows. Between 1991 and 2005 Jordan would become one of the most recognizable teams in the sport.

Although it's going too far to state that there was a carefully crafted strategy from the outset, there was certainly a distinct approach that EJ took from the start. He was different, so the team would be different, which meant challenging established ways of doing things.

The Irish traditions of being welcoming, friendly and up for a bit of 'craic' or gossip became values the team espoused. Friday morning breakfasts for the media became an important part of our weekend. For a travel-weary British press corps, a 'full English' at the Jordan hospitality unit set the weekend off. This inevitably included some banter with EJ, a running commentary on current events, and the odd bet or two. A love of music and storytelling would lead to languorous and fun-filled evenings with media, sponsors, suppliers and officials. Win, lose or draw, Jordan promised a party atmosphere, a sprinkling of celebrities, and a glass or two.

This made for a powerful combination in a sport that could sometimes take itself too seriously. We couldn't sell sponsorship on the basis of winning races and World Championships. The leading teams sold sponsorship on the basis of achieving on-track success supported by corporate hospitality and the media exposure reserved for the winners. It was an all-or-nothing strategy since there can only be one race winner on the Sunday, leaving the majority of teams and sponsors with a sense of disappointment. As McLaren's Ron Dennis used to say, second place means you are the first of the losers.

At Jordan the sales pitch was different. Eddie's approach was to have the ambition to win, but the guarantee of a successful relationship with great PR, a positive engagement with sponsors and a human touch was what stakeholders found attractive. Due to Eddie's focus on making deals the team recognized the importance of going the extra mile for its customers.

This was also reflected in Eddie's relentless work rate and an energy level that often left the rest of us wondering where it came from. As he became more financially secure and sometimes disappeared to his yacht or house in Spain for half the summer, it was also the case he was always working the phone and networking like crazy. He had never done a deal, he would say, 'sitting in the office waiting for the phone to ring'.

It was not unusual to have a day during which we would fly to three or four countries, signing new sponsorship agreements, then taking in a football match or business dinner in the evening. Eddie's work rate was high, and he expected that of anyone working for him. The demands were often intense, sometimes bordering on the unreasonable, but he was pushing the limit of what could be achieved and he wanted his staff to do the same.

If you needed to see Eddie's enthusiasm for the job, witness his reaction when the team took its first victory at the 1998 Belgian Grand Prix in Spa-Francorchamps. In doing so the team became the first in history to finish first and second on its maiden win. It also came on a day when we had the fan club, factory staff and majority of our major sponsors present. It was meant to be.

Three months later Warburg Pincus concluded a deal to purchase half the equity in Jordan Grand Prix, making Eddie a wealthy man. He and CFO Richard O'Driscoll had read the market perfectly. It was a super-successful outcome after two decades of dedication and hard work.

The following season was to be the zenith of the team's fortunes on and off the track, with two Grand Prix wins, third in the World Championship and a host of sponsorships. However, by 2000 it was clear a malaise was setting in.

The decline began for a number of reasons. The leadership team grew, and there was a loss of focus as the new shareholders sought to grow the business through diversification, including the launch of a Jordan energy drink. Board meetings were no longer focused entirely on Formula One.

The private equity deal also changed Eddie's personal ambitions, naturally so, given that he no longer had to hunger after new deals. To underline this, an ill-fated decision to sue Vodafone in 2003 led to an embarrassing High Court case. Two years later Jordan Grand Prix was sold to a Russian businessman, the deal brokered by Bernie Ecclestone. Eddie was gone from F1, a loss to the sport, but with a legacy that continues. Today the team has evolved into Aston Martin F1.

Eddie Jordan showed what can be achieved through charismatic leadership, a strong work ethic and a relentless focus on the bottom line. He inspired people, whether staff, technical partners or sponsors. Three observations can be made about his leadership style.

One was his daily sales meeting. This involved him going through a list of potential deals neatly written, edited or underlined in his Filofax. Whenever he was in the office I would receive a call to join him, usually with the head of commercial affairs, Ian Phillips. It was very disciplined and kept us all focused on what mattered: securing customers and growing the business.

A second point was his daily phone call to his mother Eileen in Dublin. Around 8 am he would phone her for a chat. In the midst of the high-tempo work rate demanded by Formula One, with constant travel, lots of pressures and deadlines, he always remembered to call her, and it did not matter who was listening. It showed a vulnerability that reminded us he was a family man, and on many occasions people commented that the team had a more human dimension to it than our rivals. It was a family business, after all.

Finally, there was Eddie's approach to management meetings in which we would often make two lists of priorities. On one side of the agenda a list of things that would make our car go faster, on the other, everything else. He knew that unless we had a fast-enough car, everything else would be much more difficult, whether it be attracting sponsors or securing the best drivers.

Formula One businesses led by individual entrepreneurs, supported by highly professional management teams, have traditionally won over top-heavy, corporate entities that have lacked the fundamental agility required to perform. It is for this reason that teams such as McLaren and Williams, with 36 World Championships between them, sport such a successful track record, unlike Jaguar or Toyota.

In both instances their leaders, Ron Dennis and Sir Frank Williams, forged their skills in the fires of disappointment resulting from early forays into the unforgiving world of running an international motor-racing team. Early trials and financial struggles often shape entrepreneurs, and in both cases they went on to run highly successful businesses.

It is also the case that both teams suffered as a result of inadequate succession planning. This led to a slump in performance, a slew of disruptive management changes and, in the case of Williams, the sale of the business during 2020.

Ron Dennis's career saw him preside over one of the most successful businesses in Formula One history. As we have seen, success can be measured by results and profitability, and in this respect McLaren was a consistent performer for 30 years. There have been successful, profitable Formula One teams in the past, so what made McLaren the standout organization was its ability to sustain long-term corporate relationships and successfully diversify the business. Today the McLaren Group includes the racing team, its applied technologies business and a successful car company.

In 2019 McLaren Automotive sold 4,662 high-performance supercars manufactured in its state-of-the-art production centre near Woking in Surrey, UK. Meanwhile its Formula One team began a resurgence that would see them claim fourth place in the 2020 World Championship, up from ninth in 2015 and 2017. Sister company McLaren Applied takes the knowledge gleaned from 50 years of race-bred technology and applies it in areas as diverse as electronics, battery technology, data analytics and lightweight structures.

The group stems from a Formula One team that owed its vision to Ron Dennis. Born in Woking in 1947, he would take over the locally based McLaren team in 1980 after cutting his teeth as a mechanic and team owner, most notably with Project Four Racing, which he founded in 1976. After securing sponsorship from Marlboro, Dennis impressed the management such that they helped engineer his takeover of McLaren, at that time the focus of their Formula One programme.

I first met Ron Dennis four years later when I applied for a job as a marketing executive at McLaren International and was interviewed by him in his pristine office in the team's headquarters in Station Road, Woking. He was businesslike and polite, and asked fairly straightforward questions of a 22-year-old Irish economics graduate with one year's experience in the advertising department at *Autosport* magazine. I wasn't the one for the job.

The next time I met him in person was for a one-to-one media interview in the McLaren motor home in 1989. Dennis was having breakfast but my hopes of a good start to the meeting ended when I fell up the step into his office and banged my head on the ceiling. Ron found that very amusing. Later his staff told me, 'Everyone does that. Ron quite likes it.'

I spoke to him at length about his team's dominant performance during a year in which they had won 15 of the 16 Grand Prix, its McLaren-Honda MP4/4 car driven by Ayrton Senna and Alain Prost. His main point was that they should have won every race, only an error by Senna robbing them of victory at the Italian Grand Prix. Dennis is renowned for his attention to detail and his quest for perfection, so it was typical of him to mention the race that got away rather than the team's 15 victories.

If the Formula One World Championship was awarded for presentation alone, McLaren would have won it every year. Everything reflected Dennis's eye for detail, his obsession with creating a clinical environment, reflecting the high standard of engineering and discipline for which McLaren became known. It was a strong message and one that proved very attractive to the team's corporate sponsors.

McLaren became the benchmark team in terms of presentation, matched only by Ferrari. Both have undoubtedly benefitted from the input of sponsor Marlboro, the brand backing McLaren between 1973 and 1994 and supporting Ferrari to the present day.

Marlboro's brand guidelines demanded clean lines, the crisp white-and-red chevron with easily read black-on-white lettering. It also funded best-in-class designs for everything from press kits to driver race suits and hospitality units. This played perfectly to Dennis's unwavering belief in the importance of presentation.

His ability to attract commercial partners was an established skill when Dennis secured a pivotal business relationship with businessman Mansour Ojjeh, a Saudi-born French national whose aerospace company Techniques d'Avant Garde (TAG) was also known for its acquisition of the Swiss brand Heuer in 1989.

In taking over the running of McLaren at the behest of Marlboro in September 1980, Dennis and Ojjeh convinced none other than Porsche to design a V6 turbo engine with which McLaren would be powered for the following three years. Funded by TAG, this unit would power McLaren to success in the World Championship for Drivers in 1984 with Niki Lauda and 1985 with Alain Prost.

This illustrated another ingredient in strategies deployed by Dennis as he focused his team on achieving competitive advantage – the desire to innovate. The 1981 McLaren MP4/1 featured the first all-carbon-composite chassis, a development that in one fell swoop changed the direction of car design, combining strength and lightness, key factors in driving Formula One vehicle performance. This was made possible by McLaren entering another partnership, this time with the US aerospace company Hercules. Under the technical direction of John Barnard the car also set new standards in terms of safety, creating the template for the Formula One cars we see today.

Another aspect of McLaren's development was that the initially successful business partnership between Dennis and John Barnard ultimately came to an end in 1989 when the pair split, Barnard leaving to join Ferrari. This helped Dennis to move away from a technical structure over-reliant on one individual, something he came to recognize as a potential weakness.

An example of the risk of overdependence on a key person can be seen at Red Bull Racing, which has achieved all of its successes under Adrian Newey's technical leadership. However, as he relates in *How To Build a Car*, a key factor in the team's success has been his ability to delegate. This is evidenced by how often he ascribes the success of individual projects or developments to colleagues.

Newey joined RBR from McLaren, lured by Dennis in 1998 after a championship-winning, seven-year spell at the Williams team. He achieved much at McLaren, including designing championship-winning cars driven by Mika Häkkinen and David Coulthard, and when he departed many felt that Ron Dennis had made an error. It would take almost a decade for McLaren to win another title, Lewis Hamilton claiming his first World Championship Drivers in 2008.

By then McLaren had moved into a new headquarters facility near Woking, a monument to Dennis's obsessive attention to detail and commitment to innovation. Designed by Britain's Sir Norman Foster, the McLaren Group campus is located on a 125-acre site, the futuristic design of the McLaren Technology Centre housing the facilities required for the design, manufacture and operation of the company's Formula One cars. Adjacent to it sits the McLaren Production Centre, home of the McLaren Automotive business.

As ever, there was a keen emphasis on presentation with a view to impressing the customers, but on a level that had never previously been seen at a Formula One 'factory'. The lineup of championship-winning cars, innovative designs and heritage models from the days of McLaren's Can-Am and Le Mans sports-car racing programmes help visitors to become immersed in a long tradition of excellence. This is underlined by the ability to see today's cars being developed and manufactured behind floor-to-ceiling glass walls. In 2013 the team celebrated 50 years since founder Bruce McLaren incorporated the company. McLaren's heritage is an extremely important part of its business story.

The fact that visitors can see precisely what the workers are doing, the culture of their work environment, the cleanliness and the immaculate presentation, underlines the deep conviction that Ron Dennis has in his business and his pride in the staff. While many companies might hide away their operations, McLaren has them out in the open, public recognition that factory-floor workers play as critical a role in the company's success as the mechanic in a pit stop, or the driver behind the wheel.

Under Dennis, McLaren's approach was not to everyone's taste, sometimes criticized for being somewhat 'bland' or 'corporate' in a sport renowned for its colour, noise and excitement. Consider the extreme sports, lifestyle marketing of Red Bull or even the colourful approach taken by Jordan. However, this rather missed the point, as McLaren's corporate clients were invariably large multinationals who appreciated the clinical environment created by Dennis and his team.

During the time Dennis led McLaren, the Formula One team enjoyed some of the longest commercial relationships in sports history, including 30 years with Hugo Boss and TAG Heuer. Those key customer relationships were sustained by the efforts of Dennis's marketing supremo Ekrem Sami, a key figure in the McLaren story. His role was to ensure that the perfection demanded by Dennis on the technical side of the team was also reflected in its commercial operations. This meant achieving best-in-class standards of customer relationship management, evidenced by McLaren's investment in marketing, client services, hospitality and communications departments.

It set out to create an image and environment that appealed to corporate clients and in which they felt comfortable doing business. This was one of the masterstrokes of Dennis's leadership, developed and executed with the help of lieutenants such as Sami.

It includes innovations such as being the first to move away from using motor homes, originally converted buses and later mobile hospitality units in the paddocks of Formula One races in Europe. Instead, McLaren created a portable building – the Communications Centre – in 1999, with a suite of offices that reflected technology, innovation, attention to detail and success.

That was replaced in 2006 by the enormous Brand Centre, a three-storey building transported on a fleet of 17 trucks – all for the five days of a Grand Prix, and only in Europe. An astonishing achievement at the time, the Brand Centre's 15-year life has to come to an end in 2021, the shift towards more environmentally sustainable operations leading to a reduction in size, with only eight trucks required to move it to European events. It came to represent McLaren's stature in the sport, and the extent of its ambition under Dennis.

His role as Team Principal at McLaren came to an end in 2009 when he promoted long-time colleague Martin Whitmarsh to the role. This came in the wake of championship-winning success in 2008, but also following the unseemly 'spygate' controversy of 2007. This involved McLaren being excluded from the World Championship for Constructors and fined US $100 million by the FIA as the result of being passed confidential design information belonging to Ferrari.

Under Whitmarsh's leadership the team did not win any further titles, although it remained a top-three team, winning Grands Prix until 2012. A slump in 2013 led to Dennis returning to lead the team, later appointing Frenchman Eric Boullier to work alongside Managing Director Jonathan Neale, but the results did not improve despite a renewed partnership with Honda. In 2016 it became evident that Dennis's partnership with long-time associate Ojjeh was at an end, and he was ultimately ousted from the business he led for over 35 years.

Nevertheless, Dennis's legacy is that of an organization that set new standards of presentation, innovation and technical excellence over a 20-year period, and that remains a major player in Formula One today. Under the leadership of Zak Brown and Andreas Seidl the team has restored its engine partnership with Mercedes, produced competitive cars for the last two years, and rebuilt a portfolio of corporate sponsors – with over 40 partners in 2021. Gone, however, are the corporate greys and silvers so beloved by Dennis, the team's vivid papaya-orange livery reflecting a more outwardly dynamic, open positioning for its brand.

As a leader Dennis belonged to a 'command-and-control' style of leadership, but his strong vision for the business ensured that the attention to detail and focus on excellence cascaded throughout the organization and provided a catalyst for success over many years. The McLaren Technology Centre (MTC) and McLaren Production Centre (MPC) stand as a reminder of how visionary a leader he was, personally overseeing every aspect of how the facility is presented and operates.

His ability to develop and retain long-term corporate relationships reflected McLaren's dedication to customer service, while the business strategy developing during his era saw the company diversify into becoming a highly successful car manufacturer and technology group.

The team's innovation mindset was not confined to its racing technology either, as evidenced by the Brand Centre. This even applied to the way in which they celebrated their successes. McLaren introduced the 'winning shirt' initiative, whereby team members would be given a rather striking shirt to wear when posing for their team photograph after winning a Grand Prix. This was subsequently mirrored at the company's headquarters, where the McLaren sign would change colour to reflect another on-track success.

This approach to recognizing that success is a team effort is by no means unique in Formula One. But as the sport has become increasingly complex and fast-paced, leadership teams have learned to place more emphasis on staff recognition, wellbeing and retention. The really successful leaders have a backstory that involves inspiring their teams, aligning everyone behind a common purpose and recognizing the role each individual has to play in helping the team achieve success.

Dietrich Mateschitz is seldom written about in the international business media. It begs the question how, in the age of Gates, Zuckerberg and Musk, the founder and owner of Red Bull has managed to remain so low-key. One reason is that Red Bull is a private company, another is that Mateschitz has no interest in standing in front of his brand. The company comes first.

When Red Bull first appeared in Formula One as a personal sponsor of Austrian driver Gerhard Berger, few imagined that the sweet, fizzy energy drink would go on to dominate a sector of the drinks industry and embarrass the automotive industry, building better, more consistently competitive Formula One cars than Ferrari.

There are two distinct strands to the Mateschitz story: the development of the Red Bull company and the manner in which he was able to take over the unsuccessful Jaguar Formula One team and turn it into a winner. I was there the day Mateschitz addressed the workforce at Jaguar in late 2004, hot on the heels of Red Bull's takeover. He told the relieved workers about his vision for the team, his ambitions for the future. If any of us doubted him, we only had to look at what he had achieved with Red Bull in the two decades since it was founded to know that this was a man who knew how to get things done.

Having worked in marketing for Unilever, Mateschitz later joined German cosmetics company Blendax, where he had an international marketing role for products including toothpaste. It was while on a business trip to Asia that he came across an invigorating tonic drink known as Krating Daeng, which a Thai company was selling widely in the region. Popular for its ability to boost energy, thanks in part to its caffeine and taurine constituents, it featured a pair of fighting gaur, or Indian bison, as a logo.

I was fortunate in 2004 to meet with Peter Huls and Roland Concin, two of Mateschitz's right-hand men, and during a day-long introduction to the world of Red Bull they explained how he had taken this regional product and turned it into a global brand phenomenon. Huls was head of engineering and technology, Concin responsible for operations, and they explained how Mateschitz had taken the original drink and modified it to appeal to a western palate before setting about production. They also explained how product differentiation was key from the start, including the choice of a slim, tall can with its cool blue and silver colours.

The Red Bull production lines at the Rauch factory in Rankweil illustrated the scale of Red Bull's success less than two decades after Mateschitz had the vision to create an 'energy drink' and, in so doing, invent an entirely new sector of the soft drinks industry. The automated production lines were busy when we walked around, each producing 90,000 cans of Red Bull an hour, or 25 per second – and there were four lines.

Later I met Jurgen and Roman Rauch, whose family business is primarily known for producing fruit drinks. They recalled the moment when Mateschitz came to them with the idea of producing his product in their factory. His initial order quantities were so small they really struggled to justify setting up the production lines, but when the original batch quickly sold out and he came back for more they realized he might be onto something.

From the outset Mateschitz's vision was to avoid traditional advertising and promote the product by creating events where customers could sample Red Bull. Event-based marketing was a core strategy from the outset and, in embracing extreme sports, motor sport and aviation, it also reflected the enthusiasm Mateschitz himself had for skiing, Formula One and flying. His story is a masterclass in entrepreneurship. Red Bull's success as a business reflects his lifelong passions.

Many people in Europe will remember the early days of Red Bull's roll-out when flat-bed Minis began appearing with a large Red Bull mounted on their rear deck. Guerrilla marketing was part of the Red Bull game plan, targeting everything from major events to traffic jams where promotional staff on scooters would hand out product to frustrated motorists.

I asked Mateschitz about this when we met in 2004. He told me that the entire focus of their marketing is to enable people to try the product. His research showed that some consumers simply did not like the taste at all – as many as 50 per cent. That left half the world's population who potentially regard a can of Red Bull as a convenient way of securing a caffeine rush. More regular users, he said, will drink four to six cans a week.

From the start Red Bull was associated with high energy, youthfulness and vitality; it was edgy. Mateschitz was very clear about the brand values. Extreme sports showed cool young people performing outlandish feats on skis and snow boards, from base jumping to free climbing. Drink Red Bull and this *is* you.

Aviation sport was by no means a mainstream activity to reach consumers, but by using base jumping and free-fall parachuting, and then extending it into the creation of the Red Bull Air Race, which visited major cities around the globe, Mateschitz was again combining high energy and under-lining the slogan adopted in their advertising: 'Red Bull gives you wings'.

Other events soon followed, from the motocross-based stadium events called Red Bull X Fighters to the very popular Red Bull Soap Box derby and amusing Red Bull Flugtag, which involves members of the public trying to build homemade, human-powered aircraft. There have been more than two dozen Red Bull-created event formats, each underlining the brand's values and putting the product into the hands of consumers worldwide. Each activity was carefully crafted so that it could travel well from market to market and be scalable.

Probably the most well-known event was Red Bull Stratos, when on 14 October 2012 Austrian free-fall parachutist and wing flyer Felix Baumgartner jumped from a special capsule floating at 128,100 feet above New Mexico. He broke the sound barrier during his free fall, reaching a terminal velocity of 833.9 mph, setting new world records for the highest free fall and highest human balloon flight. More importantly it was widely broadcast, with 80 television stations in 50 countries taking the live feed and rolling news channels replaying the jump endlessly. There were 52 million views online. It took Red Bull to new heights in terms of its message of 'energy', being on top of the world and, of course, giving you 'wings'. It also contributed directly to Red Bull's record year, selling 5.2 billion cans worldwide.

Mateschitz's prowess for creating a brand marketing phenomenon is well established, but one of his greatest achievements has been in the creation of Red Bull Racing. The team we see today was his vision, and from the very start he shared clear targets together with the approach he would take to creating a successful business.

Jaguar Racing, owned by Ford, was created following the US automotive giant's acquisition of Stewart Grand Prix in 2000. Originally founded by three-times world champion Jackie Stewart, the team had become an established challenger. As Jaguar, however, it became an embarrassment to the brand it represented. Between 2000 and the end of 2004 the team scored only two podium finishes, both in the hands of Eddie Irvine, but failed to win a single race. It never finished higher than seventh in the Constructors Championship.

Ford, frustrated by the team's lack of success and unwilling to underwrite the budget for 2005, put the team up for sale. If a buyer could not be found the team would close with the loss of 325 jobs.

I had just joined the team and found myself dispatched to China to work on a rather complex deal whereby Ford would sell the team to a Chinese entity. In so doing we would create Ford Team China, taking the Formula One liability off Detroit's desk and building a joint venture relationship with Chinese investors. Somewhere in Shanghai lies a quarter-scale Jaguar Formula One car painted in Ford Team China colours, much to the confusion of anyone who might find it.

Back in Europe a more obvious deal materialized when Red Bull, one of Jaguar's sponsors via driver Christian Klien, broached the idea of buying the team. Tony Purnell, Jaguar Racing's Team Principal and CEO, was able to conclude an agreement with Mateschitz. Red Bull Racing was born.

Those hundreds of jobs had been saved, but everyone wondered what a Red Bull Formula One team would be like. If companies of the calibre of Ford and Jaguar had failed to produce a winning car, what chance would an energy drinks company have against the likes of Ferrari, McLaren and Williams?

When Mateschitz came to the factory a few days later he addressed the staff and explained his vision for the business. He described how, in the 1960s, he had become a big fan of Formula One, following the exploits of drivers including Austrian Jochen Rindt. He liked the technology, the purity of the racing, the challenge that was involved. He said he liked the lifestyle around Formula One too, but that it had all become a little bit serious, and so Red Bull would be putting the fun back into the sport and doing things differently from the rest.

He also said that he wanted to win the World Championship, and that to do so he would put the right structure in place and invest accordingly. A clear message was that Red Bull only does things properly, and that same approach would apply in Formula One.

Christian Horner and Adrian Newey, the team principal and technical director of the Red Bull Racing that came to dominate Formula One from 2010 to 2013, were not in the audience. They had yet to be employed. This was ground zero for Red Bull's Formula One project.

With his vision outlined, Mateschitz began to make the changes that he felt necessary to turn the team from a loss-making, unsuccessful embarrassment into a team capable of winning. One of the early changes was to replace the senior management, notably Tony Purnell and David Pitchforth, with a fairly brutal 'clear your desks' approach.

New management was installed, with Horner brought in by Mateschitz's motorsport adviser Dr Helmut Marko. A successful and ambitious team boss in lower formulae, Horner was regarded as a reliable lieutenant who could be trusted to deliver on Mateschitz's vision.

David Coulthard was recruited as one of the drivers for the 2005 season, and 'DC' brought with him some vital qualities. He knew how to win and had worked with two of the most successful teams in the sport – Williams and McLaren. Understanding the culture of a winning team was important, and Mateschitz wanted to get the right people into key roles as soon as possible.

By the end of the team's first year changes had already been made to the way things were done, but some of this 'pain' was balanced by the recruitment of Newey from McLaren. As a multiple championship-winning car designer, and someone whom DC had worked with at both Williams and McLaren, his was a key appointment. He was then empowered to put in place the people, structure and technology necessary to haul Red Bull Racing up the league table.

Newey's first full design for Red Bull came in 2007, since the 2006 car was already designed when he joined, but in the meantime DC had scored the team's first podium finish in Monaco 2006. Regular points-scoring results and more podiums began to come the team's way, but 2009 became the breakthrough year with an inaugural victory in the Chinese Grand Prix. By season's end the team and lead driver Sebastian Vettel were second in both the Constructors and the Drivers World Championships, but little hinted of what was to follow: complete dominance of Formula One in the four seasons that followed, with successive titles from 2010 to 2013 inclusive.

Behind all of this success is Mateschitz's vision, outlined on that day in November 2004 when he stood in front of the relieved staff in their Milton Keynes factory. He had a clear vision of what he wanted to achieve, he put in place the right people for the job, empowered them, provided the resources necessary to invest in the areas that mattered, and used Red Bull's global marketing power to build the team into a giant of the sport both on and off the track. In so doing he created not only a winning racing team, but a winning business, which is sponsored by major global brands including Oracle, Exxon Mobil and TAG Heuer.

Working with Eddie Jordan and Dietrich Mateschitz, competing against Ron Dennis's McLaren, teaches a lot about leadership. Each had a very clear vision for their business, and was passionate about creating a successful business. They shared a single-minded determination, yet brought their own particular flavour of leadership.

Eddie Jordan was all about the deal, and investing the money in making the car go faster, while Ron Dennis was just as obsessed with achieving perfection in presentation as he was with creating innovative race cars. In Dietrich Mateschitz we had someone who combined his business with his passions, empowered the most talented people he could find and showed how to be the best in the world, from energy drinks to Formula One.

A key learning is that successful leaders in Formula One are very clear about their business objectives so that every member of the team understands the goal. Mateschitz was clear about his purpose in competing in Formula One, and that shared purpose is a powerful weapon in building a successful team. At Mercedes-Benz this includes each member of staff having a written set of goals – personal, departmental and company-wide.

The command-and-control style of leadership symptomatic of Formula One in the 1980s and 1990s has given way to a more enlightened approach to managing large teams. This includes focusing on the welfare of employees, with leading teams now investing in mental health and mindfulness for all employees. There is a realization that high-performing teams can take their toll unless support is provided.

One reason is that, as David Coulthard points out, successful Formula One teams drive an accountability culture where each person has to accept that they are being measured and made responsible for their contribution. Taking ownership for your contribution to the team effort, whether on an individual or departmental level, is critically important if a Formula One team is to avoid the silo mentality that can develop when people start to focus on their area alone. The ability to take a helicopter view of your contribution to the team plan is essential.

Since the pressure to perform requires open, honest communication about the issues facing the team, it is important for team personnel to know that they work in a safe environment. It is therefore incumbent on leaders to create a culture where personnel feel safe enough to be honest about, and avoid fear of failure. The flip side of this accountability culture is that individual team members are given recognition for their contribution, and that the team takes time out to celebrate their success.

In his book on leadership Manchester United's legendary manager Sir Alex Ferguson relates how the two most important words in the English language are 'well done'.[3] Formula One teams know the importance of celebrating their successes, whether that be an outright victory, a podium finish or – in the case of a smaller team – simply scoring World Championship points. It is important for team members to feel they are part of a successful, rewarding journey.

Succession planning can be a difficult topic for leaders who are focusing on delivering strong results at the very top of their career. In Formula One we have witnessed teams suffer significant issues when the time comes for the next generation to take over. It is noticeable how much the leadership at Mercedes is focused on succession planning. CEO Toto Wolff has made no secret of the fact that he plans to step away from his Team Principal duties, while James Allison moved on from his role as Technical Director in 2021, the team creating the new position of Chief Technical Officer. Doing this has enabled a vastly experienced member of the team to continue making a contribution, while enabling others to benefit from career development.

Ultimately the leadership focus within Formula One teams is on creating the framework within which talented people can be recruited, allowed to flourish and retained within the business as it grows. This means having a safe environment that allows trust, honesty and openness to drive an upwards trajectory of performance. One that drives sustained success.

Lessons in leadership

HAVE CLEAR OBJECTIVES FOR THE BUSINESS
Leaders such as Dietrich Mateschitz, Ron Dennis or Toto Wolff clearly identify and communicate the team's goals. There should be clarity of purpose across the organization.

SURROUND YOURSELF WITH TALENTED PEOPLE
A common factor among Formula One's most successful teams is the leadership's ability to identify and recruit the most talented people they can afford.

CONSTANTLY MEASURE YOUR PERFORMANCE
Formula One's results are clear. You win or you lose, and performance measurement has to include everyone who contributes to the team's output. The truth is in the data.

CREATE YOUR OWN STYLE
There is no one-size-fits-all when it comes to leadership. Each person is different, so while the values and behaviours of good leaders are common, we can layer our personality on top.

DO NOT WORRY ABOUT SHOWING VULNERABILITY
Eddie Jordan was not afraid to show his vulnerable, human side. Leaders cannot be expected to be 'superhuman', whether it is a question of having an off day or admitting to an error of judgement.

RESPECT YOUR RIVALS
Formula One teams spend a lot of time watching their rivals, evaluating how they are performing and learning from them. Even when winning we can ask our teams to see if there is something we are missing, a gap in our armour that the opposition might be able to exploit.

DO NOT FEAR FAILURE
Many leaders make mistakes, or suffer failures, on their way to the top. Ron Dennis, Frank Williams and Eddie Jordan all endured tough times early on in their careers. Far from putting them off, those failures became rich learning experiences that helped them to get it right next time.

CREATE THE FRAMEWORK FOR PEOPLE TO EXCEL

Considering that this is a people business, leaders need to create a framework – including a defined set of values and behaviours – that gives personnel the opportunity to be the best version of themselves.

BECOME YOUR COMPANY'S VOICE

One of the most important roles for Formula One's leader is communicating with both primary and secondary stakeholders, articulating the company's message and helping to set the tone for the business and everyone working in it.

Notes

1 Newey, A (2017) *How to Build a Car: The autobiography of the world's greatest Formula 1 designer*, HarperCollins, London
2 Dixon, E (2020) Mercedes F1 Post UK£14.7m Profit For 2019 Despite UK£333m Spend, *Blackbook Motorsport*, https://www.sportspromedia.com/news/mercedes-f1-finances-profit-turnover-spend-2019-toto-wolff (archived at https://perma.cc/M3ZQ-E7XC)
3 Ferguson, A and Moritz, M (2016) *Leading: Lessons in leadership from the legendary Manchester United manager*, Hodder & Stoughton, London

CHAPTER THREE

Building winning teams

Formula One team operations are often given as an example of world-class teamwork. Generating that level of collaboration, accountability and trust is not easy. Organizations recognize how important it is to build teamwork. For that reason alone, there is an entire industry devoted to helping companies launch initiatives, develop programmes and participate in activities that build relationships, promote positive energy and create the means for people to solve complex problems.

It all comes down to building effective working relationships supported by good communications, trust and respect among colleagues. This is essential if a team is to consistently achieve ambitious goals and have the ability to challenge each other as well as the issues they face without creating the tension and conflict that leads to underperformance.

It is right that Formula One teams are regarded as providing good examples of teamwork even if, from time to time, the human condition means that errors creep in and tensions flare. Unquestionably world-class teamwork is a defining quality among the strongest teams. The ability to perform consistently, to create that sense of 'team' in which there is a collective responsibility to get the job done, is one of the pleasures of working in this environment.

My first experience of teamwork came in late 1990 when Eddie Jordan asked me to help promote his fledgling Formula One team, Jordan Grand Prix. It was growing out of his successful Formula 3000 team, this being the category of racing below Formula One at the time, and by the time I started providing press and media services to it there was a total of 33 staff.

By any standards this was a small team of people, even back then, and the task in front of them was truly colossal. As Eddie would go on to say some years later, if he had realized quite the extent of the challenge he might have thought twice about it but, as is so often the case with self-made entrepreneurs, ignorance of the pitfalls can be a good thing.

The first Jordan Formula One car was designed by a team of three engineers: Gary Anderson, our chief designer, along with young design engineers Andrew Green and Mark Smith. All three went on to become Formula One team technical directors. Compared to the leading teams at the time, this was a tiny design group. Today a group of three design engineers would form a project team to produce a specific vehicle system or assembly.

A small group of individuals supported the design team, charged with buying, managing suppliers and ensuring on-time delivery. Everyone was multitasking. The mechanics from Formula 3000 formed the core of the new Formula One team's race personnel, and as the new car progressed so they turned to building sub-assemblies and, finally, the complete car ready for testing in the autumn of 1990.

I organized a small gathering of the press in the modest business unit at Silverstone, where the team would base itself for the first season at the highest levels of motor sport. One of those in attendance, the renowned French journalist Jabby Crombac, would famously write 'Why do they bother?' when he filed his copy. The tiny Jordan team, with its single Formula One car built in a glorified garage, did not fill the key opinion formers in the Formula One media corps with hope. They had seen it all before: dreamers hoping for Formula One glory, soon to founder on the rocks of financial hardship.

As it transpired, that Jordan–Ford 191 turned out to be one of the most beautiful and effective Formula One cars of the early 1990s. A simple, neatly packaged product that featured some clever detailing that Gary and his guys incorporated. It was also easy to work on, a facet of Gary's design philosophy that he had carried with him since the days when he too had been a mechanic.

Powered by the powerful Ford Cosworth HB V8 engine, the car would go on to score its first finish in that season's Monaco Grand Prix, and its first points with a fourth and fifth for drivers Andrea de Cesaris and Bertrand Gachot in Canada, driving the team into fifth place overall in the Formula One World Championship for Constructors. That was fifth out of an entry of 18 teams. Today such a performance in a debut season would be unthinkable.

How was that possible, given that our tiny design team was working with an unimaginably small budget and that the season was a first experience of Formula One for fairly well everyone involved?

Talent and teamwork lay at the centre of this achievement. We were able to undertake a giant-killing act by virtue of our small size. It worked in our favour. As the subsequent seasons would prove, it became more difficult to recapture the spirit and achievement of that first season. Considering that we came within a few laps of winning the 1991 Belgian Grand Prix only for the engine to fail, it would take a further seven years before we finally achieved that goal and, as luck would have it, that occurred at the same circuit, Spa-Francorchamps.

As chief designer Gary had a vision of what he wanted to achieve, and with a small group around him he was able to delegate the key systems on the car quickly and oversee progress in a typically hands-on manner. As someone who had previously designed his own Anson Formula 3 race cars he was very experienced at project-managing the design, manufacture and development of a car. The fact that this was Formula One didn't faze him, even if the pressure was intense.

So too with the rest of the team: the ability to learn quickly, relying on key relationships built between each other in the lower formulae, played a critical role. Without realizing it, we had a closely networked organization with short lines of communication and strong alignment around common goals.

The team also had talent, of course, bolstered by some experienced hands. In the main, however, Jordan embarrassed teams such as the factory Ford-supported Benetton outfit because it was a small, highly connected group of motivated individuals determined to show the world what they could do.

No one in the team could click into cruise mode, or expect to be kept in the job without delivering. The culture of the team was for everyone to work until the job was done, displaying a work ethic that ensured Jordan punched way above its weight. The candle was burned at both ends, and all of the individual team members knew that they were being completely relied upon. No one could shirk responsibility.

As the team grew in size, thanks in part to Eddie Jordan's ability to woo significant sponsors off the back of that first season's meteoric performance, it was noticeable how life became somewhat harder. The halcyon days of that first season began to fade.

The complexity of maintaining efficiency and strong teamwork in the years that followed taught us all some key lessons about business. First was that you can quickly become a victim of early success, necessarily growing to meet the demands of sustaining that performance in an environment where the experienced competition have greater bandwidth and strength in depth. That growth often stretches the systems and processes that worked at the beginning, as few small businesses have the ability to scale quickly.

The second was that people have strengths and weaknesses that come to the fore depending on team size. Someone who works superbly well in a small group may not necessarily flourish on becoming a smaller cog in a big machine. We certainly saw some of that at Jordan, where the complexity of building ever more sophisticated Formula One cars during the mid-1990s meant that the technical management would struggle to achieve the same level of success as we saw in 1991.

The third was that, at every level of the business, the shortened lines of communication that we all enjoyed at the start became impossible to sustain later on, causing significant stress in the system. It became increasingly difficult for individuals to manage the aspects for which they had previously taken responsibility. This meant developing a more complex structure, relying on more colleagues, often including new recruits who had the qualifications but not necessarily the same cultural approach. We ultimately ended up with some colleagues who regarded Jordan as 'just another job' and believed the salary at the end of every month was more or less guaranteed no matter how they performed.

What saw Jordan through that difficult growth period was the leadership provided by Eddie and key lieutenants who grew in their roles as the business progressed. Besides Gary as technical director, Trevor Foster grew from being an engineer and then team manager in Formula 3000 to directing operations for the Formula One programme, assisted by team manager John Walton. A key lieutenant for Eddie was Ian Phillips, a highly experienced motorsports manager who had previously run the Leyton House March Formula One team, while our former bank manager Richard O'Driscoll joined Jordan early on as finance director. Initially I worked on sponsorship with Eddie, joining the management board in 1998 when given overall responsibility for marketing and communications.

This tight-knit team of half-a-dozen individuals turned Jordan from being a giant-killing act in 1991 into the championship-challenging team we had in the period 1998–2000. By then we were employing upwards of 250 full-time staff, and empowering a new group of senior managers.

By then, too, we had suffered some casualties. John Walton had left the team in 1996, while Gary Anderson would depart in late 1998, almost at the very moment of winning our first Grand Prix. A strained relationship with Eddie had grown from the difficulties born of rapid growth and the increased expectation of our sponsors for the team to deliver on-track success. Growth also meant that Gary no longer led a small team; he could no longer single-handedly manage every aspect as he had done before without becoming a bottleneck. Among the new recruits employed to bolster the team's capabilities were men such as Mike Gascoyne, Sam Michael and Bob Bell, people who would themselves go on to become technical directors of teams such as Benetton, Williams and Renault in the years ahead.

Our approach to the challenges of a fast-growing team and more complex structure was to attempt to keep the key disciplines each under a single leader and to join those leaders and their teams at relevant touchpoints throughout the hierarchy. An effective management network was enormously important.

As ultimate authority within the technical, operational, commercial and financial side rested with individual leaders, they took responsibility for their areas whilst ensuring that their reports were empowered and accountable. Cross-functional communications played a vital part in stitching the team together, ensuring alignment and common purpose. This was central to Jordan's achievements and would later serve as an explanation as to why some of the very large car-manufacturer-backed teams that came into Formula One would prove incapable of matching that kind of success.

As we have seen in Chapter 2, the classic example of a failed team was Jaguar Racing, owned by Ford and grown out of Stewart Grand Prix (SGP). As an independent team it achieved a lot in its short three years of participation in F1 between 1997 and 1999, scoring a race win, a pole position and fourth place in the World Championship for Constructors in its final season. Founded by three-times world champion Jackie Stewart and managed with his son Paul, SGP had many similarities to Jordan Grand Prix. It also developed from a team that had already achieved significant success in the lower formulae.

Organic growth and the inevitable progression into Formula One were always going to be the outcome for a team owned and run by the well-connected, resourceful and ambitious Stewart family. In common with

Jordan, there was clear leadership from Jackie and a well-constructed management team of industry professionals tasked with taking responsibility for their area of the business. As a smaller team they benefitted from short lines of communication and the team culture was highly entrepreneurial. This owed much to Jackie's 30-year career as a global ambassador for brands such as Ford, Rolex and Goodyear. He knew how to construct and manage deals with large corporate sponsors.

The transition from Stewart Grand Prix to Jaguar Racing ought to have been a straightforward one: ideally, the same culture and structure bolstered by larger budgets and commercial clout. Things did not work out that way, and between 2000 and 2004 Jaguar Racing achieved less than Stewart and became something of a case study in how not to tackle Formula One. Talented staff found a top-heavy management that variously lacked clear direction, relevant experience and ultimately suffered from being a sub-division of Ford. In taking a successful, entrepreneur-led business and squashing it beneath a giant multinational that had little understanding of what was required to succeed in Formula One, the result was always going to be disappointing.

The first indication that Ford had erred was when Wolfgang Reitzle, head of its Premier Automotive Group, which included the Jaguar, Land Rover, Aston Martin and Volvo brands, assumed overall responsibility for the Formula One programme, with Neil Ressler acting as team boss. Both highly capable and experienced automotive industry professionals, they found the going difficult. In Formula One, as in any business, it is vital that the leadership understands the industry inside out. There is no time to learn in a sector as complex, expensive and unforgiving as this. The relentless pace of Formula One often catches out the unwary, and since Jaguar took over an existing team there was little time to plan.

The leadership team soon witnessed change. It was subsequently placed in the hands of US racing legend Bobby Rahal who gave way to former Formula One world champion Niki Lauda and subsequently a British management consisting of CEO Tony Purnell and Managing Director David Pitchforth. This lack of stability did nothing for company direction, morale or credibility. By the time Purnell and Pitchforth started to make progress with the team, Ford had already tired of the project's cost and poor results, and the company was put up for sale in 2004.

It would later become clear that Formula One was not the only business that Ford's senior management had struggled to come to terms with. As history shows, when the poorly performing businesses at Jaguar Land

Rover, Volvo and Aston Martin were also sold, their new owners made a success of them. Indian group Tata was able to unleash the potential in the Jaguar and Land Rover brands, long held back by the dated culture of Ford at the time. Focus groups of existing Jaguar customers in the United States had dictated the continuation of product lines that owed everything to the Jaguar brand's past, and little to the technology-centric, design-focused younger customers that it needed to lure.

The degree of command-and-control at the top of Ford had much to answer for in relation to the problems that beset Jaguar Racing. The lack of relevant experience among the senior leadership team combined with systems that prevented the team from having the agility needed to win. From a people perspective the entrepreneurial culture of Jackie Stewart's close-knit team was replaced by a focus on process rather than performance.

This is another reason why it came as a surprise to many that the same team would subsequently dominate the sport between 2010 and 2013. Transformed under Red Bull's ownership, it would bring Germany's Sebastian Vettel four consecutive Formula One World Championships for Drivers.

It is a striking reflection on the power of good leadership and team culture that the Red Bull energy drinks business had the ability to create a far superior Formula One team than Jaguar. Aligned behind Dietrich Mateschitz's goal of winning the World Championship, and led by an ambitious CEO, the team unlocked its potential.

The tendency has always been for some observers to view the Red Bull Racing story as simply that of a billionaire's obsession with Formula One and relaxed attitude at throwing hundreds of millions of dollars at his hobby. But, as we have seen in Chapter 2 on leadership, Mateschitz is an entrepreneur who understands how to invest in talent and inspire people to achieve ambitious goals. When he hosted that town hall meeting not long after buying the team, he did not see a group of people who had failed, but a team that needed the direction and support necessary to win.

Considering the top-heavy nature of Jaguar Racing and its structure within Ford, one of the key factors in Red Bull's turnaround was the way in which the reporting lines became much more simplified. These shortened lines of communications made decision making and problem solving much easier. Requests for investment in R&D facilities or fresh talent were challenged, but Christian Horner and Adrian Newey were able to demonstrate the benefits by the success the team achieved.

The appointment of Horner as Team Principal in January 2005 came as a surprise to many, since he had only run teams in the lower formulae. His team was successful, however, and as a result won the support of the head of Red Bull's motorsport programme, Dr Helmut Marko. Experienced in race team management, including dealing with sponsors, drivers and championship organizers, Horner represented an investment in the future. He was soon supported by a small yet highly capable team of senior managers.

As we have seen, another key appointment was David Coulthard, for when 'DC' joined the team he brought with him 12 seasons of testing and racing for two of the very best teams in Formula One: Williams and McLaren. DC also possessed a strong intellect, an understanding of business and a vision of the key building blocks needed to transform Jaguar into a stronger team. Recognizing that he was nearing the end of his career, he saw his role as one of helping the team to transition.

Thus it was Christian Horner and David Coulthard who played a pivotal role in persuading Adrian Newey to join the team as technical director. This included demonstrating to Newey that he would have the necessary financial support and freedom to run the technical side of the business. Ultimately this combination of Christian Horner and Adrian Newey, team boss and technical visionary, created the foundation for Red Bull Racing's emergence as a dominant force in the sport. In the same way that Frank Williams and Patrick Head created a powerful combination at Williams F1, or we experienced the benefits of a close-knit team at Jordan, part of the RBR success story came in the simplicity of its management structure.

I was very mindful of these lessons when, in 2005, I established Status Grand Prix along with Dublin businessman Mark Kershaw, with the aim of entering an Irish team in the A1 Grand Prix World Cup of Motorsport. This was a new series, the brainchild of businessman Tony Teixeira and Dubai's Sheikh Hasher Maktoum al Maktoum, nephew of the emir.

A1 Team Ireland was born with the objective of creating a championship winning team; one that could prove the concept of A1GP in which countries of all sizes could compete in a Grand Prix-style competition with equally matched cars. The winner would be awarded racing's World Cup.

The A1GP concept required that we used a standard car designed and built by Lola Cars in Huntingdon, Cambridgeshire, powered by a reliable and impressive engine from Zytek, a specialist in its field. As every team had the same car, same engine and even the same tyres, from Cooper Avon, it really came down to the 'team' of people to make the difference, and that was what really appealed to us.

The series ran to a 'winter' schedule in the northern hemisphere and in the inaugural 2005/06 season we performed reasonably well. We appointed former Formula One driver Ralph Firman to drive for us, supported by rising star Michael Devaney as test driver. Leading the technical side of the team we had a highly skilled engineer in Andy Miller together with a team of mechanics put together by a former colleague from Jordan Grand Prix.

It was clear, however, that simply banding together a group of experienced people was not enough. Although we finished a creditable eighth in the first championship, we had only scored a single podium finish. More often than not we came away with a sense of disappointment rather than achievement.

For season two we made some changes. Budgets had overrun in season one due to having insufficient controls and systems in place, so we replaced Ralph with Devaney and subsequently Richard Lyons. Both were capable drivers, but from the outset performances were poor. Not only had we failed to make progress since year one, but the competition had improved and we were falling backward. Change brought a lack of stability and, as results deteriorated, tensions emerged.

A blame culture began to develop. The drivers were complaining about the car, the engineer was confused as to why his decisions were not leading to improved performance and the team of mechanics became frustrated. In spite of everyone's best efforts our well-funded, immaculately presented car was out of contention.

Again we went through changes, including replacing our engineer, drivers and some of the pit crew, but things did not improve. We finished the second year in a disastrous 19th place, confused by our performance and recognizing that swapping people was not the answer.

What we did know was that we did not yet have a team. Some were too ready to blame others and there was a lack of accountability. I felt responsible, and although all of the decisions made thus far had been well intentioned, the team had not gelled. It called for a new approach.

We decided to start with the driver, because it is they who need to have the confidence in the car in order to deliver the required performance. If a driver feels confident, they can push the limits. Much of that confidence comes from the driver's faith in the engineer's decisions and the way they impact on vehicle performance.

The best driver in Ireland was Adam Carroll. He had been on the cusp of breaking into Formula One, even testing for the Honda team, but his career was stalling. It took some time to secure his services, but in taking him on I knew we need not worry about driver ability. Initially we partnered him with a young engineer named Dan Walmsley, the bulk of the mechanics remaining the same and benefitting from two years of experience working together. Immediately our results improved.

A series of podium finishes was followed by our first victory. We won the A1 Grand Prix of Mexico on 16 March 2008, the eve of St Patrick's Day, a notable moment for everyone connected with A1 Team Ireland.

The race win was down to a lot of things: a great performance from Adam and a stunning pit stop executed to perfection by the mechanics. Suddenly we had a team, and by the end of the year had finished sixth in the A1GP, confident that more was to come.

Unfortunately, we had to find a replacement for our engineer, a frustrating development at precisely the moment when we were on an upwards trajectory. By now, however, I realized there was no point in simply employing someone without first seeing whether they would fit into the culture of the team and work well with our driver. Trust, respect and the ability to work together in solving problems was crucial.

As a result I asked Carroll to become involved in interviewing potential engineers. It was an interesting experience. The engineer I thought might best fit the team was not the one Adam chose. Instead he selected Gerry Hughes, a hugely talented engineer with experience in Formula One, but with a personality quite different from that of our driver.

It was the right decision, because they appreciated each other's strengths. Our driver knew he had an engineer who had experience, a shared ambition to win and a determination to work together in unlocking the car's speed.

When he joined the team Hughes insisted on revising the engineering processes to ensure that we fully understand each element of vehicle performance and had a solid baseline to work from. Once he and the driver knew they had that foundation in place, they were able to focus on performance.

We won the championship, scoring five victories and three second-placed finishes, including a completely dominant performance in the final A1GP event at Brands Hatch in May 2009. Our driver and engineer formed a strong partnership, and our experienced pit crew had become a formidable team.

Those years were extremely challenging, but it taught me a great deal about building a winning team. I reflect on the fact that half the programme was wasted in trying to get a disparate group of individuals to work together simply because they had relevant experience. It was far more important to ensure that people had a similar approach, even if they brought different skills to the table. The fact that we found a combination of driver and engineer who could work well together instilled confidence throughout the team and ended the blame culture that had developed in the second year.

We achieved our objective in the end, and I learned a lot about myself as well as about other people. I came to recognize that the world-class teamwork I had experienced at Jordan Grand Prix was not easily replicated because it takes time for a team to gel.

It is one thing to surround yourself with talented people, but whatever their academic qualifications or experience, the cultural fit is critically important. Taking time to recruit the right person also means establishing how they will integrate into the team, positively adding to the network.

It is difficult to be successful in international motor racing, whatever the category. The dynamics of a racing car and the inputs from the driver means there are lots of variables to consider, and this means that a team has to be able to constantly analyse its performance, tackle problems head on and continuously drive improvements.

It is a cycle of continuous improvement in an environment of technology and teamwork. If the technology is not working, the performance will not be there, and the same applies to the teamwork. That has to work in order for problems to be solved.

Formula One teams have developed a number of approaches to build winning teams. For all that the sport can become obsessed with technology, the successful teams constantly demonstrate that success comes down to people, the way in which they work together and the values they hold.

One of the most significant developments in Formula One teams over the last 20 years has been the increasing diversity of the workforce, with gender and racial diversity contributing to diversity of thought. By employing an increasingly diverse range of people there have been significant improvements in team dynamics, creativity, innovation and cohesion. These are all important factors in helping teams facing significant challenges. Even successful ones.

James Allison, CTO of Mercedes-Benz, has spoken about the healthy scepticism that the team has about its own performance, for example, despite the fact it has been the dominant team in Formula One since 2014. Rather than rest on their laurels, Mercedes and RBR will examine both their successes and failures to see where that can improve. In his book *The*

Winning Formula David Coulthard explains how RBR will take a margin of victory and examine whether that should have been even greater. Mercedes does the same, so that a post-race debrief can appear like a catalogue of mistakes, even if they have won the Grand Prix.[1]

To facilitate this approach teams have regular town-hall meetings in which team leaders share insights, ensuring that the whole organization is aware of the issues and challenges that need to be solved. Over the last 20 years we have seen multiple world champions such as Michael Schumacher or Lewis Hamilton attending the headquarters' town hall meetings. In so doing they recognize that 'the team' is not only the crew who attend races, but the entire workforce tasked with design and developing the car as well as the administrative functions important to any business.

Having the driver talk through their weekend, explaining the reasons behind an issue or thanking the team for its support, helps to ensure that the team feels fully connected. Every employee is part of the network.

Having regular, consistent communications across the team ensures that everyone is aware of the issues facing the team. This is particularly important when ensuring that colleagues do not become siloed and have the benefit of seeing the big picture of what is happening across the business.

Problems are aired and shared. Allison and his Mercedes colleagues often mention the way in which Mercedes solves problems. A key approach is to 'blame the problem, not the person'. This plays to the objective of avoiding blame. The system has to deliver success, so if one part is struggling the team has to pull together to help find solutions. It is not 'their problem', it is 'our problem'.

One of Mercedes' initiatives was to work with former professional footballer Dr Ceri Evans, a doctor and psychologist from New Zealand who has worked with teams including the All Blacks. He developed a mantra used by the team: 'See It, Say It, Fix It'.

This cuts to the core of how a team such as Mercedes works, with team members unafraid to escalate issues with a sense of urgency. If team members see a problem affecting someone else or another department they collaborate to put a solution in place.

The preparedness to be open and honest about issues is vitally important, and Mercedes CEO Toto Wolff often describes the way that being unafraid to challenge team members is 'tough love'. The competition is going to spend their time probing for your weaknesses, so the team has to turn the mirror on itself.

The flipside of requiring team members to be open and honest about their challenges, working together to deliver solutions, is that the successful teams also drive recognition. As we saw in Chapter 2 on leadership, McLaren was one of the first teams to publicly demonstrate recognition of the whole team through their 'winning shirts' initiative, which stretched to the factory staff also celebrating the team's successes. This formalized the way in which a team celebrates its achievements, and has the added element of sharing that publicly.

At Mercedes their philosophy of inviting any team member to represent the organization when receiving the Constructors' trophy on the podium is a very effective tool. It is a powerful way of recognizing the contribution an individual has made to the team's success, and shows the degree to which the leadership is happy to step back and let everyone share in the success.

Speaking on my podcast At The Controls in 2020, Mercedes powertrain engineer Holly Chapman and mechanic Sam Bradley explained how they were shocked and delighted to be asked to represent the team on the podium at that year's Austrian and Belgian Grand Prix.

Neither had imagined that they would one day get to stand on the Formula One podium alongside Grand Prix winners Valtteri Bottas and Lewis Hamilton. Just a few years previously Sam had been a trainee mechanic, while Holly was introduced to Formula One by her stepfather when she was a teenager.

The recognition of their contribution to Mercedes has cemented their commitment to the team, and will have inspired their colleagues. This is an extremely powerful example of how leaders can tap into the motivation of team members, inspiring them to be the best versions of themselves and contributing to the overall success of the organization.

Lessons in team building

PROMOTE OPENNESS AND HONESTY IN A SAFE ENVIRONMENT
High-performance teams face ambitious goals, so it is never going to be easy achieving them. Create a safe framework within which people can collaborate, challenge one another and develop solutions.

CULTURE IS AS IMPORTANT AS QUALIFICATIONS
We want to recruit the best people, but it is vital that the 'fit' is right. Take time to ensure that new members of the team will adapt or contribute to the organization's culture.

NETWORKED ORGANIZATIONS ACCELERATE OUTCOMES
Short lines of communication facilitate improved collaboration and decision making. This is one of the reasons why start-ups work. As teams become larger and more complex, cross-functional networks provide a mechanism to facilitate collaboration.

USE INTERNAL COMMUNICATIONS TO HELP DRIVE ALIGNMENT
Town hall meetings, management briefings and consistent internal communications are important ways to ensure everyone understands the opportunities and challenges facing the business.

STAFF RECOGNITION MOTIVATES AND INSPIRES
By recognizing those who consistently deliver high performance, or who regularly go above and beyond the call of duty, we not only reward the individual but inspire the team to emulate them.

INVEST IN PERSONAL WELFARE AND AMBITION
Today's teams recognize that a small investment in mental health and mindfulness provides worthwhile returns. It is just as important as creating the opportunity for personal development and education.

BLAME THE PROBLEM NOT THE PERSON
Tensions are inevitable among any team tasked with developing world-class solutions, but it is vital that a blame culture is avoided. When issues arise, Mercedes' approach of blaming the problem, not the person, is a good starting point.

BUILD TRUST, RESPECT AND HONESTY
High-performing teams display strong values that enable personnel to come together in the face of major challenges. In a Formula One pit stop, each team member trusts their colleague to deliver their task with split-second efficiency. They respect each other's role, and have honest debriefs to assess team performance.

Note

1   Coulthard, D (2018) *The Winning Formula: Leadership, strategy and motivation the F1 way*, Blink Publishing, London

CHAPTER FOUR

The diversity challenge

On stage at the Terrou Bi resort hotel on Dakar's Boulevard Martin Luther King, I asked the audience for a show of hands. How many of them were interested in Formula One? Conscious that I was a very pale white man standing in front of a multicultural audience of delegates from a pan-African company, I expected a somewhat muted response.

Or maybe that was my unconscious bias, for the opposite happened. A sea of hands were outstretched.

When I then asked who they followed and supported the answer, when it came, was both obvious and yet enlightening. There is one individual in Formula One who has won the hearts and minds of African sports fans, and of a much broader church of supporters from black and coloured communities around the world.

His impact has been immense. His achievements and campaigns have changed the direction of Formula One, accelerating it towards a future that includes men and women of any race or background, whether as fans, team personnel or drivers of Grand Prix cars.

The audience in that Senegalese hotel had only one hero in mind.

London, 6 June 2020. The Black Lives Matter protest march edging its way through St James's Park was just one of many that took place around the world in the wake of the killing of George Floyd in Minneapolis the previous month. One of those present, unnoticed both by fellow protesters and the attendant media, was Lewis Hamilton.

Wearing a black beanie hat, yellow 'Covid' face covering and 'Black is a Vibe' T-shirt, Hamilton was three weeks away from starting the campaign that would lead to a record-equalling seventh Formula One World Championship title. Six months later he would be awarded a Knighthood in Queen Elizabeth II's New Year's Honours List.

Statistically Formula One's most successful ever driver, to many fans the greatest racer of all time, Hamilton has driven change inside and outside the industry as the sport's only ever black driver. There have been other Formula One drivers from mixed-race backgrounds, and from all over the world – indeed every continent – but it has fallen to Hamilton to become the first of black, Afro-Caribbean heritage, to break through the ranks.

That he has not only risen to the heights of Formula One but gone on to completely dominate the sport has vindicated both his and his family's efforts to break down barriers. Hamilton's achievements have caused discomfort for a sport that had never asked itself key questions about diversity, inclusion and in-built, systemic racism.

For a sport with the optics of being predominantly white, male and European, Hamilton has shone the spotlight on the complex issue of an industry that failed to mirror the richness and diversity of its global audience. Specifically, he has raised questions around the biases, both conscious and unconscious, that have resulted in him being the only black competitor in the 70-year history of the sport. While many within the Formula One industry denied that the sport was systemically racist, Hamilton's rise, combined with the global Black Lives Matter movement of 2020, forced a rethink.

The profile enjoyed by Britain's multiple world champion added to the pressure on Formula One, the FIA and other key stakeholders to consider their policies as regards to diversity, and strategies that could help tackle the issue. As the sport's governing body, the FIA represents the world's car clubs together with its global membership and Jean Todt, its president, was quick to respond to Hamilton's campaign. Under Todt's leadership the FIA had already spent a decade tackling gender diversity through its Women in Motorsport Commission.

On 5 June 2020 – the day before Hamilton joined the London Black Lives Matter protests – the FIA issued a short but clear statement in relation to the death of George Floyd and the governing body's commitment to tackling racism: 'The death of George Floyd and others has laid bare the injustice and racism in our society and the desperate need for steps to address it. We mourn with the families for their loss. The feelings of outrage, sadness and weariness are justified. We need to come together to demand meaningful change. We must end these obvious and less apparent, yet harmful, injustices happening every day. FIA's diversity initiative recognizes that our industry clearly needs increased diversity and opportunity throughout its ranks.'[1]

Less than two weeks later the FIA used its first Sport and Mobility e-Conference, attended by over 1,000 delegates from 146 countries, to announce its Purpose Driven movement, which included a commitment to fight systemic racism and prejudice and ensure equality of opportunity to succeed. Formula One responded just four days later by launching its own initiative, We Race as One, using the united front created by the battle against the Covid-19 global pandemic to condemn racism and inequality.

Chase Carey, then CEO of Formula One, clearly felt it was the right thing to do, and to be seen to do, at a time when the effects of Covid-19 and the Black Lives Matter movement were being felt around the world. Formula One's owners, Liberty Media, a US company listed on the New York Stock Exchange, recognized the importance of taking a stand – both from the perspective of corporate social responsibility and in order to bolster the reputation of its Formula One business at a time when its black world champion was demanding change.

'The #WeRaceAsOne initiative we have launched today, in support of the #PurposeDriven Movement launched by the FIA last week, is our way of saying thank you to the bravery and unity everyone around the world has shown during this unprecedented time', said Carey. 'It will also be a platform for Formula One to come together and achieve results against the most important issues facing us as a sport and the world. That is why at our first race in Austria, Formula One will stand united to say loud and clear that racism must end.'

Todt underlined the united front being taken by the FIA and Formula One: 'The FIA is guided by the Fundamental Principles of its Statutes, including the fight against any form of discrimination and notably on account of skin colour, gender, religion, ethnic or social origin. We must promote diversity in motorsport.'[2]

The message could not have been clearer and yet, in order to counteract any suggestion of the sport merely responding to events beyond its control, action was required. Again, Hamilton was at the forefront.

On 21 June 2020 he wrote a column in *The Sunday Times* newspaper in London in which he announced the creation of The Hamilton Commission with the objective of improving the representation of black people in UK motorsport. Co-chaired by Hamilton and Dr Hayaatun Sillem, Chief Executive of the Royal Academy of Engineering, the commission appointed 14 board members, comprising eight women and six men from a range of political, academic and business backgrounds. The commission was set to meet four times over a nine-month period prior to making its research findings public, along with recommendations as to how young black people could be encouraged within science, technology, engineering and mathematics (STEM) and into career opportunities across UK motorsport.

With the 2020 Formula One World Championship delayed until July as a result of the global pandemic, Hamilton's campaigning led to two very public demonstrations of change. The first came when the Mercedes-Benz Formula One team announced on 29 June that the cars driven by both Hamilton and teammate Valtteri Bottas would be painted in a black livery instead of their customary silver. This was a particularly public statement by the German firm.

The team also undertook to announced a Diversity and Inclusion programme in the current year. 'Racism and discrimination have no place in our society, our sport or our team', said Team Principal and CEO Toto Wolff, adding, 'this is a core belief at Mercedes. But having the right beliefs and the right mindset is not enough if we remain silent.

'We will not shy away from our weaknesses in this area, nor from the progress we must still make; our livery is our public pledge to take positive action. We intend to find and attract the very best talents from the broadest possible range of backgrounds, and to create credible pathways for them to reach our sport, in order to build a stronger and more diverse team in the future.'[3]

Here was a clear message combined with a call to action, and while Mercedes' competitors also supported the FIA and Formula One in relation to the campaign for greater diversity and inclusion, it was critical that the team for which Hamilton drove should support his campaign so publicly.

The wave of initiatives and statements in the lead-up to the start of the new World Championship suggested a degree of unity across the Formula One community, but not everything flowed harmoniously. Lewis Hamilton's decision to Take the Knee during Formula One's pre-race anti-racism ceremony was not met with universal approval. This gesture of protest, first used by San Francisco 49er quarterback Colin Kaepernick during the playing of the national anthem at his team's pre-season match in 2016, had previously provoked controversy in the United States. Hamilton recognized the dilemma it represented for some of his rivals.

Not all of Hamilton's 19 competitors felt comfortable to mirror his actions. Denmark's Kevin Magnussen stated that while he was against racism he did not feel able to support the political aspects of the Black Lives Matter movement. Russia's Daniil Kvyat commented that, culturally, he could only kneel before his homeland, the national flag and God. Naturally this apparent disunity caused much comment on social and mainstream media, Formula One and the FIA taking the view that they could not force every driver to Take the Knee.

Lewis Hamilton has every right to stand against racism. While some critics argue that Formula One has never been overtly racist, Hamilton's own life experience included being bullied at school and facing the kind of casual racism only too familiar among black and ethnic minorities.

Nic Hamilton, Lewis's younger brother, explained to me how the family's experiences when taking part in kart races made them feel alien in the world of motorsport: 'Being a black family in a white-dominated sport such as motorsport was not always easy. I recall going karting with Lewis at Rye House (a kart-racing track). We're all sitting there in our Vauxhall Cavalier and everyone is just staring at us, almost like "Who is this black family that has just turned up and what are they doing?"'

In a social media post published shortly after George Floyd's death, Lewis Hamilton reflected on his personal experiences at school attended by predominantly white students in Stevenage. 'I was bullied, beaten and the only way I could fight this was to learn to defend myself. So I went to karate. The negative psychological effects cannot be measured. This is why I drive the way I do, I'm still fighting.'[4]

Speaking alongside me at a corporate event in February 2020, three months before George Floyd's death, Hamilton's focus on promoting diversity and inclusion within the technology companies that compete in Formula One was already clear. With the title of the famous poem 'And Still I Rise' by African American civil rights campaigner Maya Angelou written on his race helmet, and tattooed on his back, Hamilton has lived his life and pursued his career conscious of the inequality affecting people of colour.

'Right now I'm trying to push the sport for diversity', he told me. 'It's a multicultural sport in the sense of nationalities but in an organization of nearly 2,000 people (referencing his Mercedes Formula One team) there is not a lot of colour, not a lot of minorities, so I am pushing and trying to get the sport to go in that direction.'

In light of Formula One recognizing the need for greater diversity, including encouraging young men and women from ethnic minorities and low socio-economic backgrounds to consider a career in the sport, Hamilton and Mercedes pushed the agenda throughout the balance of 2020 and into 2021.

The Mulberry Schools Trust, a multi-academy trust set up in 2016 in London's borough of Tower Hamlets, attracted a partnership with the Mercedes Formula One team in November 2020 offering students aged 7–18 extra-curricular programmes in STEM subjects through vocational training, specialized study and masterclasses.

Launched by Lewis Hamilton, Toto Wolff, Jane Farrell (Chair of the Mulberry Schools Trust), together with her colleague, CEO Dr Vanessa Ogden, the objective of this initiative is to drive equality, diversity and inclusion by offering children opportunity irrespective of gender, race or social class. The first event for the Mulberry STEM Academy took place at the end of February 2021, Mercedes hosting a virtual event during which 40 students were able to interact online with the team's chief technical officer James Allison, chief people officer Paul Mills and four graduates who have volunteered to support the programme.

'We have developed a uniquely exciting curriculum for our scholars, designed to ignite their passion for STEM and build confidence and aspirations for their future education and careers', said Mills.[5] In this way, Mercedes seeks to fill its pipeline of talent with candidates who reflect the society within which it operates, bringing with it the benefits that diversity of thought and background are known to produce.

For Hamilton, the question remains as to whether his success as a world champion, combined with his campaigning, will effect the changes necessary to ensure he does not become a one-off, the only black competitor to have reached the pinnacle of world motor sport.

'It is very, very unlikely at this current point that you are going to see another me come through in the next 10 or 20 years', he told me. 'How can we change that? My goal is really to try to work with the sport, with the governing body, and try to shift the cost of the lower categories and make it more open to working-class families, because that's what we were.'

Of the 767 drivers to have competed in an FIA Formula One World Championship Grand Prix, only two have been women. Their place in Formula One's history has been cemented as much by their ability to break the male stranglehold as by the fact that they achieved their breakthrough so early, during the first and third decades of the World Championship's history. While other forms of motorsport have seen more female competitors, most notably in sports-car racing and in American series including

IndyCar racing with its blue-riband event, the Indy 500, the pinnacle of the sport has remained stubbornly male dominated.

No woman has competed in a Formula One World Championship race since 1976, a season remembered by fans for the titanic duel between Britain's James Hunt and Austria's Niki Lauda. While their epic tale was given the Hollywood treatment in Ron Howard's 2013 film *Rush*, no mention is made of Italy's Lella Lombardi – she participated in four Grands Prix that year.

The previous season her March car had finished sixth in the Spanish Grand Prix, a result that netted the Piedmont-born Lombardi one-half of a World Championship point. To this day she remains the only woman to have scored a World Championship point in the sport's 71-year history.

The half-point came as the result of the race being halted by a fatal accident, caused when the car driven by race leader Rolf Stommelen suffered a rear wing failure and ploughed into a group of spectators, killing three. Perhaps unsurprisingly, the event is most often remembered for its tragedy rather than Lombardi's singular achievement.

Lombardi competed in Formula One across three seasons, driving six different cars in 17 events from which she made 12 starts. Failing to qualify for five Grands Prix tells nothing about Lombardi's skill behind the wheel, as anyone who worked with her recalls the passion, commitment and skill she brought to the task of being a Grand Prix driver. Beyond her World Championship appearances, she would successfully race in sports cars, touring cars, NASCAR and four non-championship Formula One races.

She made her debut, aged 34, at the 1974 British Grand Prix, failing to qualify a privately entered Brabham with race number 208 – the wavelength of her sponsor Radio Luxembourg. She was in good company, however, other non-qualifiers included highly respected drivers Derek Bell, Vern Schuppan and Howden Ganly.

Angela Webb, wife of Brands Hatch owner John Webb, recalls Lombardi's arrival and the decision to hire a Brabham from Formula One supremo Bernie Ecclestone in order to facilitate her 1974 British Grand Prix outing: 'The £5,000 we spent renting a car from Bernie was our only investment in Lella. She lived well and had little trouble getting sponsorship. She stayed in Italy and flew to each race, yet never asked for expenses. That's unusual for a racing driver.' Lombardi was gay, her partner Fiorenza seldom accompanying her to races, but Webb says that drew little comment, far less any media scrutiny.

'She did her own thing. She wasn't interested in fashion and usually wore trousers if she was in civvies. She had an image to keep: "I'm tough so don't mess with me." She was a loner, really. No entourage. She never brought a girlfriend.

'Her sex and sexuality were not topics of conversation in the paddock. She was judged purely as a racing driver. The boys ganged up and got horribly rough on the track – filthy tricks, kart-style – but she could look after herself. She was tough and had great duration.'[6]

Lombardi, a gay woman in a man's world, was breaking the mould, a trailblazer in many respects and yet these days regarded as a footnote in Formula One's history. She was ahead of her times. Today the arrival of a Lombardi into Formula One would surely cause a sensation, setting social media alight and making front page headlines.

The only other woman to compete in Formula One World Championship races was fellow Italian Maria Teresa de Filippis, born in 1926, the daughter of a wealthy Neapolitan count who split her time between palatial homes and enjoyed both tennis and horse riding prior to turning to car racing. Having started by racing a Fiat 500, she progressed to hill climbing and sports-car racing before entering the 1958 Monaco Grand Prix in a Maserati 250F.

She failed to qualify, along with half the field, including a certain Bernie Ecclestone. Undaunted, she appeared at the Belgian Grand Prix just one month later, qualifying and finishing in last place but on the same lap as Jo Bonnier, the talented Swiss driver, godfather to 1996 world champion Damon Hill. It would be her only Formula One race finish.

Three weeks later, in France, she was not permitted to compete. In a 2006 interview with *The Observer Sport Monthly* she told interviewer James Eve that the race director at Reims informed her, 'The only helmet a woman should wear is the one at the hairdresser's.'[7] Undeterred, with no less than five-times world champion Juan-Manuel Fangio telling her that, 'You go too fast, you take too many risks', de Filippis went on to compete in Portugal and Italy, retiring from both events.

In 1959 she again attempted to qualify for the Monaco Grand Prix, this time at the wheel of a Behra-Porsche but – along with teammate Wolfgang von Trips – failed to make the cut. When close friend and team owner Jean Behra was subsequently killed in a support race to the German Grand Prix in August of that year de Filippis decided to bring her Grand Prix career to a close.

Lombardi and de Filippis were the only two women who joined the 765 men who drove in Formula One World Championship events between 1950 and 2020. The sport has no rule or regulation preventing women from competing against men – notwithstanding misogynist race directors.

Three other women have attempted to race in Formula One World Championship events, but failed to qualify. British downhill skier turned racing driver Divina Galica attempted to qualify for the 1976 British Grand Prix in a Surtees entered by Nick Whiting, brother of famed race director Charles Whiting. In 1978 she failed to qualify for both the Argentine and Brazilian Grand Prix, driving for Lord Hesketh. South African Desiré Wilson failed to qualify for the 1980 British Grand Prix at Brands Hatch, while Italian Giovanna Amati failed to qualify for three Grand Prix in 1992 before handing over her uncompetitive Brabham to Damon Hill.

In the years since, women have driven Formula One cars during promotional runs, driver evaluations and in testing. America's Sarah Fisher, best known for her exploits in IndyCar racing, drove a McLaren Formula One car in the 2002 United States Grand Prix for promotional reasons, while Briton Katherine Legge tested for Minardi in Italy back in 2005. Spain's Carmen Jordá and María de Villota signed testing agreements with Renault and Marussia, the latter suffering a horrific accident during her initial test in 2012 which resulted in serious facial and head injuries including the loss of her left eye. It is believed by her family to have contributed to her untimely death a year later.

More recent are the opportunities created by Swiss racer Simona de Silvestro, Columbia's Tatiana Calderón and Britain's Susie Wolff. Silvestro competed in IndyCar racing prior to signing an agreement to test for the Sauber Formula One team in 2014, completing 112 laps of testing at Ferrari's Fiorano test track. The relationship with the team failed to develop further.

Calderón graduated through karting, starting aged four in her home city of Bogota, into lower formulae including Formula 3, GP3 and Formula 2 before being signed by the Sauber Formula One team and testing for them in Mexico in 2018. Thereafter her ambitions of racing in Formula One stalled, her career taking her into sports-car racing and Japan's premiere Super Formula category.

Susie Wolff, wife to Mercedes Formula One CEO Toto Wolff, was born into a racing family in Scotland. As Susie Stoddart, she raced in karts, climbed through the ranks to compete in Formula Renault and Formula 3 before joining the German DTM touring car series where she drove for two different AMG-Mercedes entrants over the course of seven years.

In 2012 she signed as a development driver by the Williams Formula One team. Toto Wolff was a shareholder in the team at that time. In 2014 she became the first woman in 22 years to drive a Formula One car during a World Championship event when she took part in a free practice session at that year's British Grand Prix. A repeat outing followed at the German Grand Prix two weeks later.

In 2015 Wolff took part in official pre-season testing and again drove for Williams in official practice at both the Spanish and British Grand Prix, setting 13th fastest time in the latter. She retired from the sport at the end of that season, stating that she had gone as far as she could with her career.

At the Global Edge 'Connecting the Stars' conference in Los Angeles in 2014, Wolff gave the audience a succinct insight into the challenges facing a female Formula One driver: 'When people see me for the first time, the first thing they say is "well, you don't look like a racing driver". Now I don't know what a female racing driver is supposed to look like but I can only guess that I am supposed to be quite masculine, quite big and definitely very aggressive.'

'I fight hard against that stereotype', she added. 'But the truth is I am incredibly lucky because in my sport, when my helmet's on and I'm out on a racetrack, it doesn't matter what I look like, it doesn't matter what my gender is, all that matters is the time on the stopwatch and the performance that I can show out on track.'

As the entrepreneur behind Formula One's spectacular growth, Bernie Ecclestone could often swing from one extreme to the other in expressing his opinion on the prospect of women joining the ranks of F1 drivers. 'I don't know whether a woman would physically be able to drive an F1 car quickly and they wouldn't be taken seriously', he told WPP boss Martin Sorrell during an Advertising Week conference in 2016.[8] It was a comment that drew much criticism across mainstream and social media, but this was as nothing when compared to earlier statements.

Asked for his opinion on US driver Danica Patrick finishing fourth in the 2005 Indianapolis 500 Ecclestone was reported by ESPN as saying, 'Women should be dressed in white like all the other domestic appliances.' In 2000 he reportedly told *Autosport Magazine*, 'What I would really like to see happen is to find the right girl, perhaps a black girl with super looks, preferably Jewish or Muslim, who speaks Spanish.'[9]

These comments, widely reported at the time, did nothing for Formula One's standing in the world. It underlined the impression of a sport steeped in misogyny, and yet Ecclestone could also step in to defend the right of women to compete. When the legendary Stirling Moss told BBC Radio 5 Live in 2013 that, 'the mental stress I think would be pretty difficult for a lady to deal with in a practical fashion. I just don't think they have aptitude to win a Formula One race'[10] – it was Ecclestone who spoke out.

'There's no reason why a woman shouldn't be able to compete with a man', he told *The Guardian* newspaper. 'Unfortunately, the way things are, I don't imagine a lady will ever get the chance to drive a Red Bull or a Ferrari. The only chance is with a lesser team – and they only take someone if they come with a good sponsor. Regretfully, the problem is that many ladies who could compete probably as well as the guys won't get the chance.'[11]

What the world of motorsport has learned, however, is that there is no natural reason why women cannot compete at the highest levels. The population of women drivers has always been small, but an inspirational few have been able to take on and beat the men.

Frenchwoman Michèle Mouton, now President of the FIA Women in Motorsport Commission, is the only woman to have won a round of the FIA World Rally Championship. She scored four outright victories on rounds of the World Championship in 1981 and 1982, driving for the factory Audi team. She claimed three of her victories in the latter season – in Portugal, Greece and Brazil – finishing second to Germany's Walter Rohl in the Drivers' Championship, but only after an accident on the Ivory Coast event caused her retirement. Rohl was handed the title as a result, but his response to being severely tested by Mouton lacked grace. 'I would have accepted second place in the championship to [Hannu] Mikkola', he told Hugh Hunston at the *Glasgow Herald*, 'but I can't accept being beaten by Michèle. This is not because I doubt her capabilities as a driver, but because she is a woman.'[12]

Appointed to head the Women in Motorsport Commission by FIA President Jean Todt in 2010, Mouton's remit has been to promote access and develop talent across all categories of motorsport. This applies to all the roles and functions that have lacked opportunity for women in the past. From driving to engineering, team management to fitness training and roles within the administration of the sport worldwide.

With a wide range of initiatives aimed at increasing gender diversity across the industry, it has remained the case that – in Formula One at least – women have not been able to make the breakthrough into competing head-to-head against their male counterparts. Despite the very obvious profile, publicity and commercial opportunities that would result from a woman joining the ranks of Formula One drivers, the system by which international motorsport operates has continued to fail in this regard. The absence of women drivers in Formula One is also reflected in the lower formulae. The pipeline of female talent is much smaller than that for men.

With only 20 Formula One drives available each year, opportunities are limited. In addition, the best Formula One drivers now enjoy careers lasting much longer than was the case in earlier eras. This is partly due to the fact that drivers now come into the sport at a much younger age, and also as a result of the safety improvements that mean that drivers can expect to survive, injury free.

Famed drivers who survived long careers in the past included five-times world champion Juan-Manuel Fangio and three-times world champion Jackie Stewart, both of whom competed across nine seasons. Similarly four-times world champion Alain Prost and three-times world champion Niki Lauda survived to have careers spanning 13 seasons.

Each of these greats knew many friends and colleagues who were killed or suffered life-changing injuries. Jackie Stewart recalled that he and wife Helen counted over 50 drivers whom they had personally known to have lost their lives during the course of his racing career.

By the end of 2020 Formula One had seen only a single fatal accident involving a driver during the course of the previous 26 seasons. This remarkable achievement owes much to the way in which the FIA, teams and promoters have continued to place safety at the centre of the sport's regulatory and operational environment.

Today's successful drivers can enjoy long and fruitful careers. Examples include Michael Schumacher and Rubens Barrichello (19 seasons), Jenson Button and Kimi Räikkönen (18) and Fernando Alonso (17), the latter pair continuing their careers in 2021.

With few women drivers coming through the ranks, and a lower turnover of leading drivers in Formula One than at any time in the sport's history, the likelihood of the sport ever seeing a woman competing on a like-for-like basis against men was receding. At a time when society in general, and the international business community in particular, was coming under greater pressure to address gender inequality, the pinnacle of international motor racing appeared to have created even greater barriers to entry. With the existing system guaranteed to limit opportunities for women to race in

Formula One, change was needed. Change which would see gender placed at the centre of initiatives aimed at addressing imbalance in the sport.

Unsurprisingly the first significant initiative came from Susie Wolff, for as the most recent woman to participate in a Formula One World Championship event she knew, more than most, about the challenges facing women. This included not merely the issues involving the sport's structure, including the inevitable requirement for young drivers to find significant amounts of sponsorship funding, but the often-unspoken cynicism of factions within the sport's fanbase and media.

At the Autosport International show in January 2016 she launched the Dare To Be Different initiative in partnership with Motorsport UK with the objective of promoting the participation of women across all forms of motorsport. With women holding 5 per cent of competition licences in the UK, Wolff's aim was to encourage girls to consider motorsport as a potential career, and not only as drivers. The programme addressed the challenge of encouraging women into engineering and technical roles within the sport, with activities aimed at encouraging the study and application of STEM subjects.

Initially, Dare To Be Different organized five events across the UK in which girls aged 8–14 were given the opportunity to try karting as a sport. In addition, two networking events were created to enable women involved in the wider motorsport industry to come together, sharing information and support. The entire programme quickly built an online community across social media channels using the hashtag #D2BD.

'Our main aim with Dare To Be Different is to Drive Female Talent. This is an ambitious and long-term project that will build an online community of women from all over the world', said Wolff at the time. 'It will connect them through a shared passion and empower them to become the next wave of role models, whilst also providing access to some of the most successful female names in the sport. Our UK events for young girls will boost awareness and demonstrate the varied and exciting areas of the sport – showing that they too can dare to be different.'[13]

Thanks to Wolff's profile, the D2BD programme generated significant interest across mainstream and social media, helped by an ambassador programme that included Claire Williams – Deputy Team Principal of the Williams Formula One team. Ultimately the programme gained sufficient momentum to attract the attention of Mouton's FIA Women in Motorsport Commission, such that in early 2019 the two announced a combined programme. The initial 'FIA Girls on Track – Dare To Be Different' event was held in on the occasion of a Formula E event in Mexico City in February of that year. Over 200 girls aged 8–18 were involved in a series of activities including karting, a pit stop challenge, STEM activities, road safety and environmental awareness workshops.

FIA Girls on Track is now the primary gender diversity campaign run by the Mouton's Women in Motorsport commission on behalf of the sport's governing body. In spite of the Covid-19 pandemic an ambitious four-year Rising Stars activity commenced in 2020, with one girl being selected each year to join the Ferrari Driver Academy.

The 'First Edition' of the FIA Girls on Track Rising Stars saw a group of female kart racers taken through a series of knockout events staged by the famous French Winfield Racing School. Entrants were subject to a series of closely monitored cognitive, physical fitness, technical and driving tests. Furthermore, they were interviewed by a panel, comprising men and women, to discuss their ambitions and evaluate their communication skills.

Evaluations were carried out with professional drivers including experienced French racing drivers Cathy Muller and Stéphane Ortelli, while Ferrari Sporting Director Laurent Mekies and Head of the Driver Academy Marco Matassa were fully invested in the programme. This was no low-level publicity stunt, but an expensive, well-constructed programme to identify an individual who possesses the potential to rise to Formula One.

Ferrari's Formula One Team Principal Mattia Binotto along with FIA President Jean Todt gave their direct support, and with an eight-part series streamed on YouTube, this was an initiative that demonstrated authentic, high-level support from senior leadership. The first winner, 16-year-old Dutch kart racer Maya Weug, won a single year contract to compete in Formula 4, a notable prize that will enable her to compete in a key stepping-stone category.

Until 2023 the Rising Stars initiative will be the principal vehicle through which Ferrari will develop female driving talent, and represents a significant commitment from the FIA and Formula One's most famous team to ensure that women are represented within the pipeline of talent. The merging of Susie Wolff's D2BD initiative with Michèle Mouton's FIA Girls on Track programme occurred at precisely the moment a new approach to improving gender diversity in top-level motor racing was launched, and not without controversy.

The W Series Championship was announced in October 2018, an all-female racing series for Formula 3-level cars, privately funded and requiring none of the competing drivers to bring third-party sponsorship with them. With a net cast worldwide, women of any age and experience were invited to apply to compete, an initial shortlist of 55 drivers being whittled down to a final entry of 18 drivers for the first season, held in 2019.

The brainchild of W Series CEO Catherine Bond Muir, a London-based lawyer, together with entrepreneur Sean Wadsworth, the championship attracted notable support from the outset. Former F1 star David Coulthard joined the organization as non-executive Chairman, using his network to attract former McLaren colleagues Dave Ryan as Operations Director and Matt Bishop as Director of Communications. Another former Formula One driver Alexander Wurz, Chairman of the Grand Prix Drivers Association since 2014, agreed to lead the driver selection programme, which was conducted during a series of tests to evaluate each driver's technical competence and physical fitness as well as their ability behind the wheel.

Bond Muir's vision for W Series is that it disrupts a system that has so far not produced the opportunities for women drivers to reach Formula One and other international motor-racing series. By eliminating the need to bring sponsorship, and boasting a prize fund totalling US $1.5 million per season, W Series' objective is to throw the door open to women who have the ambition to reach the top and provide them with the opportunity.

Of the 55 applicants to enter the selection process for the inaugural season, the ages ranged from 17 to 33 and included women from every continent. This also meant a series that, from a diversity perspective, included women of colour, thereby addressing another point of challenge for top-flight international motor racing.

To underline W Series' objective of providing equality of opportunity, Operations Director Dave Ryan took on the task of running all 18 race cars with a group of engineers and mechanics who work for the series. Furthermore, with the drivers being allocated a different car and group of technicians to work with each weekend, the series ensured absolute parity on track.

The inaugural W Series race was held in Hockenheim, Germany, on 4 May 2019 with victory going to eventual series winner, British driver Jamie Chadwick. She would ultimately win two of the championship's six rounds with fellow countrywoman Alice Powell, Finland's Emma Kimiläinen, Spain's Marta López and the Netherlands's Beitske Visser claiming one victory each.

When the series was announced, reaction was mixed. While many could see that positive discrimination in the form of a championship geared solely towards women might well disrupt the existing system, others decried what they saw as segregation from the men.

Michèle Mouton, for example, is a firm believer that the only way for women to compete in motorsport is directly against men – just as she did during her long and impressive World Rally Championship career. The FIA does not, through its licensing and sanctioning mechanisms, prevent any woman from competing in any series, so the concept of W Series was something of an alien concept. While the FIA Girls on Track Rising Stars programme funnels girls towards the Ferrari Driver Academy, with one winner per year, W Series enables 18 women to compete at Formula 3 level with the intention of providing a springboard into any form of top-flight motorsport.

For drivers such as Powell, whose career had stalled through lack of sponsorship while racing at Formula 3 level in 2014, W Series proved to be the catalyst for increased profile, recognition and opportunities to race in other series. This is has proven to be the case with other W Series drivers, the profile afforded by the championship generating opportunity – a key objective for Bond Muir.

Following the initial success of W Series in 2019, the 2020 Covid-19 pandemic caused the championship to be cancelled due to the fact that its international entry list was badly affected by worldwide travel restrictions. Undaunted, Bond Muir and her leadership team used the intervening months to build on its relationship with Formula One.

Ahead of 2020 it had been announced that W Series would provide a support race to the Formula One Grands Prix in both Mexico and the United States, but for 2021 that opportunity took on an entirely new dimension. It was announced in November 2020 that every W Series event in 2021 would support a round of the Formula One World Championship with eight events including six European Grands Prix plus the original US events. 'It is unbelievably exciting', Bond Muir told me. 'What's happened for W Series is that in our second year we are going to be racing on the largest global motorsport platform. It does not really get much better than that.'

As Chair of the Equality, Inclusion and Diversity committee for Motorsport UK, Bond Muir is also playing a key role at national level in driving the change that is needed, saying: 'I think it's important to look forward and see what we can be as a motorsport rather than to look back and say that motorsport is incredibly male and pale.'

What is clear from this deal is that Formula One's owners, Liberty Media, can see the very real benefit of having an all-women support race to what is currently an all-male Formula One event. With Liberty's successful growth of Formula One's audiences across social media platforms since taking over the business from CVC Capital in January 2017, the opportunity to grow the sport's appeal for girls and women is clear.

Furthermore, as part of Formula One's diversity initiative running under the We Race as One banner, W Series represents meaningful inclusion. It does not guarantee that a W Series driver will one day progress to a fully-fledged Formula One driver, but it increases the chance of one of the female competitors generating global media attention, attracting sponsors and being talent-spotted by a team. In short, it creates the opportunity that Bond Muir insists has been the issue caused by the way in which the sport's career ladder had been framed.

While the FIA Girls on Track Rising Stars programme and W Series have taken very different approaches to creating opportunities for women to compete in international motor racing, they represent an important change in the way motorsport approaches gender diversity. Mouton's philosophy is based on head-to-head combat with the men, something that she has proven during her own career, while Bond Muir feels that a larger number of women and girls need to be given the opportunity in order for one or two to emerge in a breakthrough moment for the sport.

W Series is not a case of quantity versus quality, each of the drivers having undergone rigorous evaluation tests. Each one of the competitors has an ambition to race – whether in Formula One or in other categories of inter-national motorsport. The series answers fundamental questions about increasing opportunity, removing the financial barriers to entry and creating a jumping-off point to a professional driving career.

Inaugural champion Jamie Chadwick has seen career opportunities open up, including securing a major commercial sponsor along with a role as Development Driver for the Williams Formula One team. In 2021 she was set to defend her title during W Series's second season in front of the assembled Formula One teams.

Chadwick's career progression, starting in karting aged 11, has been notable for championship-winning success in cars. The winner of a scholar-ship to compete in the Ginetta Junior sports-car championship, she would go on to become the first female and youngest driver to win the British GT Championship, driving an Aston Martin in the GT4 class in 2015.

She is typical of the new breed of young, ambitious women competing in international motor racing, but remains cautious about her own chances of reaching Formula One. 'I had to be competitive or be winning in all the levels before I could even think about getting a Formula One seat', she told a BlackBook Motorsport webinar. 'The ultimate timeline for me is within the next three years but from my perspective I don't see it as a massive rush. In my opinion there will be a female Formula One driver in the future, whether it is in the next three years like I am hoping, or in the next 10 to 15 years. I don't want to see a female Formula One driver there as a token gesture, rather five or six female drivers competing for a podium in Formula 2.'[14]

Chadwick's concern over tokenism is well made. Among the Formula One community there is widespread recognition that when a woman finally joins the ranks of drivers, she should be given the space and opportunity to carve a long-term, competitive career based on performance.

Winning Grands Prix and vying for the World Championship is invariably car and team dependent, therefore any woman driving in Formula One will not necessarily need to win races in order to sustain her career. Very few drivers who make it to Formula One do go on to become race winners and world champions, making it all the more important that a woman reaching the pinnacle should be judged by the same standards as her male counterparts.

While the search for a female Formula One driver goes on, the transformation in Formula One's approach to gender diversity and promoting equal opportunities for all has been significant. This lies at the heart of Formula One's We Race as One initiative, together with the FIA's Purpose Driven movement.

The momentum gathered over the last decade is set to build as the industry has come to recognize the myriad benefits from increasing the pool of talent, and balancing teams with men and women from diverse backgrounds. Educational programmes focused on attracting women into engineering have enjoyed marked success, while Liberty's takeover of Formula One at the beginning of 2017 has resulted in many more women being appointed to senior roles at the very top of the sport.

When the 2020 Formula One World Championship was thrown into chaos by the Covid-19 pandemic it fell to F1's Global Director of Race Promotion, Chloe Targett-Adams, to rework the entire race calendar. This involved renegotiating contracts with existing promoters, securing the use of new venues and successfully delivering a 17-race World Championship in a year when many other international sports were at a standstill.

'I do realize my role can help to inspire other women', says Targett-Adams, who worked as a solicitor prior to joining the Formula One Group as Senior Counsel in 2009. 'I came into this business when it was being run by Bernie Ecclestone, but I reported to another woman, Sacha Woodward-Hill, our General Counsel and a director of the business, and was part of a majority female team, so in many respects we have had women in senior positions within the business for some time.'

Although the proportion of women in technical roles in the travelling race teams remains low, with Mercedes admitting to having only four women from a core team of 65 race staff, it is evident that those who are employed hold senior positions. Ruth Buscombe is Senior Strategy Engineer for Alfa Romeo Racing, while at Red Bull Racing the same role is held by Hannah Schmitz, both women graduating with master's degrees from the University of Cambridge. Both moved directly into Formula One, Buscombe as a simulations development engineer at Ferrari, where she remained for over three years, while Schmitz joined Red Bull Racing as a modelling and simulation engineer back in 2009.

Rosie Wait also secured her master's in engineering at the University of Cambridge prior to starting her career at McLaren, then moving to Williams before joining Mercedes where she became Head of Race Strategy in 2018. When Lewis Hamilton scored a strategically brilliant victory at the 2021 Spanish Grand Prix, Wait was one of those credited with giving the seven-time world champion a winning advantage.

Mirroring the success achieved by this trio is Bernie Collins, Head of Race Strategy at Aston Martin Formula One. She achieved her master's of engineering at Queens University, Belfast, before joining McLaren where she remained until joining her current team in 2015.

Each of these women is a leader in their field, arguably the person upon whom Formula One drivers are most dependent for split-second strategy decisions. They have worked hard to achieve the academic qualifications necessary to do this. This underlines the importance of Mercedes' initiative in working with Mulberry STEM Academy to increase opportunities for students from every socio-economic background.

These inspirational women participated in racing or complex vehicle programmes during their university careers, Buscombe and Collins joining Formula Student and Schmitz leading Cambridge University Eco Racing, which participated in Australia's World Solar Challenge. Furthermore, Buscombe's master's thesis was to study the effect of the drag reduction system on Formula One cars, and this was carried out in conjunction with the FIA. In matching their talent and hard work with access to the Formula One industry these women have helped to create a template for the future. The foundation stones are education and opportunity.

Formula Student has been in existence for 40 years, starting with the Society of Automotive Engineers in the United States and embraced by the Institute of Mechanical Engineers in Europe since 1998. Teams of undergraduates design, develop and race a car, teaching a wide range of management and technical skills.

IMechE views Formula Student as a testing ground for the next generation of world-class engineers, with universities supporting their teams to compete in an annual competition. Not surprisingly this programme has helped to inspire engineers towards considering motorsport as a career choice. With universities working hard to attract female engineers to fill the skills gap in wider industry, this necessarily means that more women are being introduced to motorsport engineering.

Naturally, the key requirement for a woman to join her university's Formula Student team, and to move from there into Formula One or the wider motorsport industry, is that she should have chosen to become an engineer in the first place. This is where much work remains to be done, for all too often young people are unaware of the jobs that are available, and the importance of the STEM subjects in enabling them to build a successful career. Fortunately, the world of motorsport has benefitted from a programme designed to attract younger school children towards the industry.

F1 in Schools is a worldwide initiative run from the UK by founder and CEO Andrew Denford, the objective being to offer children aged 9 to 19 the opportunity to engage in STEM subjects with a motorsport programme at its heart. Each team has to design, manufacture and develop a small model racing car, learning important skills including fundraising, project management and marketing.

Over 20,000 schools around the world have participated in F1 in Schools to date and, with the top-down support of Formula One, the annual finals are held at a Grand Prix with judges and prizes awarded by senior figures. Red Bull Racing's Chief Technology Officer Adrian Newey is notably a patron, along with Claire Williams, former boss of the Williams Formula One team.

The audience facing me in a conference room at Birmingham's Edgbaston Cricket Ground was daunting. It was not that large, perhaps 50 or 60 faces staring back, yet I could feel my hands clammy, my throat a little dry.

I could tell this was not going to be easy. No one had said hello when they came into the room, all too busy chatting to show any interest in this morning's 'keynote speaker'. Suddenly this event no longer felt like a great idea. Me, a middle-aged white man in a two-piece suit, standing in front of an audience consisting entirely of 14-year-old schoolgirls from British-Asian families.

Forty-five minutes later they were standing in a circle, bombarding me with questions and asking how they could get a job in Formula One. I had taken them on a journey, starting with cricket and football, sports that they and their families loved, through to Formula One, introducing them to the variety of roles that go into making a team competing in the World Championship.

Designers, engineers and mechanics working alongside colleagues in marketing, finance and hospitality, factory-based roles ensuring the cars are built on time, through to travelling roles in the race team. One girl told me she loved to cook, but had no idea that a racing team employed chefs, while another said she was really good at maths but could not see how that would lead to a real job 'earning decent money'.

For the Formula One industry the role of education is not only simply to inspire students into studying the right subjects but showing them what is possible. So few students are aware of the range of roles that exist in a modern organization, and as technology companies Formula One teams offer an extraordinarily rich opportunity for talented young people, irrespective of gender, ethnicity or people with disabilities.

David Coulthard's media production company, Whisper Films, has a 50/50 balance between men and women in its 120-strong workforce, and a number of staff have physical disabilities. As a former Formula One driver, President of the British Racing Drivers Club and Chairman of W Series, Coulthard has become a strong advocate of diversity and inclusion in the broadest sense.

'Our journey through diversity and inclusion has been one of the best experiences of my career', he says. 'Having grown up and raced in the male-dominated environment of motorsport in the 1980s and 1990s, it is refreshing to see how strong our teams are because we have a balance, men and women from a wide range of backgrounds working together, bringing the best of themselves into the team. We are interested in talent, irrespective of that person's sex or ethnicity, and the team dynamic is made far richer by virtue of having such diversity. It also helps us to ensure that our creativity matches the interests of the audiences we serve. In that respect it plays very directly to our strengths as a business.'

Lessons in diversity and inclusion

Change demands leadership and vision
Lewis Hamilton is driving change in Formula One, being not only the first black driver but also the statistically most successful in the sport's history. He has been able to take a stand against racial inequality, galvanizing the sport and leading initiatives.

ACTIONS ARE MORE IMPORTANT THAN OPTICS
The Mercedes-Benz Formula One team changed its livery colours as a mark of support for Lewis Hamilton's campaigning, but its action in partnering with the Mulberry Schools Trust promotes opportunity irrespective of gender, race or socio-economic background.

INITIATIVES DEMAND TOP-DOWN SUPPORT
FIA Girls on Track promotes gender diversity across all roles and functions within motorsport. It is sanctioned by the president and – through its Rising Stars programme – supported at the highest levels by Scuderia Ferrari.

CONSIDER DISRUPTING THE SYSTEM
W Series was founded to disrupt a motorsport system that, in the opinion of its founders, was failing to create a pipeline of female talent. Its use of positive discrimination is geared towards addressing a fundamental imbalance in opportunity for female drivers.

EDUCATION IS KEY TO INSPIRING TALENT AND PROMOTING OPPORTUNITY
Through programmes such as Formula Student and F1 in Schools the motorsport industry is benefitting from introducing school children, young adults and undergraduates to the opportunities that exist within the industry.

BUSINESSES SHOULD REFLECT THE SOCIETY THEY SERVE
As a successful entrepreneur David Coulthard's experience is that teams are made stronger by employing talent irrespective of gender, race, sexual orientation or disability.

Notes

1 FIA (2020) FIA Statement on Racism and Inequality, 5 June 2020, https://www.fia.org/resources/fia-statement-racism-and-inequality (archived at https://perma.cc/ZG87-BKTR)

2 Formula 1 (2020) Formula 1 Launches #WeRceAsOne Initiative to Fight Challenges of Covid-19 and Global Inequality, https://corp.formula1.com/formula-1-launches-weraceasone-initiative-to-fight-challenges-of-covid-19-and-global-inequality/ (archived at https://perma.cc/S8T6-HR4Y)

3 Mercedes AMG Formula One (2020) Silver Arrows Return to Racing With Renewed Purpose, https://www.mercedesamgf1.com/en/news/2020/06/silver-arrows-return-racing-renewed-purpose/ (archived at https://perma.cc/JA2T-AHMN)

4 Hamilton, L (2020) lewishamilton, *Instagram*, https://www.instagram.com/p/CBEXRiXA9Xj/ (archived at https://perma.cc/K94C-L5DP)

5 Mercedes AMG Formula One (2021) Mulberry and Mercedes Host First STEM Academy Event, https://www.mercedesamgf1.com/en/news/2021/02/mulberry-mercedes-first-stem-academy-event/ (archived at https://perma.cc/F6WZ-AD3P)

6 Fearnley, P (2015) Lella Lombardi: She Made Her Point, *Motorsport Magazine*, https://www.motorsportmagazine.com/archive/article/april-2015/110/she-made-her-point (archived at https://perma.cc/UTF2-U9YN)

7 Eve, J (2006) Maria Teresa de Filippis, *The Observer* https://www.theguardian.com/observer/osm/story/0,,1720870,00.html (archived at https://perma.cc/NA26-DYYQ)

8 Critchley, M (2016) Bernie Ecclestone Risks Fresh Sexism Storm With Claim Female F1 Drivers 'Would Not Be Taken Seriously', *The Independent*, https://www.independent.co.uk/sport/motor-racing/bernie-ecclestone-risks-fresh-sexism-storm-claiming-female-f1-drivers-would-not-be-taken-seriously-a6992926.html (archived at https://perma.cc/7HDB-UXYT)

9 ESPN (2005) F1 CEO Compares Women To 'Domestic Appliances', https://www.espn.co.uk/racing/news/story?series=irl&id=2089257 (archived at https://perma.cc/KP8F-Y5JM)

10 Gow, J (2013) Women in F1, *BBC Radio 5*, https://www.bbc.co.uk/programmes/b01s77h0 (archived at https://perma.cc/E6LB-X38L)

11 Guardian (2013) Sir Stirling Moss: Women Lack the Mental Aptitude to Compete in F1, *The Guardian*, https://www.theguardian.com/sport/2013/apr/15/sir-stirling-moss-women-f1 (archived at https://perma.cc/5GFF-C97T)

12 Hunston, H (1982) Women Drivers Out to Beat the World, *The Glasgow Herald*, https://news.google.com/newspapers?id=yvc9AAAAIBAJ&sjid=LEkMAAAAIBAJ&pg=3914,5843531&dq=mouton&hl=en (archived at https://perma.cc/Y76F-U7UW)

13 Esler, W (2016) Susie Wolff's Dare To Be Different Aims for More Females in Motorsport, *Sky Sports*, https://www.skysports.com/f1/news/12433/10129679/susie-wolffs-dare-to-be-different-aims-for-more-females-in-motorsport (archived at https://perma.cc/RQ3C-PWTR)

14 Chadwick, J (2021) BlackBook Motorsport Virtual Summit, Using Your Platform for Positive Change, *BlackBook Motorsport*, https://app.livestorm.co/blackbook-motorsport/bbm-virtual-summit-1400-gmt-the-impossible-task-how-f1-pulled-a-calendar-together-during-a-crisis (archived at https://perma.cc/KYQ9-U8XJ)

CHAPTER FIVE

Teamwork – the pit stop

Considering the millions of dollars spent on designing, manufacturing and developing a modern Formula One car it can appear paradoxical that one of the most important parts of a Grand Prix comes when the car is stationary. Pit stops are mandatory, and a pivotal moment in each race.

It is unsurprising that pit stops have come to be regarded as an example of high-performance teamwork. It requires a collective effort while under constant scrutiny to perform – a carefully choreographed process, backed up by relentless training. Everyone who takes part also knows that the team's performance can easily be compromised. The stop will last as long as the slowest member of the team.

At the 2019 Brazilian Grand Prix Max Verstappen's Red Bull came into the pits on lap 21. In just 1.82 seconds the Red Bull Racing pit crew had his car fitted with a set of brand-new tyres, the front wing adjusted and sent on its way. He won the Grand Prix, and his team had set a new world record for teamwork.

For two seconds the car sits at rest, the driver composed within their cockpit, while up to 23 mechanics and technicians set to work. In just two seconds they have to deliver a world-class performance: complete a pit stop during which all four wheels and tyres are changed, and the aerodynamics of the car adjusted.

The modern era of pit stops began in 1982 when the Brabham Formula One team under technical boss Gordon Murray decided to use pit stops in order to optimize race strategy. Starting their cars on low fuel loads meant they were potentially much faster than the opposition, and a mid-race stop to refuel also allowed them to fit new tyres. Those first stops took up to half a minute.

Today, in two seconds, each member of a Formula One pit crew does something remarkable. These men and women know precisely what is expected of them. They also know their performance is critical. They have a set of processes to follow using bespoke equipment, and they have trained hard to ensure the performance is consistent. You really don't want to be the mechanic who drops the wheel nut and watches as it rolls across the pit lane, or fumbles with the wheel gun while trying to remove the wheel – with your colleagues looking on.

Consider the task facing them. Two mechanics are required to operate the front and rear jacks, and in case of any issues with the complex, quick-release jacks they are typically supported by two backup crew. The front jack mechanic is standing in the pit lane waiting for the Formula One driver to stop precisely at the required point: effectively at the jack mechanic's feet. This is not a job for the faint hearted, as we have seen accidents in the past. The front jack mechanic then slides the jack under the centre of the front wing, engages it positively and levers the car into the air. Having watched as colleagues perform their tasks, stepping back and raising their hands when finished, the front jack mechanic must drop the car back on to the ground. Stepping out of the way by pivoting the jack, the mechanic then removes it from under the car.

The rear jack is engaged as soon as the car is stopped and, since the operator has to wait for the car to enter the pit stop box, comes a fraction of a second after the front jack has been engaged. The rear of the car carries most of the weight, including the engine and gearbox. With it being levered into the air the two rear wheels, larger and heavier than the fronts, can be slipped off and replaced. Again the rear jack operator has to wait until the rear wheels have been fully located on their hubs, the crew moving back, before dropping the car to the ground. For the rear jack mechanic there is the added complication that the rear wheels are used to transfer the 1,000 bhp produced by the engine to the track, so it is vital that the wheels are back on the ground before the driver drops the clutch and wheel-spins into the pit lane.

Then we turn to the two personnel whose job it is to stabilize the car which, balanced on centrally mounted jacks front and rear, can be in danger of rocking on either side. They step forward, grabbing the central roll hoop, clearing any debris from radiators and watching as their colleagues change the wheels.

Each wheel requires three personnel. First comes the wheel gun operator, whose job it is to locate the powerful pneumatic gun on to the wheel nut. This has to be drilled off the threaded spline on the hub to enable the wheel to be removed, and then reattached and driven home into a locked position once the new wheel has been placed on the car. A spare wheel gun sits behind the operator in case of problems.

Engaging the gun, with its pneumatic line running towards the overhead gantry, is by no means straightforward; you need to engage smoothly and squarely and press it fully home. The movement has to be very accurate, and wheel gun operators extend the gun towards the wheel centre as the car comes into position. This sweeping motion allows them to prepare and align prior to the car coming to a halt.

As they do this, the second member of the wheel crew has to step forward, pulling the wheel off the car in one seamless manoeuvre and out of harm's way. Ideally the crew member will take hold of the wheel in the very moment it stops rotating. The tyre is hot, its surface of molten rubber at over 100 degrees C, while the wheel itself has been heated by the 800-degree brakes.

The third crew member now has the task of placing the new wheel and tyre onto the hub, locating the wheel so that the wheel gun operator can set to work and redrill the nut on to the hub. Locating the wheel squarely on the hub, considering the all-up weight of the cumbersome wheel and tyre comes to 9 kilograms, is never an easy task. Any error in locating the wheel can result in having to make a second attempt.

For each wheel the three crew members have four tasks to perform in around two seconds: wheel nut off, old wheel off, new wheel on, wheel nut on. That works out at 0.4–0.5 seconds per task. This is split-second teamwork in action. When you multiply that operation by four, you have 12 personnel each facing the same extraordinary challenge. For those working in the most competitive teams in Formula One, they fulfil their task with the added pressure that their performance really does make the difference between winning and losing.

At the front of the car we have two crew members responsible for stabilizing the front wing, clearing any debris from between wing elements and making small aerodynamic adjustments. This is carried out by means of quick-adjuster mechanisms that allow for the angle of the wing to be increased or decreased.

Another colleague carries out the same task on the rear wing, cleaning the elements and sometimes removing a Gurney flap, a thin strip of material attached to the trailing edge of the wing. This can be used to trim the aerodynamic balance of the car.

Once every member of the crew has completed their task and the jacks drop the car back on to the ground, the crew chief flicks the traffic-light signal to green, the signal for the driver to return to the track. This is not the final task, however, for a colleague monitors the pit lane to ensure the fast lane is clear. This person can ultimately hold the traffic light on red until safety is assured. It requires a steady nerve.

The traffic-light system replaced the previous 'lollipop' means of signalling the driver. This used to involve the crew chief holding a long pole with a 'Stop' sign on the end, which he would lower in front of the car, then turn to reveal a '1st Gear' sign. Finally, he would raise it when the pit stop was finished. It was a cumbersome system, and prone to error, hence the adoption of simple red and green traffic lights.

The pit crew's two-second window to carry out a 'normal' pit stop can turn into something much more complex if the car has sustained damage or a technical failure that requires more than the four wheels to be replaced and the wings adjusted. A damaged nose section, which includes the front wing and its protruding wing endplates, is a frequent occurrence, and teams plan accordingly. A significant structural component accounting for around 20 per cent of the car's structure, the nose sections come equipped with a quick-release mechanism. This enables the crew to change them in around 12 seconds. In some respects this is even more impressive than the achievement of changing four wheels in three seconds. It increases the number of personnel working on the car and involves additional processes, including jacking up the car from the side whilst the front-wing jacking point is replaced.

There can be other reasons for lengthy pit stops. It is also not uncommon to see the steering wheel replaced if the team suspects that its electronics have developed a fault, whether through component failure or rainwater getting into the system. Open cockpits packed with electronics can lead to problems when faced with heavy rain.

In 2012 much comment was made when Lewis Hamilton drove his McLaren to a strong fourth-place finish in the Indian Grand Prix in spite of a pit stop for all five wheels: four new tyres and a new steering wheel. The speed of that change was 3.1 seconds. While the four wheels and tyres were being replaced Hamilton disengaged the steering wheel using its quick-release mechanism while a mechanic slid the new wheel into place. Hamilton was able to flick the car into gear instantly, ready for the off.

While the performance of the personnel working in the pit lane is the primary focus of attention during pit stops, the driver has a pivotal role to play. They are the part of the pit crew.

Drivers have to deliver the team's race strategy, including conserving their tyres and fuel and ensuring they drive their car to its optimal position in the race. Naturally their starting position determines the degree to which they may be helped or hindered by traffic during the race, and becoming trapped behind a slower car can play havoc with the best-laid plans.

Weather is another variable that has to be taken into consideration, for a fundamental change in conditions will again necessitate a strategy rethink. Then there is the competition. Using analytical tools we can simulate our race and model what the competition's strategy might be. But we have to allow for the fact that a clever or unexpected move on their part might necessitate an instant response. Flexibility is vital. From the moment the race starts the best strategies are the ones that can adapt to circumstances, particularly since no strategy can predict the opposition's tactics with 100 per cent accuracy.

Good two-way communication with drivers is essential, for although they are driving the car they are by no means in possession of the full picture – in fact, quite the opposite. Looking out of the narrow visor of their race helmet they can see relatively little apart from the information on the steering wheel read-outs, a few hundred metres of tarmac directly ahead, and fleeting glimpses of the car behind in the tiny, vibrating wing mirrors situated on either side of the cockpit. Faced with a paucity of information about how the race is playing out, drivers are heavily reliant on their race engineer supported by data analysts and strategists to advise them as to what is happening: to their car, the competition and the big picture of how the race is unfolding.

Once a pit stop is called and drivers know they are going to be making a stop, they start working through a procedure. It starts with them making sure to drive a good 'in' lap. The drivers will push hard on the 'in' lap to ensure that they maintain maximum performance over the first and second parts of the three-sector lap, knowing that in the third sector they will lose time when they peel into the pit lane. They are typically reminded by their engineers to 'push' over this all-important 'in' lap.

Driving into the narrow, often twisty, pit lane entrance, drivers have to maintain performance, because they do not have to achieve the pit lane speed limit of 80 kph until they reach a designated line within the pit lane itself. Driving the initial part of the pit lane as though it is a continuation of the race track is essential in order to minimize lost time. Although the team knows the car's position on the track, and can see from the data its reduced speed as it enters the pit lane, a backup procedure of having drivers radio a short 'I am in the pit lane' message also prepares the team for what is to come, particularly if a stop has been hastily rescheduled in reaction to some unforeseen event.

Once in sight of the pit lane speed-limit zone, drivers have to be ready to brake hard, engage the pit lane speed limiter by using a button on the steering wheel, and then motor down the pit lane to the correct 'box' where the pit crew will be waiting. It is important for drivers to ensure they are within the 80 kph speed limit. One of the reasons drivers can incur speeding penalties is the failure to be under the 80 kph limit before hitting the limiter.

The crew will have been advised by their team manager that the pit stop is about to happen. They will not rush into the pit lane immediately, thereby giving the competition additional information about their strategy plans, but wait until they hear over the pit crew radio channel that the driver is now in sector three and about to come into the pit lane. The crew now know they have 20 to 30 seconds to prepare for the pit stop.

Obviously drivers should know precisely where their pit stop box is located in the pit lane. After all, they will have driven the car in during three practice sessions and qualifying. However, the pit lane can become confusing to drivers during pit stops, particularly with the 10 pit crews and their equipment blocking the normal line of sight. For this reason the teams will have a set of visual aids that drivers will look out for.

At the 2013 Malaysian Grand Prix the importance of the driver's role within the pit stop process was brought sharply into focus when Lewis Hamilton forgot that he was now driving for the Mercedes-Benz team and steered his car perfectly into the McLaren team's pit stop box. They had been stationed in the pit lane waiting for their driver, but Hamilton saw them and appeared to forget that he had changed teams the previous winter. Cue much amusement, but some significant embarrassment for Hamilton.

To assist drivers in locating their team's pit box a member of the crew will stand on the pit wall, often the driver's own pit board operator, and hold an arrow or marker board out into the fast lane of the pit lane to remind of the pit box location. The team itself will have designed both the pit lane gantry and colouration of the markers on the pit lane surface to provide further visual guidance.

Once they have found their box, drivers have to swing the car into location, taking care to avoid the pit box of the competitor immediately adjacent to their own pit garage, and ensure that they line the car up straight and squarely to stop 'on the marks'. These 'marks' are the lines marked on the pit lane surface. Using tape or paint, these illustrate precisely where all four wheels should stop and the front wing line up so as to match the body positioning of the front jack man and the wheel gun operators.

A few centimetres either way can make all the difference, adding tenths of a second to the commencement of the wheel change. To aid post-race analysis the marks are calibrated in 5–10 centimetre increments, enabling the team to review how accurately the driver positioned the car. Should a driver stop 40–50 centimetres before or after the centreline marks, the entire pit crew will need to shuffle that distance in order to carry out the stop. To further aid the driver in lining up the front wheels, two members of the crew will often have signs or marker boards to give the driver precise aiming points.

Judging the car's braking to be inch-perfect is part of a driver's skill set, and the team will have practised stopping 'on the marks' throughout practice. Since the pit stop boxes often feature a combination of tarmac and cement surfaces, the drivers need to be sure of the level of grip available. It is for that reason we see drivers asked to perform a fast pull-away during practice, spinning the rear tyres within the pit box where they must make their stop during Sunday's race. This wheel-spinning burnout helps to layer as much rubber as possible on this vital few metres of pit lane.

Once the car is halted, correctly positioned in its box, then and only then can the pit crew swing into action. The clock is ticking.

It is all too easy to get it wrong, and over the years we've seen pretty well every combination of how not to do it: wheels not ready when the driver comes into the pits; the wrong set of tyres prepared or still in their tyre-warmers; jacks misaligned and requiring a second or third attempt to jack up the car; a driver unable to stop 'on the marks'; drivers missing their pit box entirely or stopping at the wrong team.

At the 2011 Chinese Grand Prix Jenson Button relinquished the lead of the race when he was distracted after flicking the wrong button on his steering wheel and accidentally steered his McLaren into Red Bull Racing's pit box. It was a mistake his team boss Martin Whitmarsh called 'fairly disastrous'.

Then you have the really serious mistakes, with cars released from the pits before the crew have completed their task, always dangerous and never more so than when F1 pit stops include refuelling. A car accelerating with the fuel rig still attached can lead not only to a fire but to physical injuries suffered by crew from flailing lines. Refuelling rigs have been pulled out of position and we have even seen refuelling lines ripped away from the gantry entirely.

Then there are the moments when the wheels have not been reattached correctly, as with Nigel Mansell's Williams in Portugal in 1991. I recall having to jump out of the way as his right rear wheel bounced towards the Jordan garage, ending his race in ignominious fashion. It turned out to be a pivotal moment in that year's championship.

What can be more damaging to the reputation of a world-class team than the wheel literally falling off the car? And all because of a failure of team-work and process. If the wheel nut hasn't been put on the car properly, there is no point in the car being released, and yet this is what we have seen happen on so many occasions. In the case of Mansell's race in Portugal, one of the tyre operators on the wheel had indicated to the team manager that their 'wheel' was fine by raising an arm, when in fact a colleague was still trying to drill home the wheel nut. The process was not adhered to, and the result was terminal.

It can also be comical. In the early 1990s I recall one of the smaller F1 teams in the next garage to ours, its crew looking panic-stricken as their car came in for an unscheduled pit stop. As one of the rear-tyre operators pulled the wheel from the car he flung it over his shoulder into the path of the new wheels that were being rushed from the back of the garage. Sure enough, one of his colleagues got rather confused and put the old wheel back on the car. Cue the sight of a car with three new tyres, one very old one, behaving like a table with one leg shorter than the others.

The point is: pit stops require perfect teamwork in order for the team to have any chance of success. Get it right, and it can give you a competitive edge, even if usually no one notices. Get it wrong, and the results can be a failure that is public and embarrassing. Get it badly wrong, and someone could be injured or worse. It is not a job in which you can hide your mistakes.

When I started Status Grand Prix I recall one of our excellent mechanics being unable to execute a pit stop properly, and not for want of trying. He simply couldn't do it consistently, and the more frustrated he became the worse things got.

His task was to act as wheel gun operator and, although he was physically strong, the reality was that he wasn't placing the gun on to the hub squarely enough. This was causing the gun to spin off or, worse, jam the nut on the splines. As the physical errors mounted, the psychological effect became evident as he could see that all eyes were on him. His composure disappeared, and his focus drained away as he rushed to do the job.

'Less haste, more speed' or 'Slow down to speed up' are common phrases. As a team we found that the more you got the crew to relax and focus on their tasks, practising over and over again, the faster they became. In the end our team became among the very best at pit stops. Indeed it was a perfectly executed stop that brought us our maiden win in the A1GP World Cup of Motorsport in Mexico City in March 2008.

At Jordan Grand Prix I witnessed our dedicated crew raise their game steadily, aiming to match the very best teams in the world – at that time Ferrari, Williams and McLaren. Between 1991 and 1997, when we had been the young pretenders, a pit stop mishap might have cost us a points position – a top-six finish. By 1998, however, we had recruited Damon Hill, the former world champion, tasked with helping us to make the break-through into the winner's circle. Partnered by Ralf Schumacher, we had a strong driver line-up, but the question remained as to whether we had a team capable of beating the best in the world.

As Damon Hill pointed out, our Jordan 198 was basically a good car, with a strong engine and plenty of potential. It wasn't a McLaren and Ferrari beater in a straight fight every weekend, but on the right day it could challenge them. This was when the pit stops would need to go from being good to great. In the event that Hill could somehow manage to position himself in front of McLarens driven by Mika Häkkinen and David Coulthard, or the Ferraris of Michael Schumacher and Eddie Irvine, the Jordan crew would need to produce a pit stop performance every bit as good or better than these champion teams.

The right day came, and with it came faultless teamwork, including four pit stops for Damon Hill and Ralf Schumacher during a 1998 Belgian Grand Prix affected by torrential rain.

Fans and media remember our famous 1–2 victory in that race, the first-ever maiden 1–2 by a team in Formula One history. They remember it for the dramatic start-line accident, the restart and a subsequent collision between Michael Schumacher's Ferrari and David Coulthard's McLaren, which sent the German into a rage. It is also recalled for the team orders voiced by Eddie Jordan over our radio system requiring Ralf Schumacher to hold station behind Hill in the closing stages of the race.

But I remember that weekend for two things: the first was a formidable performance by Hill in qualifying, which saw him outperform Michael

Schumacher over the same lap, the cars split by a few hundred metres. The second was our pit crew, delivering those perfect performances on a day when they were faced with the pressure of helping deliver a race victory.

Formula One's official logistics supplier DHL has sponsored the Fastest Pit Stop Award since 2015. Ferrari won the inaugural award, with seven fastest pit stops across the season and a best time of 2.2 seconds. Williams won in 2016, its crew achieving a record-equalling best of 1.92 seconds in Azerbaijan. Mercedes won the accolade in 2017, but since then Red Bull Racing have upped the ante, with speed and consistency winning the award for three years in succession.

With pit stop refuelling banned after 2009, it was evident that Formula One's pit stops were about to become much faster. The limiting factor had always been the length of time it took to refuel the cars, for the FIA-regulated refuelling rigs delivered fuel at the rate of 10 litres per second. With the average stop requiring 55–60 litres of fuel, the context within which the stop had to be made was six seconds, even if the wheels could be replaced in less time.

Looking back, the wheel operators could effectively take their time, as a five-second wheel change set against a six-second refuelling window meant it was fast enough. With refuelling banned, however, suddenly it was the wheels that became the focus along with the realization that there was a new battle to be won.

Soon after the ban was introduced I recall analysing a three-second pit stop executed by the Ferrari team in the Korean Grand Prix in 2011. By then the top teams had found a number of ways to reduce the stop time. It came down to people, process and technology; all three were examined and revised and changes implemented.

Fast pit stops are all about marginal gains. Take the front jack, for example. The front jack operator not only has to stand in the pit lane and wait for the car to arrive at their feet, but on completing the stop must disengage the jack from the car and then step out of the way to avoid being run over. Ferrari's elegant solution was to have the jack redesigned in such a way that, once the car had been jacked up, the operator could move out of the way by swivelling the handle and then use a quick-release trigger to drop the car on to the ground before pulling the jack out of the way. This small change meant that the stop became faster whilst also reducing risk.

Another aspect of the stop was the way in which the Ferrari mechanics engaged very directly on to the car, trusting the driver to stop on the marks, and how their training meant that the three-second process became one seamless movement. The front wings were trimmed using the quick adjusters, which required a simple click up or down depending on the wing angle required. The Gurney flap on the rear wing was removed entirely during the stop; the need to reduce downforce had been condensed into a neatly designed rip-off strip.

With three-second stops now standard it was interesting to see the targets shifting even higher in 2012. McLaren tasked newly signed operations director Sam Michael with helping them to break into the two-second bracket. During the first half of the season we witnessed several issues with the McLaren pit stops, but as with many step-changes in performance you cannot expect everything to go smoothly. Change is never easy, and in the arena of Formula One mistakes are not only very costly but extremely public.

At the German Grand Prix, however, everything clicked perfectly into place, Jenson Button's McLaren benefitting from a 2.3-second pit stop en route to a second-placed finish. McLaren's target was a sub-three-second pit stop every time, and the times were dropping inexorably towards the magical two-second marker.

Red Bull Racing, not content with dominating Formula One in terms of race victories and championship titles between 2010 and 2013, decided to redouble its efforts to regain the high ground in the pit-stop battle in 2013. This is a typical behaviour among winning teams. They are never satisfied until they are number one in every area of operation.

Just as Ferrari and McLaren examined every detail of the human performance, process and technology used within a pit stop, Red Bull Racing did the same during the winter of 2012–13. On lap nine of the second round of the 2013 season in Sepang, Malaysia, Mark Webber pitted from the lead. We witnessed his wheels being changed in an astonishing 2.05 seconds, a full quarter of a second faster than McLaren's record.

A replay of the stop shows that trust is such an important part of teamwork, the four mechanics responsible for removing the wheels grabbing hold of them as they complete their final rotation and the car comes to a halt. As they begin to pull at the wheel their colleagues responsible for the wheel nuts have already begun to drill them off. Reducing the number of turns required by the wheel nut to remove it from the hub has helped to speed up this task enormously. It also means that the nut can more easily relocate and spin back on.

Suddenly two seconds was the new benchmark, making the three-second stops that we were admiring back in 2011 seem decidedly second-rate – a full 50 per cent slower!

For the balance of the 2013 season Red Bull Racing, McLaren and Ferrari continued with their average stops around three seconds and their best-in-class stops in the mid-to-low two-seconds bracket. Surely this was the moment of peak performance for Formula One pit stops?

Red Bull Racing did not think so; not satisfied with their world record performance in Malaysia back in March, nor even in winning their fourth consecutive World Championships for Drivers and Constructors, the team achieved a 1.923-second stop for Mark Webber on lap 28 of the 2013 United States Grand Prix. It was a record Williams would come to match in 2016, and it took Red Bull Racing seven years to knock a further one-tenth of a second off that time and claim the current record.

By constantly reviewing their performance and using the data from past pit stops to help deliver marginal gains, Formula One's teams never give up in the quest for improved performance. Their competitive spirit drives them on, together with the knowledge that every previous record has been beaten.

The teamwork, training and ambition to achieve new records is ingrained. It is only a matter of time before a new benchmark is established.

CHAPTER SIX

Formula One's safety revolution

Finishing ninth in a Grand Prix may not seem like much of a career highlight, but to finish in the top 10 in the 2014 Monaco Grand Prix, scoring two World Championship points, felt like victory for the Marussia Formula One team. After five years of hard work team bosses John Booth and Graeme Lowden were ecstatic, while Russian owner Andrei Cheglakov felt it was a breakthrough moment. They celebrated accordingly.

Their driver, Jules Bianchi, had driven brilliantly that day. A member of the Ferrari Driver Academy, he had been Ferrari's test and reserve driver as early as 2011. He was on a career trajectory that would almost certainly lead to him racing for the famous Italian team.

He had been a multiple champion in junior formulae and came from a family steeped in racing. His grandfather Mauro had been a racing driver in the 1960s, and his great uncle Lucien had raced in Formula One and won the 1968 Le Mans 24 Hours. Lucien's career was cut short by a fatal motor-racing accident, the kind that happened all too often in those days.

Little could anyone have known that afternoon in Monaco that Jules was destined to meet the same fate just months later. Suffering a severe head trauma as the result of an accident at the Japanese Grand Prix in October 2014, he would remain in a coma for nine months before succumbing to his injuries. He passed away in his home town of Nice, not far from the scene of his triumph in Monaco a year earlier.

His death shocked the world of Formula One, prompting an outpouring of tributes and much soul searching. He was the first driver to be killed during a Grand Prix since Ayrton Senna's tragic accident in Imola 1994, and it brought to an end a 20-year hiatus in driver fatalities.

It came as a stark reminder that Formula One remains a dangerous sport, and that although the risks have been mitigated through advances in technology, together with improvements to safety systems and processes, risk has not been eliminated.

As is often the case with catastrophic accidents, Bianchi's death was the culmination of a series of decisions and occurrences that compounded the risk. A sequence of events breached the defences that had kept Formula One safe for two decades.

A powerful tropical cyclone, Typhoon Phanfone, hit Japan that weekend, bringing torrential rain, wind, low cloud and poor visibility to the Suzuka circuit. The race started behind the safety car and was then halted for 20 minutes to allow conditions to improve. With the October afternoon light already beginning to fade the race finally got under way, drivers struggling to cope with a wet, then drying circuit.

On lap 42 Adrian Sutil's Sauber went off the track at the Dunlop Curve, marshals rushing to the scene and calling for a crane to assist them in lifting the car to a safe location. As a result that section of the track was subject to waved double yellow flags, a signal to drivers that means you must reduce speed, not overtake and be prepared to change direction or stop.

On the following lap Bianchi arrived on the scene but did not slow sufficiently, leaving the track at the same point, his car submarining beneath the crane. His helmet, unprotected in the open cockpit, struck the crane, causing the major head trauma that would ultimately take his life.

A 10-person accident panel headed by the president of the FIA Safety Commission, Peter Wright, presented a 396 report on the accident to the World Motor Sport Council two months later. Their conclusions included the fact that a river of water running across the drying track had played a role in both drivers losing control and that Bianchi had not slowed down enough considering that double yellow flags were being waved.

They also found that his car's brake-by-wire system had not allowed a fail-safe system to operate, whereby Bianchi's application of both the brake and throttle meant that the car was continuing to try to accelerate as well as brake. This meant that the impact speed was high, 78 mph (126 kph). The energy generated by the 700-kilogramme car hitting a 6-tonne crane had catastrophic consequences.

A series of recommendations were made to improve signalling, revise driver training, improve drainage and ensure that all Grands Prix take place within a four-hour period so as to avoid running into dusk.

The most important learning was the reminder that safety is never assured, that complacency is our biggest enemy and the quest to eliminate injuries and fatalities never ends. Bianchi, still at the beginning of his career, perished in a sport that many had thought to be no longer dangerous.

Risk waits for us to drop our guard.

The car behind us was clearly anxious to overtake. My driver, Keith Wiggins, owner of the fledgling Pacific Grand Prix team, was in no mood to let him past. We sped up. Our car, a Honda, leapt forward, but our pursuer remained fixed to its tail, matching each manoeuvre, trying to find a gap to pass. It was no easy task. The road into the Autopolis circuit in Japan was a single track, winding its way through the low hills, neatly terraced crop fields either side, smoke rising from the rural homes dotting the landscape.

We were there for the Pacific Grand Prix, so named because the owner of Autopolis had convinced Bernie Ecclestone to grant him a race even though the well-established Japanese Grand Prix at Suzuka was also on that year's calendar. Never one to miss an opportunity, Bernie had elected to grant him his race, and given it the 'Pacific' title.

The eponymous race team was to be rather like the race: one man's dream, short-lived and soon to become a distant, unloved memory. But on this morning, with 'Wiggy' anxious to get to the track and see his cars – driven by Bertrand Gachot and Paul Belmondo – take part in practice, the mood was light. He was not about to let the driver behind beat us to the track.

As we entered the circuit the guards checked our passes and directed us into the car park marked 'Formula One Team Personnel'. The driver behind tried to follow but the attendants blocked his path, directing him into the waterlogged and pot-holed overflow car park. We had taken the last available slot.

When, a few minutes later, the door to our paddock office burst open to reveal the driver of the car we had beaten to the last parking place, we knew he was angry. He was shouting, remonstrating with us for daring to block him and, worse, take the final parking spot. What was surprising was his identity. Ayrton Senna, three-times Formula One world champion, was not a happy man.

I had seen an Ayrton Senna angry before, also in Japan, when he had railed against the FIA president, Jean-Marie Balestre, in the post-race press conference at Suzuka in 1991. Unhappy about his treatment by the FIA at the 1989 and 1990 title-deciding races at the same circuit, he had not held back.

He was at it again, asking Wiggy what the hell he was doing blocking him on the way into the circuit. We looked at each other, Wiggy beginning to formulate an explanation before we noticed something change in Senna's demeanour; he was smiling, then laughing. He wasn't angry at all. This was one of his little jokes – he had thoroughly enjoyed the 'race' into the track.

We chatted for a few minutes, Ayrton asking us how things were going with the team. He offered to come and meet any potential sponsors we had in order to endorse our efforts. He had known Wiggy for a dozen years since he had been one of Senna's mechanics in the Rushen Green Formula Ford 2000 team back in 1982. The young Brazilian had been living near Snetterton Circuit in Norfolk, having become good friends with Ralph Firman, owner of the Van Diemen racing-car business, and he knew all the local racers well. For him, Wiggy was part of his enjoyable early years in racing.

To have Ayrton Senna offering to provide a helping hand, to endorse the efforts of the underfunded Pacific team, was remarkable. It was an insight into the nature of a man who could give no quarter while racing, yet be among the most sensitive and compassionate when outside of the cockpit.

Two weeks and two days later Ayrton Senna was dead, killed in a 190 mph accident when his Williams-Renault FW16 speared off the track and into the wall whilst leading the San Marino Grand Prix at Imola. Formula One had lost its superstar.

Senna lost his life in front of a live television audience estimated at 115 million. He was the only multiple world champion still racing in Formula One at that time and arguably the greatest natural talent of his generation. He was killed in an accident that would not only change the sport, but contribute to far-reaching changes in car safety design that reverberate to this day. What is more, he died the day after fellow competitor Roland Ratzenberger lost his life during qualifying.

For those of us who have made our career in professional motor racing, none will forget that weekend nor fail to wonder at its legacy. The deaths of Ratzenberger and Senna continue to influence the sport today, since it led to changes that meant no drivers lost their lives in the 20 years that followed. Considering that Senna was the 47th driver to have been killed at the wheel of a Formula One car since 1950, it could so easily have become just another tragic milestone. Instead, it marked a turning point in a business that finally determined safety should come above all else.

San Marino 1994 was Formula One's Lehman Brothers collapse, BP's Deepwater Horizon or Costa's Concordia. Risks were taken, processes incomplete, attention on other priorities; in each example the outcome was catastrophic. In the case of Formula One it generated a deep desire to ensure that such an occurrence would never be repeated.

The ability of the sport to react to this one death by setting out to eliminate Formula One driver fatalities stands as testimony to what can be achieved when people reset their priorities. Safety was elevated overnight, becoming the sport's primary focus from a regulatory and technical perspective. Everything would be done to provide the technology and support infrastructure required to ensure that those competing in this sport would have the physical risks mitigated as far as humanly possible.

The most important change was cultural, however. No amount of changes to technology, training or compliance was going to save lives if people did not practise placing safety at the centre of their decision making. The effect of the tragedies at Imola was that no one wanted to witness a repetition.

While Ratzenberger's death affected those who knew him, he was relatively unknown outside of motor-racing circles. The 1994 San Marino Grand Prix was only his third Formula One race.

By contrast, Senna's death made headline news around the world because of his fame. As a three-times world champion he was one of the sport's superstars. In analysing the Senna tragedy, it is sad to reflect on the fact that none of the 46 drivers to have died before him triggered the wide-ranging changes that needed to be made.

As one example, the Swiss driver Jo Siffert was killed in a non-championship event at Brands Hatch in 1971, his car failing as a result of accident damage. He died of smoke inhalation, none of the circuit's trackside fire extinguishers working correctly. This prompted a review of extinguishers, fireproof overall design and provision of oxygen supply to drivers. It was one of a multitude of accidents that resulted in changes, but it was often a case of too little too late.

Senna's accident led to a step-change due to his fame and notoriety, but also because his death came towards the end of a weekend already marred by tragedy. On the Friday the Imola circuit had witnessed Rubens Barrichello suffer a horrific accident when his Jordan was launched into the air by a kerb, clearing the safety barrier. It was only prevented from entering a public area by the presence of high-level debris fencing. The Brazilian suffered a concussion, swallowed his tongue and was fortunate to receive emergency treatment at the track prior to being airlifted to hospital.

The Saturday brought disaster in the form of the fatal accident involving Ratzenberger, driving for Simtek, during qualifying. The 34-year-old from Salzburg was a popular driver, enormously charismatic and talented. I had met him first in 1987 when he was competing in Formula 3 in the UK, but we got to know each other better still when he raced in the British Formula 3000 series in 1989, in which he finished third. Tall, good-looking, with an infectious smile and ready wit, Roland was at the beginning of a promising career. He had everything to live for.

As with so many Formula One hopefuls he was underfunded but worked hard to establish his career in the sport. In 1994 he had signed an initial five-race deal to drive for Simtek. This was his big chance and, although the car was not competitive, he was determined to prove himself. This determination to make the most of the opportunity may have contributed directly to his accident, for he had gone off the track on the previous lap, damaging the front wing. The usual protocol, universally understood, is to return to the pits after an off-track excursion in order to check for signs of damage.

On this occasion Ratzenberger elected to continue on to the next lap, pushing hard. On the fast section through and beyond Tamburello corner the front wing appeared to fail, sending the Simtek into the barriers at 195.68 mph (314.9 kph). Suffering a basal skull fracture and ruptured aorta, Ratzenberger died instantly. Television cameras broadcast images of his head lolling in the cockpit, the driver lifeless as the car slithered to a halt.

Naturally there was a horrified reaction to Ratzenberger's death, including from Ayrton Senna, a man whose compassion towards others had been noted before.

At the 1990 Spanish Grand Prix in Jerez, Northern Ireland's Martin Donnelly suffered a catastrophic accident while practising his Lotus. Catapulted from the disintegrating car, Donnelly's body lay on the track, his shattered legs bent at seemingly impossible angles. Senna was one of the first on the scene, and he was deeply affected by what he saw. Donnelly would recover from the worst of his injuries, but never race in Formula One again. There is no question that this accident played on Senna's mind, and now, in San Marino, the knowledge that Ratzenberger had lost his life seemed to have a profound effect on the Brazilian superstar.

The events of the next day have been well chronicled; another accident occurred at the race start when JJ Lehto's Scuderia Italia stalled on the grid and was hit from behind by Pedro Lamy's Lotus, sending a wheel high into the crowd, debris injuring eight spectators and a police officer. A safety car was deployed and the field, led by Senna, who started from pole position, circulated for five laps while the debris was cleared.

When the race got under way Senna pushed ahead to maintain and extend his lead over the coming man of Formula One, Michael Schumacher. Entering Tamburello on lap seven, Senna's Williams appeared to turn into the high-speed left-hander before stepping out of line, hopping on to a different trajectory, one that took him off the track at 190 mph (310 kph) and into the wall at 135 mph (218 kph). The impact was severe, the right front wheel slamming up and back towards the cockpit, suspension impacting on the former world champion's helmet, contributing to fatal injuries.

Senna's life and death can be witnessed in the award-winning documentary *Senna*, directed by Asif Kapadia and written by Manish Pandey. It is an extraordinary piece of filmmaking that provides deep insight into a driver who, 25 years later, is still revered as Formula One's benchmark talent.

I was not in San Marino on the day Senna met his end. Instead I was in Nice en route to a round of the World Rally Championship in Corsica. That night my wife and I headed to Monte Carlo for dinner, and as we wandered along the streets of the principality I pondered on how the world of Formula One would react to the day's events. I considered, too, how appropriate it was to be in Monaco, a venue Senna made his own, winning the Grand Prix six times and famously beating teammate Alain Prost to pole in 1988 by 1.4 seconds, an almost unheard-of margin around the shortest track in Formula One.

Some of the initial reactions to the deaths of Ratzenberger and Senna were both understandable and predictable. An outpouring of grief within the sport among fans worldwide, and for Senna at a national level in Brazil. He was given a state funeral, a crowd estimated at 3 million lining the route.

The Williams team found itself under scrutiny, with Italian prosecutors keen to apportion blame. Senior team figures including Frank Williams, Patrick Head and F1 design legend Adrian Newey found themselves at the centre of a protracted legal investigation that only ended in 2007. A team with a hugely impressive track record, who prided themselves on achieving success through world-class engineering, found themselves quite literally in the dock. They were forced to answer questions about their product design, the integrity of components such as the steering that was alleged to have broken, and their management's approach to safety.

Adrian Newey would later admit that the steering column, which was the focus of much of the accident investigation, had suffered fatigue cracks and was poorly engineered. The precise cause of the accident has never been determined.

Much as occurred on previous occasions, many in the sport expected the furore over Senna's death to subside over time. Had that happened, Formula One would have been no better than, and certainly no different from, the many human activities where safety issues rear their head from time to time but remain an 'accepted' fact. It becomes all too easy to say that accidents will happen and fatalities are inevitable in any high-risk arena.

On this occasion, things were different. Not least because the aftermath of San Marino included a serious accident involving Austria's Karl Wendlinger in Monaco just two weeks later. This helped spur the leadership of Formula One into taking action.

Wendlinger suffered a serious concussion when his Sauber crashed at the chicane that follows the famous Monaco tunnel. Although he would return the following season, he never returned to form, and few doubt that the Monaco shunt took a heavy toll.

For the sport's leadership, most notably Max Mosley as President of the FIA and Bernie Ecclestone as the CEO of Formula One, there was a sense of disbelief. Wendlinger's accident underlined the need for change, coming so soon after the San Marino tragedies. With their support a small group of engineers and experts were given the remit to change Formula One, providing a template to the world on how to address the fundamental question of safety management and risk mitigation.

For the next 20 years we were able to enjoy the benefits of their work and reflect on what had been achieved. How a culture can be changed, priorities reconfigured and the combined effort of an industry made to focus on ensuring that, whatever happened during a race, competitors would return safely to their families each evening.

In the wake of the Senna and Ratzenberger fatalities the FIA under Mosley set out to harness the brainpower of Formula One. To tap into its ability to deliver results focusing on a clear target – in this instance to eliminate fatal accidents, to 'innovate to zero' the likelihood of people losing their lives in the course of attending a Formula One event.

That Mosley was joined in his quest to revolutionize safety by Ecclestone was key. The sport had the benefit of both its regulator and commercial leader being fully aligned behind the team of people tasked with solving Formula One's safety challenges. This team included people such as Charlie

Whiting, Formula One's race director and safety delegate, and senior medical adviser Professor Sid Watkins. Supported by a range of able lieutenants and expert advisers, they were at the vanguard of the revolution that unfolded in the months, years and decades ahead.

Whiting's overarching role as technical delegate meant that he was already at the epicentre of creating the rules and regulations governing Formula One car design, so when safety was pushed to the forefront of the agenda he was able to effect the changes needed.

Watkins, a neurosurgeon at the Royal London Hospital, had worked in racing since the 1960s, including when he lived in Syracuse, New York, attending races at Watkins Glen. But it was in 1978 that he started a new role helping Ecclestone to improve the medical facilities at Formula One races, commencing at that year's Swedish Grand Prix. He personally witnessed the debacle surrounding the response to a serious accident at the Italian Grand Prix that would claim the life of Ronnie Peterson, a death that was entirely avoidable.

In the years that followed, Watkins worked tirelessly to ensure that rapid response teams were on hand at each Grand Prix. This included mandating the presence of air ambulances to transfer injured drivers to local trauma centres, which he personally checked in the days before each event. He made sure that the right skills were available: trauma specialists and anaesthetists instead of the nutritionists and psychologists who simply wanted to work at their local F1 event.

Watkins passed away in 2012, but part of his legacy is two excellent books, *Life at the Limit* and *Beyond the Limit*, which tell the story of his role in the safety revolution, starting with treating the effects of these awful accidents, but moving in the post-Senna era to injury prevention. Accidents in Formula One are inevitable, so the achievements of Whiting, Watkins and their associates have been to ensure that the drivers walk away while team personnel, media and spectators do not get caught up in the incidents when they occur.

It is Watkins who recalls how the FIA harnessed the expertise of Dr Harvey Postlethwaite, a noted Formula One designer, to review all the circuits used by Formula One. A total of 27 high-risk corners were identified, particularly those where lateral G-force exceeded a factor of 4. Through changes to car design regulations alone, slowing the cars by around three seconds per lap, the number of high-risk corners was reduced to 13, and these were then tackled by other means, including corner redesign and the implementation of improved safety systems.

This work had one aim. To end Formula One's catalogue of disasters.

The list is long, and some of the accidents so horrific that you can only wonder what today's rolling news channels would have made of them. Lorenzo Bandini died three days after suffering severe burns as the result of an accident in his Ferrari at the 1967 Monaco Grand Prix; a similarly fiery fate befell Roger Williamson at the 1973 Dutch Grand Prix. The film of Williamson's car, upside down, with ineffective fire marshalling and fellow driver David Purley desperately trying to tackle the blaze, is the stuff of nightmares. Tom Pryce, another great British hope, was killed at the South African Grand Prix when two marshals elected to run across the track. One, a 19-year-old volunteer named Frederik Jansen van Vuuren, was killed instantly when hit by Pryce's car. Van Vuuren's 18-kilogramme fire extinguisher then struck Pryce in the face, causing fatal injuries including partial decapitation.

Whilst every fatality was bitterly regretted, there was an acceptance that Formula One motor racing was dangerous. Loss of life was somehow inevitable.

I recall meeting the late Innes Ireland, a six-times Grand Prix winner in the 1950s and 1960s, and being regaled with stories from that era, including the occasion when he realized his Lotus had suffered a failure at 120 mph and was going off track. 'That got my attention, because there was a huge earth bank and wall in front of me and I didn't fancy hitting it', he said. 'So I stood up in the cockpit – we didn't wear seat belts in those days – and I simply jumped out at about 80 mph. Best decision I ever made; broke a few bones, you know, but the car was destroyed and that could have been my last day on earth.'

It was Ireland who was later credited with suggesting in 1979 that a medical car driven by a professional driver should follow the opening lap of each Formula One race, statistically the time when most accidents will occur.

In Ireland's era the cars were regarded as a death trap in certain accidents. Made of steel and aluminium, they often featured a cockpit located between the fuel tanks. Crashing in a bathtub of fuel was to be avoided. If the fuel didn't ignite then the car would concertina around the driver. Broken legs, head and chest injuries were common, internal injuries often the outcome.

Interviewing Stirling Moss in his Shepherd Market home in central London in 1987, I couldn't help but notice the mangled steering wheel of his Cooper car mounted on the wall of his office. This was the wheel that had buried itself against him in the accident that ended his professional motor-racing career at Goodwood in 1962, the nation watching and waiting in the days and weeks that followed to see if the sport's greatest hero would survive his injuries. Survive he did, but he would never race in the top flight again.

If death or permanent disablement was to be avoided, the simplest solution was to retire early, even if few had the luxury of being able to make that decision. One such was Jackie Stewart, three-times world champion, who stepped from his car during qualifying for the 1973 United States Grand Prix and called it a day. He had just witnessed the aftermath of the fatal accident that befell his teammate and close friend François Cevert, a prodigious talent with film-star looks, whose Tyrrell submarined under an Armco barrier, killing him instantly. For Stewart, who was personally able to count over 50 drivers killed during his career, it marked a watershed. He would never race again.

Stewart's decision came after years of lobbying for safety improvements. His pleas often fell on deaf ears and he was regularly criticized for his campaigns for mandatory seat belts, full-face helmets and improved race-track safety. He was a man ahead of his time.

The trajectory of a racing car in an accident is something that can be forecast. The angle of attack of a car veering off the track during an accident, whether as a result of a punctured tyre, hitting a kerb or a collision with another vehicle, can be predicted.

Circuits are now designed to have walls as far away from the track as possible. Where this is impossible for reasons of topography and track boundaries, the likely impact points are designed to ensure that the car will hit at as acute an angle as possible rather than head-on. Another key objective has been to ensure that the cars slow down as much as possible to reduce the energy involved in an impact.

Among the early initiatives to de-risk accidents was the introduction of catch fencing, sand and gravel traps. These initiatives brought their own problems, however. Catch fencing involved wire mesh strung between poles imbedded in soft ground, the idea being that the cars would become caught, bringing them to a controlled halt. It was counterproductive as the netting trapped drivers and made extraction more difficult, while the catch fencing poles could cause injury.

Gravel traps became popular during the 1970s and 1980s but, while they slowed cars down, lateral impacts with the gravel often resulted in cars being overturned. This happened to Ayrton Senna at the 1991 Mexican

Grand Prix when, in the long fast Peraltada Parabolica, the Brazilian lost control of his McLaren which spun backwards into the gravel trap and flipped upside down when its wheels dug into the very material introduced to improve safety. It was a shaken Senna who emerged, but this was only one of many such incidents in motor racing.

Car design was radically altered thanks to the FIA's forensic analysis of previous accidents, working together with the teams to ensure that the best brains were focused on improved design. Front suspension mountings were altered to prevent them from folding backwards towards and into the cockpit. Wheels were fitted with extremely strong Kevlar ties to reduce the likelihood of them flying into the crowd, as happened during the fateful 1994 San Marino Grand Prix.

Side impact protection was introduced as one of many measures to strengthen the carbon fibre monocoque within which the driver sits. The seating position was lowered to reduce the potential for the driver being hit by debris, and the driver's head was protected by the introduction of deformable structures mounted on the cockpit either side of the helmet. This Confor foam, covered in Kevlar skin, was demonstrated by the Motor Industry Research Association in the UK to dramatically reduce the effects of impacts to the head and neck. Seat belts were widened to help spread the loads involved in an accident more evenly across the torso of the driver involved.

The invention of the head and neck safety device, known by its acronym HANS, was another significant development. Imported from the United States, it had been developed by Professor Bob Hubbard at Michigan State University for use in power-boat races. It helps tackle the issues associated with significant rotational, whiplash-style injuries and the more serious concussions caused by the brain impacting on the inside of the skull as a result of high G-force accidents.

What was perhaps more impressive than the design changes carried out on F1 cars was the manner in which the race car's environment was altered to ensure that, when the inevitable accident occurred, the circuit would itself help to protect the driver. This was achieved through adopting a wide range of initiatives based on the lessons learned and the hard data collected from multiple accidents.

Given the manner in which a car's trajectory during an accident can be calculated, circuit design has evolved significantly since the Senna era. Gravel traps have been abandoned in favour of very large tarmac run-off areas that enable drivers to slow the car using the best device available: its own brakes and the tyres in contact with the ground. As a result, all the new circuits designed by Formula One's lead architect Hermann Tilke feature wide run-off zones and walls set far back, angled away from the likely trajectory of cars losing control in an accident.

Gravel traps do still exist, notably at older, traditional tracks where the topography makes it difficult to relocate walls back several metres, but the size of the gravel is carefully calculated so as to slow the cars and make it more difficult for them to dig in sideways and roll over. Handled correctly, a driver can drive across a gravel trap and rejoin the race, but in the event of a significant accident the trap will degrade the car's speed before it can impact the circuit wall.

The walls themselves have changed. Although tracks are surrounded by armco barrier, these are typically lined with towers of tyres, bound together and sealed in a protective, unifying cover.

Debris fencing has been a feature of motor-racing track safety for decades, but the height, location and construction have been greatly improved in the last 25 years. This helps to prevent spectators, media and track marshals from being struck by debris. It also prevents the cars themselves being at risk of entering spectator enclosures.

Senna's death was not the last fatality at a Formula One event prior to the Bianchi accident. Three track marshals were killed in tragic accidents at the 2000 Italian Grand Prix, 2001 Australian Grand Prix and 2013 Canadian Grand Prix. In the first two cases the marshals were struck by wheels flung from cars during accidents, whilst the 2013 fatality was more typical of an industrial accident, no less serious and just as alarming.

In Monza in 2000 an accident involving my own team's Jordan cars, driven by Heinz-Harald Frentzen and Jarno Trulli, resulted in a rear wheel being violently ripped off at right angles, striking a marshal, Paulo Gislimberti, who had left the safety of his marshal's post to find a better vantage point from which to watch the start of the race. In Melbourne it was the BAR Honda of former world champion Jacques Villeneuve, which suffered a high-speed accident after colliding with the Williams driven by Ralf Schumacher. Launched into the air, Villeneuve's car slewed to the left and slammed into the wall and debris fencing, a wheel passing through a gap in the fence, normally left for photographers to have an unimpeded view, but resulting in fatal injuries to track marshal Graham Beveridge.

In Canada in 2013 marshal Mark Robinson succumbed to injuries caused when he stumbled and fell under the wheels of a crane being used to recover one of the Formula One cars after the race. He had dropped his radio, but fell when he stooped to pick it up. The crane driver, unsighted, was unable to avoid running over him. It was the kind of incident that could occur on any industrial site, but it shocked the Formula One world that a volunteer track worker should meet such a fate.

Whether a track marshal or a Formula One driver, training and safety awareness are critical. In a sport where drivers race wheel to wheel at 200 mph, it might seem odd that stringent efforts have been made to make drivers understand that certain risks are unnecessary and unacceptable. The FIA now moves quickly to penalize driving that is deemed unsafe.

By and large the drivers have welcomed this, since the benefits of accident avoidance are many. Not only do drivers want to survive accidents, but more than that they want to avoid them entirely so that they can keep on racing and give themselves the chance of a good result.

Complacency was always going to be the enemy of safety in Formula One, and so it has proven, as the increased safety of cars and circuits has enabled a new generation of drivers to avoid injury entirely and walk away from the kinds of accidents that used to result in serious injury or death. This is particularly the case since the FIA ensured that many of the safety lessons learned in Formula One were cascaded into lower formulae of racing, meaning that today's drivers can race cars from the age of 16 or 17 and never once encounter a truly life-threatening accident.

This has led in some cases to a deterioration in driving standards, with drivers taking more risks, safe in the knowledge that the worst that could happen would be retirement from the race. It is natural that some veterans of the sport, including Jackie Stewart, have pointed out that drivers today can take risks that would have been unthinkable in the 1960s.

The challenge facing the FIA has been to find ways to penalize poor driving standards. To police the drivers in a manner that does not prevent racing yet at the same time ensures that competitors remain mindful of their obligations as regards safety.

The way in which races have been conducted has also been reviewed, with the use of the safety car now commonplace when the race director decides that the risks associated with racing at full speed are too high. As a result, safety cars are used when cars are abandoned in a dangerous location, an incident occurs that requires the medical teams and marshals to be in attendance, or heavy rain causes the track conditions to deteriorate as a result of standing water, which can promote aquaplaning. Halting a race is also more commonly used, as in the Canadian Grand Prix in 2011 when torrential rain forced a mid-race delay of 2 hours 20 minutes. Frustrating as that was for all concerned, notably a hard-pressed media and worldwide television audience, the reality was very clear. Unable to guarantee the safety of the drivers, the sport preferred to wait for better conditions to arrive. Nothing is so important that safety should be compromised.

The safety car has been just one means of controlling events, reducing risk and promoting safety. Equally important is the presence of the medical car, driven by a professional driver accompanied by qualified medical personnel and able to reach the scene of an accident within 20 to 30 seconds. Sometimes referred to by the media as the world's fastest ambulance, the presence of the medical car is a proven life saver.

Most recently this was made clear when the Swiss-French driver Romain Grosjean suffered a dramatic, high-energy impact at the end of the opening lap of the 2020 Bahrain Grand Prix. His life was saved both by the safety structures on his Haas F1 car and the rapid intervention involving the crew of the medical car.

When Grosjean's car collided with Daniil Kvyat's Toro Rosso his Haas speared into the barriers at 119 mph (192 kph), sustaining a 67g impact that broke the car in two and caused a large fire. Trapped in the fireball for 27 seconds, Grosjean was aided in his escape by Dr Ian Roberts, the medical car having arrived on site 10 seconds after the impact.

Roberts was being driven by regular medical car driver Alan van der Merwe, a former British F3 champion, in their specially equipped, 550 bhp Mercedes-AMG C63 S Wagon. Arriving on scene he was able to direct a fire marshal to spray his extinguisher towards the cockpit area, allowing Roberts to move towards Grosjean and help him to safety. It was a perfect case study for an emergency response system, which Professor Watkins first trialled at the 1978 United States Grand Prix. It is far from the only benefit to come from Formula One's unrelenting quest to improve safety.

An unexpected outcome of the Ratzenberger and Senna tragedies transpired when the FIA turned to the car industry, hopeful of finding a sophisticated crash-testing and vehicle safety programme. What Max Mosley and his colleagues on the FIA Safety Commission discovered was a car industry that regarded safety legislation as something of a necessary evil, an additional cost that aimed to meet minimum standards. Crash-testing procedures had not been reviewed since 1974, when car technology and speeds were very different indeed.

After successfully lobbying for support within the European Union (EU), and gaining the support of key automotive executives including Renault's CEO Louis Schweitzer, the FIA suddenly found itself at the forefront of a safety initiative that went far beyond Formula One motor racing. Using the knowledge gained from previous accidents the FIA developed robust crash-testing procedures for racing cars and became involved in developing the European New Car Assessment Programme (EuroNCAP), during which vehicles are crash tested and awarded a safety rating.

Using some of the proceeds from its US $360m 100-year lease of Formula One's commercial rights to Bernie Ecclestone in 2000, the FIA set up a charity that has invested heavily in initiatives including EuroNCAP and GlobalNCAP, ensuring that the safety lessons learned in motor racing benefit wider society. Car manufacturers soon discovered that a high safety rating was a useful marketing tool, hence the move to promote air bags, impact protection and technologies designed to keep drivers and their passengers as safe as possible.

That Formula One has witnessed only one further driver fatality in a Grand Prix since 1994 is a testimony to what can be achieved when an organization decides to make safety a number one priority, direct its energies accordingly and support the programme with a cultural shift.

The average person does not associate Formula One motor racing with safety, so it comes as a surprise to many to discover that in the new era words such as 'safety' and 'reliability' come before performance. Unfortunately it took the deaths of Senna, Ratzenberger and Bianchi to reinforce the need to remain vigilant, and never allow complacency to set in.

When safety is compromised, accidents occur and we witness injuries and fatalities – and this becomes an intensely personal matter. San Marino in 1994 made safety a priority because that weekend was an emotional experience, not only for those directly involved but for the entire world audience of Formula One. The scale of that incident has ultimately made it easier to educate future generations about the importance of safety and why we do things the way we do.

Securing the support needed to modify the technical and sporting regulations in order to put safety first was the easy part. Much more difficult was the cultural change in an environment that sees an influx of young, talented staff year on year, keen to work in the exciting world of Formula One, a world in which risk is ever present.

The 20 years that elapsed between the tragedies in Imola 1994 and Suzuka 2014 also emphasized the importance to the sport and its constituent teams in developing a corporate memory. Many of the drivers and team personnel working in Formula One at the time of Bianchi's accident had never experienced the loss of a driver or team member. The 2014 Toro

Rosso driver Daniil Kvyat was five days old at the time of the Senna and Ratzenberger fatalities. These new generations needed to be educated as to why safety was such a priority, and the reasons why Formula One operated in a certain way.

What was clear was the need for regulations and processes to be backed up by continued training, and by the example set by the leadership team whether at the factory or on site at events. When safety is uppermost in everyone's mind and backed up by the systems and processes in place, new recruits soon adapt. It becomes second nature to them. Safety leadership requires setting an example, practising what we preach.

Ultimately the conclusion from Formula One's experience of safety and risk management is that technology, processes and systems can go so far, but ultimately the cultural change across the industry is key. The leadership identified the need to change, and the clear message was cascaded down throughout the sport, its constituent teams and its stakeholders. Once the need for change was experienced, and the decision made to do something about it, it became a question of developing the systems and processes to effect that change and then – most importantly – sustain the benefits.

The fact that Formula One was serious about safety was evidenced when all the teams, normally ultra-competitive, came together with the sport's governing body to create an industry-wide approach to creating solutions. Looking outside Formula One was also an important part of that journey, for whilst we were unable to learn from the automotive sector, the airline industry gave us an appreciation of the advantages of using on-board computers as accident data recorders to help build knowledge about accidents and their causes.

Formula One's successful drive towards eliminating driver fatalities over the last 25 years is testimony to what happens when safety is put at the centre of the agenda. The sport's leadership created a clear vision of what the target, the systems and processes were put in place to deliver. Most critically of all, the sport has rigorously cultivated a safety culture.

Charlie Whiting's role in framing the sport's technical and safety regulations meant that he remained passionate about ensuring driver safety in the decades that followed the Senna and Ratzenberger tragedies. Safety was always uppermost in his mind, which made the events at the 2014 Japanese Grand Prix so traumatic.

In the wake of the Bianchi accident Whiting tested and then introduced in 2015 the virtual safety car (VSC), a system by which a race could be instantly brought under control using electronic signage at marshal posts around the track. The advantage of this system was that, in the event of an incident that did not require full safety car deployment, the VSC could be used to bring the race under control with drivers required to slow down and achieve a lap time around 30 per cent slower than normal racing speed. VSCs do not lead to the cars bunching up, as they do when running behind a safety car. Typically a VSC will only last for one or two laps instead of the three or four that are typical of a full safety car, and this improvement is typical of the approach the FIA takes to implementing changes whenever accidents occur.

Whiting was also a prime mover behind the introduction of the halo device, which was made mandatory in 2018. This is a structure mounted over the cockpit with the objective of preventing large pieces of debris from impacting on the driver. Although it would not have protected Jules Bianchi, given the highly unusual nature of his car's collision with a crane, that tragedy helped accelerate the FIA's focus on improving cockpit protection.

The sport had already witnessed fatal accidents involving debris entering cockpits. These included Justin Wilson, killed in an IndyCar race in the United States in 2015 when a large piece of debris impacted with his helmet, and Formula 2 driver Henry Surtees who died as the result of being hit by a wheel at Brands Hatch in 2009.

In the same year Formula One's Felipe Massa suffered serious eye and head injuries as the result of a suspension component from a car driven by fellow Brazilian Rubens Barrichello coming loose and hitting his helmet. Fortunately he made a full recovery, but Whiting and his colleagues at the FIA started to experiment with screens and canopies before settling on the halo design.

Made from titanium and weighing 7 kilogrammes, the halo forms a protective ring around the top of the open cockpit, enabling the driver to enter and exit in the normal way, but providing a last line of defence against large pieces of debris. It has to meet rigorous standards, including being able to withstand the impact of a 20-kilogramme wheel hitting it at a speed of 140 mph (225 kph).

The introduction of the halo met with criticism due to its aesthetics, but any resistance dissipated when a series of accidents demonstrated the significant benefits. This culminated in the Grosjean accident in Bahrain 2020, when his car speared through the barrier as a result of its 67g impact. The halo unquestionably saved the driver's life.

Sadly, Whiting did not live to see that superb example of the safety research that he had championed. He died suddenly while attending the 2019 Australian Grand Prix, robbing Formula One of one of its most important figures, a pioneer of the safety standards that the sport enjoys today.

Lessons in safety and risk management

Success in Formula One is as much about risk management as it is about optimizing performance. We spend a great deal of time managing the risks inherent in our business, whether that be commercial, operational or technical.

One of the reasons the sport has become so data-centric is to enhance our ability to improve the quality of decision making and outcomes, with effective risk management and safety uppermost in our minds. The risk most closely associated with Formula One is the very personal risk associated with young drivers battling wheel to wheel at 200 mph (320 kph).

In a sport where fatalities were all too common between 1950 and 1994, the change in culture, technology and systems associated with safety has been profound. In early 2014 the sport was able to commemorate 20 years since the last driver fatality in a race. Later that same year the Bianchi tragedy served as a reminder that the risks remain, complacency our greatest enemy.

Formula One's safety record is a worthy case study in how we can tackle risk head on, and the lessons are very clear:

MAKE SAFETY AND RISK MANAGEMENT A CENTRAL PILLAR OF YOUR BUSINESS
This is what Max Mosley and Bernie Ecclestone did in the wake of the Senna and Ratzenberger fatalities.

COMMUNICATE YOUR OBJECTIVE VERY CLEARLY, AND MAKE IT A HIGH AMBITION
The FIA has placed safety at the centre of its compliance, ensuring that competitors behave safely, have clear processes to follow and use state-of-the-art safety technology and processes.

SAFETY AND RISK MANAGEMENT IS ALL ABOUT PEOPLE
Systems, processes, checklists, regulations and legislation are important. But they mean nothing unless they are underpinned by a strong safety culture.

WE KNOW THE RISKS, SO BE REALISTIC AND ROBUST IN TACKLING THEM

In Formula One we know that accidents will happen. We prepare for all the negative scenarios and work backwards to eliminate or mitigate the risks.

THE TRUTH IS IN THE DATA

Not only do we know what types of accidents occur, we also know when. The medical car follows the field at the start, providing immediate intervention, as in the case of the Grosjean accident.

TAKE A HOLISTIC, THOROUGH VIEW OF THE RISKS AND THE STEPS REQUIRED TO MITIGATE THEM

Formula One's safety involves the cars, tracks, personnel training, equipment and provision of emergency services and the trauma facilities.

ACCEPT THAT ACCIDENTS WILL HAPPEN

It is a fact of the human condition. It is inevitable, which is why Formula One aims to mitigate the effects of an accident in addition to ensuring they don't happen in the first place.

USE THE POWER OF REGULATION, LEGISLATION AND ENFORCEMENT

Just as a Formula One driver's safety equipment is clearly specified and mandatory, so too is the safety performance of the car. Adherence is non-negotiable.

Note

1   Spanish Formula One test driver María de Villota suffered a serious accident during a private test session for the Marussia Formula One team at Duxford airfield on 3 July 2012 when her car ran into the back of the tail-lift of a support vehicle parked in the car's holding area. The team was using the airfield for 'straight-line' testing, and it is not an accredited Formula One venue. It was also her first time in a Formula One car, although she was a very experienced and capable racing driver. She suffered serious head and facial injuries, which led to the loss of her right eye. In spite of making a good recovery, 15 months later she was found dead on the morning of 11 October 2013 in a hotel room in Seville, and an autopsy found she had suffered a cardiac arrest. Her family was informed that this might have been caused by the brain injuries suffered in her testing accident.

CHAPTER SEVEN

Managing change

Most people don't like change, and certainly not the thought of it. So many times I have heard someone say 'It's always been done this way' in some aspect of business. Inevitably one of the attributes of the great leaders and innovators is their use of change as an effective business tool. As Red Bull Racing's CTO Adrian Newey recalls in his book *How To Build a Car*, an early experience was having a colleague who had worked for the team's previous owners Jaguar explaining the way things had to be done. For an innovator like Adrian, this was a red rag to a bull.

Given that his car designs have won no fewer than 10 Constructors' World Championships for Williams, McLaren and Red Bull Racing, he does not typically follow the pack. He relishes change because it drives innovation.[1]

As I cover in Chapter 8, all the major step-changes in Formula One design technology have driven new levels of performance, even if this has meant legions of production staff, engineers and mechanics coming to terms with the latest technologies and new ways of doing things.

I am quite sure that when John Cooper decided to put the engine behind the driver, or McLaren's John Barnard decided to manufacture a chassis entirely from carbon fibre, they were met with scepticism and resistance.

Change is a good thing, mainly because change comes hand in hand with continuous improvement and innovation. Formula One cars are changed by means of relentless development season to season, race to race, and even from one practice session to the next. The mindset of people working in Formula One is that avoiding change, trying to keep everything just as it is, is a guaranteed way of failing. The moment we are not changing, be it evolving our product, adopting new technology or improving our processes, the competition will leap ahead.

The ability to manage change and make the most of new challenges can deliver great rewards. When I look back at the changes within Formula One, it is striking just how much has changed and why, and the effective way in which it has been managed.

The changes wrought by Bernie Ecclestone on the sport during the 1970s dragged Formula One into the modern era of commercialized sport. He was the trailblazer, and not everyone could see the big vision Bernie had for the sport. Today he is remembered for building Formula One into a global sports business and, although his style was often controversial, his entrepreneurial strength and business instincts were clear. He recognized value, and he knew how to develop a highly profitable business model around it.

It is more than four years since Ecclestone was effectively sacked from the top job. The sale of Formula One to Liberty Media was inevitably going to lead to change, but the most significant was their early decision to appoint a new CEO.

There was much scepticism, for although Ecclestone was now in his eighties and had endured a recent bribery scandal in Germany, Liberty's appointment of Chase Carey raised the obvious point that he was a media executive who knew nothing about Formula One. Here was fear of change stated in simple terms.

Yet Carey was soon driving the business forward, tackling issues and pursuing opportunities as he outlined Liberty's vision of the business they had bought. That vision included not only growing the business but embracing a new way of doing things, including a more collegiate, open and transparent approach. He also promoted the need for the sport's stakeholders to confine any disagreements to private meetings.

'We have been very clear that one of the things the sport has not been well served by is a continued short-term focus and what we are going to do next week', Carey told the Press Association after 100 days in office. 'We care more about where the sport is going to be three years from now than three months from now. Bernie [Ecclestone] was always very focused on the short term, and our focus is on building long-term value.'

Carey's new strategy differed from Ecclestone's but in many respects both men had much in common. Both came into Formula One recognizing the need for change. The only difference is that 40 years after Ecclestone first drove the revolution that transformed the sport, the world itself had changed dramatically.

When Ecclestone bought the Brabham Formula One team in 1971 and realized that Formula One did not have a sustainable business his strategy became based on change. Examples included securing the commitment from all of the teams to compete in all of the races. Another was moving Grand Prix events to a Sunday, a day on which many sports were either banned or restricted for traditional religious reasons. These two changes alone helped him to create an offering that was appealing to television broadcasters and promoters. He packaged the sport for the TV age.

With a star line-up and fixed start time, Formula One was able to start charging broadcasters rights fees, and by introducing competition between circuit owners Ecclestone built a second source of revenue. Alongside television deals, race promoter fees would become the foundation stones of the Formula One business model.

Change has made Formula One the business it is today. If you accept that innovation is vital to business success, then you must also acknowledge that change is highly desirable. The world of business means that no one can afford to stand still because change is inevitably driven by outside sources.

Competition drives change, which is one of the reasons Formula One teams have a keen interest in watching and monitoring what the opposition is doing at all times. It is for this reason that technical departments closely analyse the design details of rival's cars, learning as much as they can from video, photography or any means of scrutinizing publicly available data.

This is also why we see teams closely guarding their design secrets when the bodywork is removed from the cars, and why it is always amusing to watch the senior technical staff checking out the opposition's car on the starting grid. It is the one time in the weekend when you can attempt to have a close look at the opposition.

When we see a competitor deliver a sudden step-change in performance, there is an immediate realization that something has changed. Someone has questioned established thinking, taken a new idea and run with it.

These kinds of changes are exciting, and it is very much better to be the team delivering them rather than following in their wake. Over the years we have seen many such examples.

One of the most famous came in 1997 when one of McLaren's engineers, Steve Nichols, had the idea of fitting a second brake pedal to their car. This would have the effect of braking the inside rear wheel in corners, dramatically improving cornering and stability as drivers Mika Häkkinen and David Coulthard accelerated out of a turn.

This change, an innovation based on how tracked vehicles such as military tanks and earth movers steer, was dreamt up by Nichols in an unlikely location. 'It was Christmas time and I was on holiday at my parents' house and lying in the bath', he recalls. 'We typically set up the cars with quite a lot of understeer – at the time we had fairly skinny rear tyres and fairly meaty front tyres – and I had this idea to put a rear brake on in the corners, to sort of dial out the understeer.

'Paddy Lowe was head of R&D at the time, and this would be considered an R&D project. So I told him I wanted to try this thing where we have an extra pedal in the car, and we put the right-rear or left-rear brake on to balance the car. Eventually he sanctioned the project. It sat on the test truck for months waiting to be tested, and finally we'd exhausted every other test item. At 5 pm or something, at a Silverstone test, they said let's try that brake thing!'

The components required to carry out this modification cost around £50 – a pedal, master cylinder and some brake hose – and when Häkkinen started to use it the performance advantage was half a second per lap.

Nichols admits that 'brake steering' and the adoption of a 'fiddle brake' was created with Coulthard in mind. 'I had thought of it specifically for David', says Nichols. 'Because he used to say he didn't like oversteer. I thought this would give him the opportunity to set up the car with quite a lot of understeer, and then balance it with the fiddle brake.'

Coulthard was initially sceptical about using it, particularly as he already had three pedals as he preferred the traditional throttle, brake and clutch set-up. Teammate Häkkinen used a hand clutch, having adapted to left-foot braking. With the improvement in performance proven, Coulthard's car was fitted with a fourth pedal, and he quickly saw the benefit.

'It was a brilliantly simple piece of engineering that worked', he recalls. 'We had to learn how to work with it, because you had to accelerate while you braked, otherwise you just locked the wheel.

'You could feel it was an advantage, because it yawed the car. So instead of riding over the front tyre, you could rotate the car without having to put steering lock on. And steering lock affects the aerodynamics quite a lot, so there was an advantage aerodynamically in having that. We could use it also to control a bit of wheelspin on the inside wheel, coming out of tight corners. Independently Mika and I both worked that out.'

The competition could see how quick the McLaren was in corners, but no one quite knew how they were doing it. Attention fell on the novel braking system thanks to photographer Darren Heath capturing an image of the footwell of Häkkinen's car after it retired from the Luxembourg Grand Prix, held at the Nürburgring.

His scoop, published in *F1 Racing Magazine*, had the competition convinced that McLaren had spent millions on developing a complex piece of trickery and, furthermore, that it was illegal. Ultimately the system would be banned during 1998 on the basis that it was a four-wheel steering system, but not before McLaren had started the season in dominant form.

The 'fiddle brake' innovation was all about questioning established ways of doing things, promoting change and daring to take the risk of trying new solutions. A desire to drive change lies at the heart of Formula One's innovation mindset.

Compliance also played a role in that story, for since the system was not specifically covered by the sport's regulations Nichols and McLaren felt confident in deploying the solution. Formula One politics and their unfortunate decision to name the system 'brake steering' led to its subsequent ban.

New regulations are another reason for Formula One's acceptance of change and for teams to regard change as a catalyst for innovation. When the entire industry is subject to rule changes, everyone has equal chance to make the most of the opportunity.

The FIA is responsible for developing Formula One rules and regulations, and these days works closely with the Formula One Group and the teams to ensure that the rules benefit the sport. This was not always the case due to differences in priorities between key stakeholders, witnessed by the conflicts that were a feature of the sport's political landscape from the 1970s through to the 2000s.

Since the 1990s the FIA's approach to compliance has been to ensure Formula One represents the pinnacle of world motorsport in terms of performance, yet is safe, road relevant and attractive to car manufacturers. However, decisions taken by the regulator have often led to unintended consequences for the sport's other stakeholders.

A recent example of that disconnect was the 2011 decision to introduce complex hybrid engines for the 2014 season, a decision made by the FIA based on their focus on the development of energy-efficient technologies across motorsport. This was, in turn, driven by the realization that the car industry was moving towards the use of hybrid and electric engines. Change in the automotive industry was driving change in Formula One.

The wider implication of this significant change was also to address another complaint from existing and potential customers about our sport: that it was ecologically damaging and did not promote environmental sustainability.

Burning large amounts of fossil fuel in front of a live global television audience was not going down well with multinational companies, whose own corporate social responsibility and environmental programmes were regarded as sacrosanct. The new powertrains, producing the same performance with a reduction in fuel consumption of almost 40 per cent, not only addressed that issue head on, but promoted the capability of Formula One to develop solutions that could benefit society.

This decision was essentially a technical one, however. It largely ignored the wider implications, including the sheer cost involved in developing these units together with the impact that their low noise levels would have on a spectacle enjoyed by both spectators and television audiences. Ultimately it drove one of the engine manufacturers, Cosworth, to leave the sport, while increasing costs significantly for teams faced with leasing expensive units from the remaining suppliers.

For fans and media used to hearing screaming racing engines, the arrival of lower-revving, petrol-electric hybrid engines prompted much comment, and subsequent changes aimed to reinstate some of the noise. It was an example of how technical rules made in isolation could have a profound commercial impact in terms of cost and the sport's appeal.

One of the changes that has occurred since Liberty's takeover of the Formula One Group is a more collaborative and constructive approach to working with the FIA under its president Jean Todt. This included appointing Todt's former Ferrari colleague Ross Brawn to create a technical department that would work with the teams and the FIA to ensure that rule changes would benefit the sport commercially as well as technically.

Three sets of regulations cover the governance of Formula One, and full compliance with them is a non-negotiable for teams wishing to complete. The 2021 Sporting Regulations run to 88 pages with 46 major clauses and 10 appendices detailing the rules that have to be followed in order to compete. The Financial Regulations, first introduced in 2021, detail the ways in which teams must operate under the terms of a strict budget cap.

The Technical Regulations are covered by a 137-page document with 23 articles covering every facet of the car design requirements and the technologies that are permitted. These are supported by five appendices.

The sporting and technical rules change every year. Sometimes the changes are small, on other occasions they can require the teams to design a completely new car. The reasons for the changes are many, but can include the adoption or banning of certain technologies or innovations, the need to further improve safety or address the quality of the racing. Whatever the case, these changes to compliance are ever present and a fundamental aspect of the sport.

For the 2021 season the Technical Regulations saw 21 sections changed. Due to the effects of the Covid-19 pandemic the decision was made to retain the same cars as 2020, but required the teams to carry out modifications aimed at limiting aerodynamic downforce. This very much played to the FIA's remit to control speeds and ensure continued safety.

Against early expectations the result of those apparently minor changes was significant. They had a negative impact on the design philosophy of Formula One's most dominant team, Mercedes-Benz, and contributed to Red Bull Racing entering the 2021 season with a faster car – a classic example of how marginal changes in compliance can lead to significant change.

Meanwhile, for 2022, every Formula One team has to design an entirely new car. The FIA, Formula One Group and teams agreed upon a set of rules designed to reduce costs, improve the quality of racing and, in theory, give more teams the opportunity to be successful.

As ever, the innovators within the sport will read the rules in two ways – for what they do say, and what they don't say. For the chief technical officers at Mercedes and Red Bull Racing, James Allison and Adrian Newey, this will mean exploring the opportunity to innovate, approaching changes in compliance from the perspective of how it can be explored. It is in this way their teams have dominated Formula One since 2010.

It was Red Bull Racing's concept of using high front-to-rear rake and harnessing 'blown diffuser' technology – using the exhaust gases from the engine to create an aerodynamic advantage – that helped it to gain an edge over rivals for a four-year period. Mercedes saw the adoption of hybrid engine technologies as an opportunity to develop a highly innovative turbocharger that gave improved performance and better packaging, triggering their dominance of Formula One since 2014.

Dominant teams see change as opportunity. Along with their rivals, they will approach 2022 with the objective of exploring the possibilities generated by a fixed set of rules. Much will depend upon the creativity that lies within their teams to advance solutions that no one else has thought of.

This approach can also be used in the development of new business models as old ones change or break entirely. The speed of technological change has disrupted business and will continue to do so. In this regard leaders have similar decisions to make as Newey and Allison. Do you innovate and lead, or wait to see what others do and follow? Either way, change is coming.

The change in Formula One's business model is a case in point. As the sport found its commercial feet in the 1980s, the business model developed under Ecclestone's leadership. Television companies were by now spending significant sums on TV rights resulting in those same broadcasters elevating Formula One to the top of their sports schedules to ensure they drew in the largest audience possible. Meanwhile race promoters were motivated to sell as many tickets, hospitality and event sponsorships as possible in order to fund their race fees.

With vastly increasing television audiences and well-promoted events, the teams found it possible to attract a larger and broader range of commercial sponsors. The tobacco industry continued to pump hundreds of millions of dollars into the sport but new sectors such as clothing, electronics, IT, telecommunications and energy arrived. By the 1990s, to walk through the Formula One paddock was to gain an insight into the industries, sectors and brands that were successful and keen to be associated with a globally recognized sport.

At Jordan Grand Prix between 1995 and 2000 we saw tobacco sponsorship from Benson & Hedges augmented by significant multimillion-dollar deals from brands such as MasterCard International, Pearl Assurance, Hewlett-Packard, Lucent Technologies, Infineon, Deutsche Post, DHL, Danzas, Brother Industries, Total Oil and Repsol. These companies represented global payments systems, insurance, IT, telecommunications, computer chips, freight logistics, computer printers and the energy sector.

This was reflected across the sport, with established teams sporting a strong portfolio of backers. But change was coming.

A number of things began to happen at the same time. The campaign against tobacco advertising and sponsorship was gaining pace. France's 1991 law, the Loi Evin, unilaterally curbed tobacco and alcohol sponsorship and gave a glimpse of things to come.

With tobacco under threat it was also noticeable how commercial sponsors were beginning to evaluate sponsorships on a more scientific basis, driven in part by increased choice. In the 25 years since Bernie had taken over the reins of Formula One, sports such as soccer, golf, rugby, cricket, snooker and sailing had carved out their own significant offerings. Commercial sponsors had a wider range of options than ever before.

It also became apparent that new types of sponsors did not have the staying power of tobacco, partly because their own industries were subject to disruption. As an example, the dotcom bubble of 2000 hit Formula One. Sponsors such as Lucent Technologies and Nortel Networks suddenly upped and left.

We also saw some deals end because of an increasing emphasis from shareholders on improved corporate governance. This exposed some of the old-style deals whereby a CEO had driven a commercial sponsorship simply because they liked Formula One. At Jordan we saw one sponsor embroiled in a corruption scandal, another pull out in the wake of inappropriate behaviour by a senior executive accused of using the Formula One activity for personal gain.

Against this background it was interesting to watch Formula One teams regress towards tobacco funding at the precise moment when it was under threat. In 1999 British American Tobacco started its own Formula One team, acquiring the entry previously owned by Tyrrell Racing. Six other teams were already funded by tobacco companies.

Given this reliance on one sector, the 2002 announcement by the EU that tobacco sponsorship and advertising would end in July 2005 was a highly significant moment. I recall sitting in my office and wondering where Formula One teams would find a replacement for tobacco. The EU's ban felt like an existential threat to the whole Formula One industry.

Vodafone's deal to title sponsorship of Ferrari in 2004 before moving to McLaren in 2007 suggested that some of the emerging technology sectors might replace tobacco. It was a false dawn and, even when the banking sector started to invest, we quickly came to realize that disruption was the new order of the day.

Even the move to attract funding from financial services and banking turned out to be short-lived. HSBC had been involved in Formula One since 1998, and NatWest supported Jordan's MasterCard programme, but in the mid-2000s there was an avalanche of deals. ING, Credit Suisse, Royal Bank of Scotland, Santander and UBS arrived en masse. To some, it looked as though we had found our tobacco substitute.

The financial crisis of 2008 put paid to that. The Royal Bank of Scotland was a particularly high-profile casualty. Its CEO Fred Goodwin was a

Formula One fan whose ambitions for RBS and close friendship with Jackie Stewart had led to a title sponsorship of the Williams team. ING joined Renault F1 in 2007, but were gone within three years, while Credit Suisse's deal with Sauber went the same way.

Only UBS and Santander stayed in, the former as partner of Formula One itself. The latter developed its relationship with McLaren into a UK-specific focus following its takeover of Abbey National, using British stars Jenson Button and Lewis Hamilton in their advertising.

In the post-tobacco world it was evident that Formula One's teams were facing a significant threat to their business model. Sponsorships were harder to find, those that did emerge were from companies primarily interested in supporting top teams with a winning record. For the less competitive teams this meant relying even more on Formula One's prize fund, sponsorship generated by their drivers and shareholders' funds paid directly or indirectly, often through associated businesses dressed up as sponsors.

As if the dotcom bubble, tobacco legislation, the banking crisis and economic turmoil in F1's heartland of Europe were not enough, the sport also witnessed a sharp correction as four major car manufacturers exited with little notice. The decisions by Ford (2004), Honda (2008), Toyota and BMW (2009) to turn their back on the sport came as a further blow. Each gave their reasons, but the fundamental takeaway for Formula One was that it was ultimately at the mercy of factors far beyond its control.

The first decade of the new century had shown that economic cycles, government legislation, changing business priorities and governance could have a profound effect on the sport. The certainty of the old days, when tobacco sponsors or friendly CEOs would queue up to support teams, were gone.

For the teams facing a much more demanding sponsorship environment the winners, at teams like Ferrari, McLaren, Williams and Benetton, were those that offered ever more diverse services to existing customers and repackaged their offerings to new ones. The old model of selling sponsorship based primarily on the brand awareness generated by TV coverage combined with corporate hospitality at events was replaced by a much more sophisticated offering that provided the customers with value 365 days a year.

Factory visits, team-building events, driver appearances, technical case studies and product launches became the focus of sponsorship activation as Formula One sought to engage more closely with their remaining customers. Teams had to work far harder than before at driving value.

As we saw in Chapter 1, Bernie Ecclestone's response to growing the revenues of Formula One was to begin a process of harnessing the power of the sport's appeal to an entirely new type of customer. This would include governments, sovereign funds and private promoters. Just as he had understood the potential in packaging Formula One for the television age in the 1970s, so he recognized that governments were interested in using global sporting events to promote their nationhood.

Compared to the ritual of the International Olympic Committee and FIFA awarding the rights to stage the Winter or Summer Olympics and the Football World Cup to a different country every four years, the appeal of Formula One was clear. Generating a global audience whose cumulative figures each year could stack up favourably against the quadrennial Olympic Games and World Cup, Ecclestone's proposition did not involve running a long, drawn-out tender process before awarding an event.

Malaysia was the first to come to the table, its government under Dr Tun Mahathir undertaking to build a state-of-the-art Formula One facility adjacent to the brand new Kuala Lumpur International Airport and sign up to a long-term contract. I remember arriving at the Sepang Circuit for the first time in 1999 and wondering in awe at the sheer scale of the place, ultra-modern garages, enormous paddock, covered grandstands, well-equipped media centre and medical facilities.

Malaysia worked well as a case study for 'new era' Formula One, so much so that the model was repeated within three years and contracts signed with Bahrain and China. By 2004 they had built their venues and were staging the inaugural Formula One races in the Middle East and most populous nation on earth respectively. This triggered a surge in new opportunities: Turkey (2005), Singapore (2008), Abu Dhabi (2009), Korea (2010), India (2011) and Russia (2014) would join together with Azerbaijan (2017) and Mexico (2015). More recently former European venues including Austria (2014) and the Netherlands (2021) have returned to the calendar, while Saudi Arabia has signed up to a 10-year deal commencing in 2021 and a second race in the United States will join the calendar in 2022.

In 20 years Ecclestone's decision to expand the sport far beyond its European heartlands has been a staggering success. Particularly when you consider that the appeal of these races came not from the popularity of the sport among the population of the countries concerned, but primarily from the demand from nations to attract prestigious events.

In particular the drive eastwards helped address the changes impacting on the traditional business model of the sport in Europe. New markets meant new opportunities for existing sponsors and the potential to acquire new ones eager to access an expanding global footprint. It also played to the strategy of some of the sport's key players.

As an example, Ferrari opened its first dealership in mainland China in a downtown Shanghai location in 2004, the same year as the first Grand Prix was staged just outside the city. With some 25 per cent of China's trade being driven through that one city, it came as no surprise that the Shanghai dealership proved to be a success, and by 2013 Ferrari had expanded to 30 dealers in the country. Ferrari's Chinese customers are younger than in any other market, and the number of female customers has been another notable shift, requiring Ferrari to change its accessories range to suit.

Unsurprisingly China is now well established as a key market. In 2019 Ferrari enjoyed a bumper year, selling over 10,000 cars for the first time in its history, of which 836 were shipped to China, Hong Kong and Taiwan. This marked a 20 per cent increase year on year, confirmation that Formula One's move into China has helped position the Italian company as an aspirational purchase among the nation's wealthy.

The evolution of Formula One's current business model is characterized by change, and that has been reflected by the way in which individual teams have evolved. With commercial sponsorship harder to find, team owners began to explore new opportunities.

In a similar way to which Ecclestone rethought Formula One as a global event, individual teams also began to play to their inherent strengths as technology businesses. That Formula One teams can bring a high-technology product to market each year is well proven. So too their expertise in aerospace-quality engineering, producing complex, lightweight, high-performance structures.

Add to this their inherent understanding of race-car design and technologies, allied to their understanding of data connectivity and telematics, and Formula One teams offer a suite of skills with a wide range of applications. Teams such as McLaren and Williams have undertaken work beyond Formula One throughout their long and successful history.

McLaren Composites and TAG Electronics were selling technologies solutions to a wide range of customers long before they merged in 2004 and are today known simply as McLaren Applied. As the name suggests, this business unit applies capabilities developed in Formula One into a range of applications both inside and outside the world of motorsport.

Every Formula One car has used McLaren's electronic control units (ECUs) since 2008, while in 2018 it won the FIA tender to supply temperature and pressure sensors. Every car that races in NASCAR and IndyCar in the United States utilizes McLaren ECUs, while the company has also provided batteries on an exclusive basis to the all-electric racing championship, Formula E. Beyond motorsport McLaren Applied has worked with companies including GSK, Heathrow Airport, Singapore's SMRT trains and Birmingham Children's Hospital, playing to core strengths in relation to data acquisition, analytics and real-time monitoring.

Meanwhile Williams designed cars for rallying in the 1980s and touring cars in the 1990s prior to the creation of Williams Advanced Engineering (WAE), selling technology solutions to sectors including automotive engineering, aerospace, defence and renewable energy. The success of this award-winning business has been reflected in an extremely diverse range of projects, products and clients. Among the most notable was the development, in partnership with Aerofoil Energy, of a device that, when retrofitted to supermarket fridges, keeps the cool air inside the cabinet and reduces energy consumption by up to 30 per cent. The Aerofoil tapped into Williams F1's understanding of aerodynamics, the product being inspired by the design of the wings on a Formula One car.

Other WAE projects have included production of the Babypod – a lightweight, portable baby incubator for newborn babies requiring emergency transportation – and working with Airbus on its Zephyr programme. This is a solar-electric unmanned aircraft that can operate in the stratosphere.

Formula One rivals Red Bull Racing have also been busy providing high-end capabilities to clients, most notably in the design and development of the Aston Martin Valkyrie supercar. Designed under the guidance of Adrian Newey, this is a hybrid, high-performance supercar that promises customers Formula One levels of performance. It is powered by a Cosworth V12 engine and an energy storage system developed by Integral Powertrain and Rimac, together producing 1,160 bhp.

Red Bull Advanced Technologies is now partnering with French motorsport company ORECA to design the prototype chassis for the hydrogen class that will compete in the Le Mans 24 Hours race in 2024. This is a perfect example of how a Formula One team's capabilities can be deployed for the rapid development of products that have the potential to benefit wider industry and society. At a time when much of the automotive industry is wedded to battery electric vehicles, the development of hydrogen-powered vehicles is seen as a more environmentally sustainable, long-term solution to the decarbonization of transport.

These are just three examples of Formula One teams responding to change by diversifying their businesses, and it has come as no surprise to see the Mercedes F1 team follow suit. Their Applied Science business was announced in 2019 – initially working with partner Ineos in its international sailing and cycling teams – to apply the best in motorsport and aerospace engineering to 'performance across the domains of land, sea and air.'

Mercedes-Benz Applied Science has developed its offering based around the use of a dedicated wind tunnel facility, simulation capability, composite manufacturing and engineering expertise. CEO Toto Wolff has ambitions for the business, including a £100 million revenue target by 2025.

One of the major reasons Formula One teams have been able to pursue this diversification strategy is the degree to which they have embraced digital transformation. In so doing they have armed themselves with the inherent ability to interrogate problems and rapidly develop solutions for clients across a wide range of sectors.

The changing face of business brought about as a result of digital transformation is one of the major headaches for many traditional industries, and yet opened up new opportunities for many start-ups. The demise of Blockbuster Video and rise of Netflix is one typical example of how digital technologies have driven significant change, and Formula One's willingness to embrace a data-driven ecosystem has been a strength. That teams can monitor their cars real time, optimize strategies by using software to analyse millions of potential outcomes, and remote-manage races from their headquarters, are examples of the ways in which the sport has become fuelled by data.

Starting with rudimentary hard-wired telemetry systems in the 1980s, Formula One teams quickly progressed to using wireless data acquisition just as vehicle design moved from the drawing board to computer-aided design systems in the early 1990s. The sport very quickly fell in love with the possibilities made available by increased processing power, perhaps best exemplified by the Williams-Renault FW15C with which Alain Prost won the 1993 World Championship. This car featured a number of complex technologies including computer-controlled active suspension, first used the previous season.

In the latter half of the 1990s teams began to explore 3D scanning and printing, accelerating their rapid-prototyping capability so that the time from design office to racetrack fell from weeks to days. The digital journey was enabling faster, more accurate outcomes, a strength that Formula One teams could readily benefit from and quickly appreciate.

Today's Formula One teams have the benefit of a 35-year digital transformation journey, one that has proven time and again to help drive positive outcomes. Fear of change has been quashed by the recognition that digital tools enable teams of people to achieve extraordinary outcomes, and a quick look at any one of a key number of metrics illustrates this perfectly.

In 2000, for example, Formula One car reliability had remained relatively unchanged since 1950, whereas in the last 20 years that has been transformed. Lewis Hamilton's Mercedes suffered not one single technical failure during a Grand Prix in 2019 or 2020 and encountered only one major technical issue in a four-year period.

Since teams can design, develop and prove their technologies in the digital space, they only commit to manufacture once they know systems will achieve the necessary performance, reliability and durability. The use of simulation tools means that teams can accurately predict outcomes, while technologies such as computation fluid dynamics, when combined with wind tunnel data, have helped to transform the field of aerodynamics. The sport's digital transformation journey means that engineers are no longer dealing with unknowns, rather they are able to make decisions based on knowledge.

Digital transformation has improved performance, revolutionized safety, reduced costs, increased efficiency and ultimately helped Formula One to engage more effectively with its customers. Diversification has enabled the sport to grow in new markets and provided teams with growth as they play to core strengths as technology companies.

Disruption caused by legislation, compliance and new technologies has ultimately led to the sport developing an inherent resilience, the ability to adapt to change. In the days of tobacco sponsorship no one in the sector was developing energy-efficiency solutions for the wider industry. The ban of one forced the development of the other.

All the great innovators in the sport's history have questioned established ways of doing things and driven change by taking risks, trying new things. They have often looked outside the industry for inspiration, and in taking a wider view of the world given themselves the benefit of a more diverse way of solving problems. Leading teams through change is essentially an ongoing process that should be relished because it gives rise to opportunity. The world never stops changing, and change management is therefore an important skill.

In *The Future Business Formula* published by change management consultancy Sullivan & Stanley, there are three ways to lead people through change. The first is the rational approach, where you take time to explain the change that is coming, communicate it across the team and undertake skills training. This works if everyone in the team is more or less on board with the change, but is problematic if people's intuition or experience causes them to resist.

The second is coercive, the leadership simply dictating how things are going to be and demanding that everyone falls in line. This 'command-and-control' approach is old school, more stick than carrot, and seldom wins the hearts and minds of the people you need most – your team.

Formula One teams are much more inclined towards the third approach to managing change, partly because the sheer technical challenge involved in the sport forces people to share challenges and develop solutions by working together. Sullivan & Stanley describe this as the normative approach. This approach to dealing with change requires a high level of collaboration, the team taking the time to study the new system or challenge together. This is about the people, the processes you have in place, the inter-actions that take place and the policy the team has towards change and problem solving.

People will study problems and find solutions if they are given the place and support to do so. They become much more receptive to change. In fact, they go looking for change themselves.

The fact that Formula One teams have skills that can be deployed to the benefit of wider industry and society now seems obvious, yet it took some existential challenges to create the impetus for change. Colin Chapman, founder of Lotus and one of Formula One's design geniuses, famously said that 'to innovate you must imaginate'. A slightly clunky portmanteau but one that has an important message for business leaders. Whatever the challenge, our imagination and creativity will always help us develop solutions, so long as we create the environment within which teams can be given the time and space to do so.

Lessons in change management

Change is ever present, and the modern world of business presents all of us with fresh challenges every day.

Compliance is a fact of life in many industries, and as regulations change we can take one of two approaches – see these as obstacles or opportunities.

Technology has created a wide range of improved outcomes and opportunities, but it has also reduced barriers to entry in many industries. Disruption is all around us as a result.

Formula One has been able to play to its strengths, adapting to business challenges quickly. This includes packaging the sport as a global entertainment platform, and teams learning how to sell their capabilities across a wide range of industrial sectors.

Ultimately Formula One's leadership teams have learned the importance of teamwork and collaboration in respect of change.

Key takeaways

CHANGE IS NOT AN OPTION
Whether we like it or not, change is not only inevitable but in fact an essential part of business.

AVOID A BUNKER MENTALITY
In an ever-shrinking world, and whether we are 'local' or 'global', our businesses will be affected by what happens elsewhere.

PLAN FOR CONTINUOUS TECHNOLOGICAL INNOVATION
Technology is going to continue evolving at a meteoric rate, giving our customers ever greater choice, driving disruption but also creating opportunities to innovate.

COMPLIANCE IS A NON-NEGOTIABLE
It is a basic requirement in order for Formula One teams to compete, but it need not stifle innovation.

RESISTANCE TO CHANGE IS NATURAL
To avoid resistance to change we must enable our teams to analyse the system and collaborate in determining solutions.

CUSTOMERS CHANGE, SO SHOULD WE
In a customer-centric business, make time to listen to what customers want, examine how their demands are changing and find out where we can add value.

Note

1   Newey, A (2017) *How to Build a Car: The autobiography of the world's greatest Formula 1 designer*, HarperCollins, London

CHAPTER EIGHT

The climate race

One of the privileges that comes with working in a Formula One race team is international travel. Having to spend up to one week each year in Melbourne, Montreal or Monte Carlo can only be described as a pleasure, and even the less attractive destinations have their upsides.

It is not always glamorous, and can often become exhausting, but there is always the recognition that this is something many people would love to experience. It means that you see the world, often from the window of an aeroplane, but also during quick breaks taken between the usual Groundhog Day routine of airport–hotel–racetrack in some far-flung destination.

Formula One races have taken place on every continent. Africa is not currently on the sport's schedule but Formula One did include the South African Grand Prix in Kyalami, Johannesburg, until 1993, and there are hopes for a return.

This privileged life of travel enables Formula One personnel to meet, work and engage with peoples from diverse backgrounds and cultures. Inevitably that means Formula One's travelling staff have a world view, an understanding of how similar we all are together with the impact that humankind is having on the planet. This includes witnessing first-hand the damaging effects of climate change driven by global warming, the destruction of wilderness, environmental pollution caused by industrialization, urbanization and overpopulation.

The recent global expansion of Formula One that commenced with the Malaysian Grand Prix in 1999 allowed us to witness the effects of deforestation in a country that lost 14.4 per cent of its wilderness between 2000 and 2012.[1] In Borneo, one of Malaysia's remaining wildernesses, illegal logging together with the expansion of palm oil and pulpwood plantations has reduced its forests to 50 per cent of their original size in 2019, down from 75 per cent in the mid-1980s.[2]

The approach to Kuala Lumpur International Airport, and the adjacent Sepang Formula One circuit, is marked by mile after mile of regimented palm oil plantations. This is an important source of wealth and employment for the country but one with a well-known impact on wildlife diversity thanks to loss of habitat. For visitors, it is a clear indication of how one country's environment and biodiversity has been dramatically changed in just a few years. It is far from the only one.

The inaugural Chinese Grand Prix in Shanghai in 2004 involved a one-and-a-half-hour journey from the city centre to the brand new Shanghai International Circuit in Jiading. This town was entirely independent from Shanghai until redesignated as a district of China's commercial capital in 1993.

By the time the circuit celebrated the 10th anniversary of its Formula One race, journey time from Shanghai had been reduced thanks to new motorways. The trip bore witness to Shanghai's increased, uninterrupted urban sprawl, the city having undergone a fourfold increase in size since 1984. In 2004 there were 16.4 million inhabitants, but by 2021 that figure was almost 28 million.[3]

Closer to home, the changes in the environment are sometimes less obvious than in the fast-developing nations and cities of Asia and Latin America. This does not mean the changes to our environment have been any less dramatic.

Prior to the advent of low-cost air travel in Europe in the mid-1990s, choosing to drive to Grand Prix events was not uncommon, often followed by a late-night dash back to the channel ports. For people of a certain age, therefore, the Windscreen Phenomenon is a familiar concept as drivers across Europe have noticed a substantial reduction of the number of insects killed on car windscreens, grilles and lights during long journeys – particularly at night.

Whilst the phenomena was initially dismissed as purely anecdotal and unsupported by science, that view changed dramatically with the widely reported publication in 2017 of a study by the scientific, peer-reviewed journal *Plos One*.[4] The key finding was that over a 27-year period, analysis of 63 protected nature areas in Germany revealed a decline of more than 75 per cent in the flying insect biomass – topped by a startling mid-summer decline of 82 per cent. The decline in insects suggested a collapsing eco-system with potentially catastrophic effects on wildlife populations, crop pollination and food production.

Further underpinning the Windscreen Phenomenon, detailed evidence was provided by the Danish ecologist Anders Møller in his 2019 paper, which studied the number of insects killed on the surfaces of cars over a 20-year period, 1997 to 2017, concluding that insect numbers had fallen by 80 per cent or more.[5] Part of his research involved an analysis of the local bird populations, the reduced number of insects having a significant impact on their feeding patterns and reproductive capability.

If deforestation, urbanization and the destruction of wildlife are significant causes for concern, the impact of global warming tips us towards an existential crisis. One that demands a profound reworking of humanity's way of treating the planet, its finite resources and the delicate ecosystem upon which our survival depends.

Michael Mann is an award-winning US climatologist and geophysicist, a key figure on the scientific world when it comes to demonstrating human-kind's impact on the environment, and particularly the effects of global warming since the Industrial Revolution. He was one of eight lead authors of the 'Observed climate change and variability' chapter of the Inter-governmental Panel on Climate Change (IPCC) report of 2001. His work contributed to the 2007 Nobel Peace Prize being awarded to the IPCC and former US vice president Al Gore, the latter's 2006 film *An Inconvenient Truth* having sought to educate audiences about the causes and impact of man-made global warming.

To climate change sceptics, Mann is portrayed as someone with a vested interest in promoting the idea that humans have caused changes to the climate and the earth's environment. Some are so bitterly opposed to the data and arguments he presents that he has faced threats.

However, Mann's work is based on data analysis, using a combination of actual environmental data such as temperature measurements together with proxy data – information gleaned from natural recorders of climate data including tree rings, ice cores, fossil pollen and ocean sediments. In 1998 he co-authored a paper analysing climate data over a 600-year period. The following year they went a step further, showing data covering the past 1,000 years.

This gave rise to the famous hockey-stick graph that showed a long-term cooling trend in global temperatures followed by a pronounced upward rise, most notably during the second half of the 20th century. In other words, since 1950, coincidentally the year in which the Formula One World Championship first took place.

Despite subsequent criticism of the methodology used by Mann and his colleagues, ultimately their findings were supported, and over the last two decades he has continued to publish research, contribute to the discussion of climate change in the media and campaign against those who dispute either the existence or extent of global warming. Mann advocates an end to the use of fossil fuels, and argues that the oil industry has not only known about the effects of emissions on human health and the global environment, but that it has actively spread disinformation.

He even argues that climate exchange extremists who preach what he calls 'climate doom porn' play into the hands of the oil industry, creating the impression that there is no point in trying to stop global warming. In effect, it's too far gone for us to do anything about it. This promotes inaction at precisely the time when change needs to occur.

In reality many of the solutions to preventing a further escalation in global warming already exist. In the same way that the Covid-19 vaccines were not developed in just one year, but as the result of many years of advanced research, Mann argues that we have the solutions to switch off our dependence on fossil fuels. All that is required is the commitment to do so.

Formula One has a very public role to play in this, providing an example of just how quickly a sector that has been so reliant on fossil fuels can change. The sport's role in the politics of climate change may appear peripheral, but as we explore later in this chapter, the platform provided by Formula One for both technological development and the marketing of products by both the automotive and energy sector make it entirely relevant. A significant number of people watch Formula One, observing it on social and mainstream media. Ultimately the sport's audiences are influenced by what they see.

In 2019 Formula One's cumulative television audience across the year totalled 1.9 billion viewers, and although this comprised repeat viewers, it represents an indication of the sport's impact on a global population of 7.8 billion people.

Up to 104 million individuals watched each Grand Prix in 2020, with video views on social media reaching 4.9 billion and notably strong growth in China. The world's most populous country is a key market for the sport given that it is the world's largest automotive market and responsible for 41 per cent of the world's electric car sales in 2020.[6] It is also a barometer of the changes taking place in the world as a result of the effects of environmental pollution and climate change. Despite the continued use of coal within its energy sector, China has committed to limiting peak emissions by 2030 and achieving carbon neutrality by 2060.[7]

The Covid-19 pandemic demonstrated humankind's vulnerability, our interdependence and the degree to which the world truly is a global village – the term first used by Canadian author Marshall McLuhan back in the early 1960s when air travel was a tiny fraction of what it is today. In the face of a rapidly moving, existential threat, humanity responded with a series of unprecedented measures aimed at mitigating risk and putting in place scientific solutions to the virus in the form of vaccines.

Initially healthcare professionals were quick to point out that vaccine development would take many years, perhaps up to a decade. The previous record for producing an effective vaccine was four years, the length of time it took to produce a vaccine for mumps in the 1960s. Yet the coronavirus pandemic resulted in multiple vaccines being developed, proven and deployed within a calendar year of the World Health Organization's pandemic declaration on 11 March 2020.

While some questioned how this had been made possible without compromising the usual rigour that goes into testing the efficacy and safety of vaccines, the lessons learned have profound implications when it comes to humanity dealing with a significant threat. Two factors contributed to this dramatic turnaround: the vast resources provided by governments and industry to fund research and development of a vaccine, and the prior decades of research into vaccine development along with the tools that could be used to create them.

Dan Barouch, director of the Centre for Virology and Vaccine Research at Harvard Medical School in Boston, Massachusetts told nature.com, 'It shows how fast vaccine development can proceed when there is a true global emergency and sufficient resources.'

Tackling the coronavirus pandemic so effectively was 'a good example of what science can do very quickly', says Akiko Iwasaki, an immunologist at the Yale School of Medicine in New Haven, before adding, 'but it didn't happen overnight'.[8] She points out that research on DNA vaccines started in the 1990s, and that the specific type of vaccines used to tackle Covid-19 came as the result of more than a decade of intensive work. Fortunately for humankind, Covid-19 turned up just when we had developed the capability to respond quickly.

Having the necessary resources made available in order develop solutions based on existing knowhow was critical. Yet those resources were only made available once society came to recognize the extent of the threat and developed an ambitious goal aimed at tackling it.

In addition, the solution was not provided by focusing on a single vaccine, instead more than a dozen individual pharmaceutical companies and collaborative partnerships worked on solutions. Ultimately several vaccines proved to be effective and, along with rapidly developed treatments, provided the means by which society could return to near-normality.

There is much that society's response to the global pandemic can teach us about ways in which the environmental crisis can be resolved, particularly in respect of the forces behind man-made climate change. This includes the ability of an R&D-intensive sport such as Formula One to develop, trial and implement solutions that will not only enable it to become sustainable, but for those solutions to be transferrable into wider society.

On the basis that tackling the root cause and impact of climate change will require a multilayered approach, Formula One has an important role to play in determining just some of the solutions.

Given that road transportation of all kinds is responsible for 28 per cent of the world's annual emissions of greenhouse gases,[9] and that 45 per cent of that figure comes from passenger vehicles,[10] Formula One's prominence as a technology and marketing showcase for both the automotive and energy sector gives it an important role in framing society's quest for solutions.

In 2021 four automotive companies supply engines in Formula One, but eight automotive brands use the sport as a marketing tool. As part of the Daimler Group, Mercedes-Benz produced just over 2.8 million cars and vans in pre-Covid 2019, while Daimler's trucks and buses business unit saw over 500,000 vehicles leave its production lines. In the same year the Renault Group sold 3.4 million vehicles globally, although its collaboration with Nissan and Mitsubishi drove the total sales from their alliance to 10.3 million units. Meanwhile, Honda sold 5.3 million cars, and almost 20 million motorcycles. In the luxury sport-car marketplace Ferrari sold over 10,000 units, while McLaren Cars produced 4,765 and Aston Martin – a partner and sponsor of Red Bull Racing – delivered 5,800.

Ferrari was spun out of its parent Fiat Chrysler Automobiles (FCA) in 2016, the owner of automotive brands including Chrysler, Dodge, Fiat and Jeep. That move started when 10 per cent of FCA's shares in the Italian sports-car company were floated on the New York Stock Exchange in 2014.

Ferrari's largest individual shareholder remains Exor NV, the investment vehicle of the Italian Agnelli family. This holding company owns 22.91 per cent of Ferrari's stock, but controls 35.8 per cent of the voting rights. It also owns 14.4 per cent of Stellantis, the entity created by the 2021 merger of Group PSA – owners of Peugeot, Citroën, DS, Opel and Vauxhall – with FCA. With Stellantis also owning Alfa Romeo, an FCA brand that has been the main commercial and technical partner of the Sauber Formula 1 team since 2018, this further illustrates the closely networked nature of the global automotive industry – with common shareholders, technical alliances and partnerships the order of the day.

Added together, the automotive groups involved in Formula One directly, or via shareholder relationships, sold over 27 million cars in 2019, representing slightly more than 40 per cent of the global market. Further integration within the industry is likely to occur in the near term. With Formula One playing a key role in the global marketing of so many brands its influence remains high.

When the 2021 Formula One season kicked off, commentators were tipping Mercedes to face tough opposition from the Honda-powered Red Bull Racing team, while it was hoped that Ferrari would stage a resurgence thanks to an improved engine that would also benefit the Alfa Romeo Racing team. McLaren was also hoping for greater success, thanks in part to its new supply of Mercedes-Benz engines.

Meanwhile, the German manufacturer was also hoping to achieve success with its new-found customer at Aston Martin, a partnership in Formula One that reflects a rather deeper business relationship. All Aston Martin sports cars now feature AMG Mercedes engines, and Daimler has acquired a 20 per cent stake in the quintessentially British sports-car firm. New arrival Alpine was sporting its French-race-blue livery, powered of course by engines from parent company Renault.

Commercial sponsorship of these teams came from a diverse range of companies, many of them from new and recently emerged sectors. One, however, has remained a consistent supporter of Formula One since the commencement of the World Championship in 1950. The oil industry has used the technical showcase and marketing power of motor racing to develop and promote fuel and lubricant brands since car racing began more than a century ago.

Shell enjoys the longest-standing partnership in Formula One history, having suppled Enzo Ferrari with its products when he was driving for Alfa Corse back in 1924, and then partnering with his eponymous team from 1947 onwards. Following a hiatus in the relationship in the 1970s and 1980s, during which time Ferrari was supported by Italian oil company AGIP, Shell returned to the team in 1996.

Royal Dutch Shell is the world's fourth largest oil and gas company measured by revenue,[11] one of the so-called 'supermajors'. Its next largest competitors are British giant BP, the US's Exxon Mobil and Saudi Arabia's Aramco, each of which has a significant Formula One involvement. Another state-owned oil company, Malaysia's Petronas, has been the title sponsor of Mercedes in Formula One since 2010, and prior to that backed the Sauber team. Polish oil company Orlen sponsors Alfa Romeo Racing through its personal association with national racing hero Robert Kubica.

BP is partnered with Alpine and Exxon Mobil with Red Bull Racing while Aramco became a sponsor of the Formula One World Championship in 2019. Within months of the Aramco deal being announced Formula One finalized an agreement with the Saudi Arabian government that will lead to the oil-rich country hosting a World Championship event for the next decade.

As the pinnacle of world motorsport, Formula One remains the go-to category for car manufacturers eager to promote their products in global markets. Meanwhile the automotive and motorsport industry's reliance on the internal combustion engine means that they have inevitably become close bedfellows of the oil industry. 'First fill' deals between oil companies and car manufacturers means there is a high degree of leverage in their business relationships, with 'approved lubricants' and 'recommended fuels' deals highly sought after.

The sponsorship relationships in Formula One are a very public demonstration of the degree to which the oil industry regards the motorsport programmes of car manufacturers as a central marketing channel.

When Carl Benz famously applied for a patent for his vehicle 'powered by a gas engine' in January 1886, he not only heralded the dawn of the car but the start of mankind's love affair with gasoline and its denser, slower evaporating relative, diesel.

In the very same year a Scottish businessman named David Cargill founded the Rangoon Oil Company to develop oil fields in the Indian subcontinent.[12] Later renamed Burmah, the discovery of oil in Iran's Khuzestan Province in 1908 led to the creation of a new entity known as the

Anglo-Iranian Oil Company, the forerunner of British Petroleum (BP). By the 1940s BP was one of the famed 'Seven Sisters' oil companies that dominated global supply alongside Shell, Esso, Mobil, Texaco, Gulf and the Standard Oil Company of California (SoCal).

By the time the inaugural FIA Formula One World Championship began in 1950, the automotive world knew precisely who to do business with when it came to finding fuel and lubricants, and little has changed today. A casual glance through Formula One's history books acts as a snapshot of oil industry brands over the years, from José Froilán González winning the 1951 British Grand Prix in his Shell-supplied Ferrari to Lewis Hamilton clinching a seventh world title in his Petronas-emblazoned Mercedes, and every point in between.

It is hardly surprising that motor-racing fans are referred to as 'petrol heads' or Formula One cars described as 'gas guzzling'. Dramatic pit stops to refuel the cars made a spectacle out of the need to replenish a fuel tank after only 30 or 40 minutes, sometimes leading to a fiery incident of the kind that befell Jos Verstappen during the 1994 German Grand Prix.

The message delivered by Formula One, simply by virtue of the need to push the limits of performance, was that the excessive use of fuel was to be encouraged. Whether the drivers were burning fuel, rubber or risking themselves, it was all part of the drama, risk and appeal of Grand Prix motor racing.

Then, in 2009, two minor announcements were made that raised little in the way of interest in Formula One circles. In August of that year Nissan's ambitious CEO Carlos Ghosn announced that deliveries of the all-electric Nissan Leaf would commence before the year was out. Meanwhile, in November, a small showroom was opened in Monte Carlo to display a small two-seater sports car, based on a Lotus Elise but entirely re-engineered as an electric vehicle. As a result, Formula One racegoers attending the 2010 Monaco Grand Prix would find themselves momentarily distracted by the sight of a wine-red Roadster sitting in the window. The world's first Tesla.

Ten years after the launch of the Nissan Leaf and the arrival of Tesla's tiny showroom on the streets of Monte Carlo, Formula One announced plans to become carbon neutral by 2030. In addition, Pat Symonds, Formula One's Chief Technical Officer, made it clear that Formula One cars would no longer be powered by refined fossil fuels, turning its back on gasoline by 2025.

'In the interests of getting the ball rolling and to keep costs down, we've specified 10 per cent advanced sustainable ethanol for 2021', said Symonds at the time. 'But our ambitions go beyond that and, as I say, we want to get to 100 per cent advanced sustainable fuel.'[13]

In just 10 years the end of Formula One's love affair with fossil fuels is within sight. Starting with the introduction of kinetic energy recovery systems (KERS) in 2009 and followed by the development of highly complex hybrid petrol-electric powertrains in 2014, energy efficiency and waste-energy recovery has been part of Formula One's technological mix for over a decade.

The decision to move towards a future in which Formula One's cars will be powered by sustainable fuels represents just one part of an ambitious plan to address the sport's generation of greenhouse gases and environmental pollution. The November 2019 announcement of Formula One's plans to achieve a net-zero carbon footprint by 2030 covered the Formula One cars, on-track activity and the full operations of the World Championship. It also committed to a key milestone in 2025, namely that all its World Championship events would be sustainable, with single-use plastics eliminated and all waste reused, recycled or composted.

Chase Carey, then CEO of Formula One, outlined his vision for the sport's environmental target. 'In launching F1's first-ever sustainability strategy, we recognize the critical role that all organizations must play in tackling this global issue. By leveraging the immense talent, passion and drive for innovation held by all members of the F1 community, we hope to make a significant positive impact on the environment and communities in which we operate. The actions we are putting in place from today will reduce our carbon footprint and ensure we are net zero carbon by 2030.'

As has become the norm, F1 and its regulator spoke with one voice, FIA President Jean Todt stating that, 'Our commitment to global environmental protection is crucial', later adding that, 'With the involvement of the teams, drivers, F1's numerous stakeholders and, crucially, the millions of fans around the world, the FIA and Formula One are committed to driving development and ensuring motorsport grows as a laboratory for environmentally beneficial innovations.'[14]

The message was clear. Formula One's ability to develop innovative technology solutions against tight deadlines would now be deployed in the race to save the planet. The FIA's Environment and Sustainability Commission, headed by Felipe Calderón, gave teeth to Todt's move to place motorsport at the vanguard of environmental technologies. Formula One teams can now apply to the FIA for Environmental Accreditation, Mercedes Grand Prix achieving the optimal three stars in November 2020.

Counterintuitively, a sport associated with environmental destruction aims to pivot into one that has a net-zero impact on the environment. Furthermore, it will develop and showcase solutions that will be both transferable and scalable in other sectors, ultimately helping society in its fight to protect the environment and head off the worst effects of climate change.

To support the announcement, Formula One revealed its current impact on the environment in terms of emissions of carbon dioxide. In 2019 Formula One's carbon footprint through direct, indirect and supply chain impact was estimated to be 256,551 tonnes of CO_2, broken down into five key areas of operations.

The Formula One cars themselves contributed only 0.7 per cent of the sport's emissions. Across a full World Championship season, the 20 cars burn around 150,000 litres of fuel, the same quantity that a single, four-engined Boeing 747 uses on a 10-hour flight. In overall terms, both the consumption and emissions of Formula One cars are small, even if the external optics are of a sport enjoyed by gas-guzzling petrol heads.

Of far greater concern, but hidden from view, are Formula One's global logistics operations together with the business travel that is an inevitable consequence of delivering a World Championship. Logistics accounts for an estimated 45 per cent of F1's carbon emission, by far the largest single contribution to the sport's environmental impact.

Official logistics supplier DHL is responsible for coordinating all of the freight to the long-haul events outside Europe, with 40–50 tonnes of equipment per team – cars included – added to the 150 tonnes of broadcasting equipment that go into providing the live digital broadcast feed from each event. This includes 60 kilometres of cabling and up to 120 cameras.[15]

Additionally, Formula One's Paddock Club corporate hospitality set-up has to be transported to each event in order to ensure a high-quality, standardized offering to the sport's corporate clients. This can take up to 30 containers of hospitality equipment, including everything you would expect for a five-star service to be guaranteed irrespective of destination.

Tyre supplier Pirelli is an example of a critical supply chain partner, responsible for bringing 1,600 tyres to each Grand Prix along with the equipment needed to service them. For European events Pirelli mirrors the teams in transporting freight by road, but for long-haul events sea-freight is a preferred method, and this is also used by teams to transport non-critical items.

Business travel is estimated to contribute 27.7 per cent towards Formula One's carbon footprint, comprising not only air travel but ground transportation together with hotel accommodation. The 10 teams take 800–900 personnel to events, while the FIA, Formula One and key contractors take this number to well over 1,000. While senior leadership and management are split between first class and business, the majority of travelling personnel fly economy.

With 23 Grand Prix events in 2021 the volume of travel has increased enormously as the result of Formula One's growth in relation to the number and geographical location of events. Twenty-five years ago there were 16 Grand Prix, 11 of which were in Europe and five in long-haul destinations. On the provisional (non-Covid-affected) calendar for 2021, 9 of the 23 events take place in Europe, requiring team personnel to travel to no fewer than 14 long-haul destinations.

Formula One's headquarter facilities in London and broadcast centre in Biggin Hill, combined with the teams' headquarters and factories, contribute a further 19.3 per cent towards Formula One's emissions of greenhouse gases. While Formula One's offices consume energy for heating, cooling, lighting and powering the usual array of IT equipment, team facilities produce significantly more emissions from R&D and manufacturing activities.[16]

This includes the operation of wind tunnels, a critical piece of R&D equipment since the arrival of aerodynamics as a key discipline in Formula One car design during the late 1970s. A typical wind tunnel consumes around 10,000 kilowatt hours per day in order to operate the giant fans, rolling roads and maintain the correct air temperature. This means that a single facility can consume the same amount of electricity over the course of one year as 250 family homes.[17]

Manufacturing operations include complex machine tools, autoclaves used for curing composite structures, together with the rigs and testing equipment used to prove systems and assemblies prior to deployment. In the case of a Formula One engine manufacturer, of which there are currently four, this includes running dynamometers. These allow both individual engines and powertrains to undergo static rig testing. With physical track testing dramatically limited in recent years, and totalling only three days in 2021, greater emphasis has been placed on using rig testing and simulation tools.

In the case of Formula One's powertrain manufacturers, the requirement for each driver to use no more than three engines over the course of a season means that engine life cycles have increased from 500 kilometres in the 1980s to 10 times that today. This means that durability testing has increased, while the ongoing requirement to work with oil companies to develop new fuels and lubricants means further rig testing.

Typically, the introduction of a new fuel will require three full engine cycles on dynamometers, for example, large extractor fans being used to expel engine emissions from the test cells. Once again, energy use is significant and the source of that energy is now the focus of Formula One's 2030 carbon neutral strategy.

A clue as to the speed with which Formula One is addressing its ambitious strategy can be found in how it used the global Covid-19 pandemic to accelerate a multi-year programme to run its global broadcasting operation remotely. The sport's operations previously included a mobile broadcast facility that housed the vast production and editing suites needed to beam Formula One to over 190 countries and territories around the world. This 'TV Village' had to be transported around the world, was energy-hungry and required a large team of travelling personnel to operate it.

When combined with Formula One's corporate hospitality operations, support race operations, circuit energy and generator usage, the broadcasting facility contributed an estimated 7.3 per cent of the sport's carbon emissions in 2019. A long-term plan to start operating the broadcasting facility remotely had already been in the pipeline, but the Covid-19 outbreak and restrictions on global travel forced Formula One to bring that change forward. With the 2020 Formula One World Championship delayed by four months, the decision was made to immediately build a large-scale, remote operation.

'We completed this multi-year project in just over seven weeks, under lockdown conditions, something we're very proud of', said Dean Locke, Formula One's Director of Broadcast and Media. 'Going remote has allowed Formula One to reduce travelling freight by 34 per cent, while the number of travelling staff has also been reduced by 37 per cent.'[18]

Instead of moving freight and people, Formula One has instead opted to move large quantities of data – over 160 terabytes – to the Media and Technology Centre in Biggin Hill, near London, each weekend.

The initial move towards remote operations began six years earlier, in 2014, with a digital technical team, data analysts and social media editorial team. To that has been added technical operations rooms to support the trackside broadcast including, for example, the on-board camera production that forms such an important aspect of the sport's content. All the team radio feeds are now curated and produced remotely, while the distribution of the global television feed has also moved to Biggin Hill with a master control room managing up to 140 sources from the track.

Meanwhile the main Technical Centre, which until 2020 was based trackside, has been moved back to base. Although the acquisition of media and data continues to be carried out trackside, the editing and production of the final content is now conducted remotely.

Supported by 53 operators monitoring over 400 screens and a vast array of computers being used to process the sport's digital content, the main director and producers take the remote feed from 90 cameras and 170 audio sources, creating the live, delayed and highlights coverage. They are supported by teams responsible for the graphics, telemetry systems, IT systems, media management and the official timing system.

This shift towards remote operation is not new to Formula One but will play an increasing role in reducing the number of people needing to travel to events while reducing the quantity of freight needing to be transported by air, sea and road. Examples of this approach already exist. For more than a decade and a half, race teams have run race strategy remotely, with race strategists, aerodynamicists and performance engineers working from mission control centres back at base.

Looking like mini versions of the Mission Control Centre in Houston, which has managed flight control for US manned space travel since 1965, Formula One's remote operations rooms allow teams of engineers to use data analytics in order to drive rapid decisions that are then communicated to their colleagues trackside. Measured in milliseconds, the delay in data being received from countries such as Australia is inconsequential.

To visit Red Bull Racing's AT&T Operations Centre in Milton Keynes is to get a glimpse into the benefits of remote working. Aside from reducing travel and freight, decision making is improved by being away from the raw emotion of race, and there is a significant benefit to staff being able to maintain a better quality of work–life balance.

In the coming years the recognition that moving data is a lot easier and less damaging to the environment is going to play a major part in reducing Formula One's carbon footprint. Formula One, the FIA and the constituent teams will continue to examine ways in which remote operations can be adopted. This is also being reflected in the way the media will cover the sport, as instantaneous access to video, audio and data feeds mean that commentators and journalists no longer need to attend events on the far side of the world in order to report on and analyse the sport in depth.

The optics of Formula One, particularly for those who are not fans of the sport, have seldom been positive. Writing in *The Guardian* newspaper back in 2008, British writer and comedian David Mitchell had this to say: 'It is noisy, environmentally unfriendly and ends with people wasting champagne. There is a vogue for banning things these days, which I am not keen on, but, if we are going to ban lots of activities that people wrongly enjoy – smoking, drinking on the Tube and so on – then surely motor racing is a candidate.'[19]

Four factors have driven Formula One's change of direction: regulation, competition, customer demand and public opinion. Burning fossil fuels for sporting entertainment is no longer regarded acceptable to the sport's stakeholders.

Shortly after his election to the presidency of the FIA, Jean Todt asked fellow Frenchman and former Ferrari powertrain engineer Gilles Simon to commence work on creating a new set for Formula One engine regulations that would place an emphasis on energy efficiency. This would be achieved by taking the existing Kinetic Energy Recovery Systems, first deployed in 2009, and combine them with road-relevant technologies to create a hybrid powertrain that would optimize the performance derived from a fixed amount of fuel.

These discussions began with a technical working group comprising the existing engine manufacturers together with other interested parties, and lasted throughout 2010 and into 2011. Present throughout the process were Ferrari, Mercedes-Benz, Renault and Cosworth, but other manufacturers including Toyota were involved in the early discussions.

With energy efficiency the core objective, the working group considered ways in which the new Formula One powertrain could be made to use less fuel in outright terms, to make better use of the fuel in terms of combustion efficiency and to recover waste energy such that it could be harnessed and redeployed. Focus quickly shifted to defining a hybrid engine featuring a small internal combustion engine and battery-powered electric motor.

The first decision was to reduce the capacity of the engine significantly, bringing it down from the 2.4 litres used by the existing V8 engines to a modest 1600cc. To enable sufficient power to be produced by such a unit, turbocharging would be permitted by means of a single unit.

Then came a set of decisions about the type of fuel injection system to be used, port injection being replaced by direct injection. This would run at high pressure, up to 500 bar.

The quantity of fuel to be used for a race distance was fixed, at 100 kilogrammes, and furthermore the maximum flow rate had a ceiling 100 kilogrammes per hour at 12,000 rpm. Although the subsequent rev limit would be set at 1,5000 rpm, the fact that the fuel flow could not increase beyond 12,000 rpm rendered the rev limit somewhat irrelevant.

These measures, when combined, sought to reduce the amount of fuel used by a Formula One powertrain by a figure of around 35 per cent when compared to its predecessor – a significant reduction in the amount of fossil fuel used by a Grand Prix car during the course of a race weekend. The reduction in the supply of fossil fuel energy would be offset by the development of a sophisticated energy recovery and storage system. This was to be housed behind the driver, below the fuel cell, with complex control systems enabling the battery to be recharged and the energy released according to the driver's requirements over the course of a lap.

The energy recovery system was always going to feature a KERS unit, but the discussions within the technical working group quickly concluded that the exhaust gases could also be used to drive a turbine that would charge the car's energy storage system. The combination of KERS system with the 'e-turbo' would mean that each powertrain would feature two electrical motors capable of generating electricity. Known as the motor generator unit-H (heat) and motor generator unit-K (kinetic) these units would recycle waste energy, charging an energy storage unit. This battery is permitted to deploy up to 120 kilowatts (161bhp) of power, a cap that was agreed at the time the rules were drawn up in 2011.

Throughout 2010 and into 2011, up to and including the World Motor Sport Council (WMSC) meeting held on 11 June that year, the new engine was to be a four-cylinder unit, a marked shift away from the multicylinder era of Formula One marked by the use of V12, V10 and V8 units. After the June WMSC meeting, however, Ferrari began to lobby for the number of cylinders to be increased in line with their desire for Formula One to reflect the multicylinder units that are a feature of their road cars. With the help of McLaren's Martin Whitmarsh, who set about calling the relevant parties in order to secure the necessary buy-in, a move towards a V6 engine was finally agreed and voted for on 29 June 2011, with an introduction deadline set for the 2014 Formula One World Championship.

Two and a half years after that decision was taken, Formula One entered its hybrid racing era, its powertrains achieving that unprecedented 35 per cent reduction in the quantity of fossil fuel being used, and the complex waste energy systems achieving their targeted power of 120kw/161bhp.

What was unforeseen at the time of the 2011 vote was that one manufacturer, Mercedes-Benz, would come up with a series of innovations that would enable their hybrid powertrain to start the new era with a significant performance advantage. This included a highly compact split turbine and compressor, joined by a shaft running at speed of up to 125,000 rpm through an integrated MGU-H. This had the benefit of improving packaging, efficiency and outright performance.

In addition, and contrary to initial thoughts that the energy recovery and storage systems would be the primary forces of development, Mercedes quickly began to exploit combustion improvements in the tiny 1.6-litre V6 internal combustion engine. By focusing on combustion chamber design and technologies that would ensure optimized combustion for the fuel and air mixture in the engine, Mercedes-Benz was able to confirm in 2017 that it had achieved more than 50 per cent thermal efficiency. Acknowledging that 100 per cent thermal efficiency is impossible, Mercedes cleverly marketed this significant engineering achievement as being 'Halfway to Impossible'.

Achieving 50 per cent thermal efficiency means a level that is 60 per cent more than the average road-car engine. In 2013 the thermal efficiency of an average road car was 29 per cent,[20] meaning that more than 70 per cent of the fossil fuel pumped into a car is being wasted on heat, noise, friction or simply being blown straight down the exhaust pipe and into the environment.

Dr Nigel McKinley, Mercedes' team leader for powertrain performance simulation, explained the background to this achievement and the potential implications for the wider automotive industry: 'The success of the combustion process determines how much fuel energy propels the car. Our engineers made developments to the geometry of the combustion chamber and also numerous developments to other areas of the power unit, which optimized the precise condition of air fuel mixture leading to efficient combustion. This means that half of the fuel is now being used to propel the car, and if road-car engines achieved a similar step this would have a major effect on CO_2 reduction.'

A significant part of Mercedes' progress was made possible by working with the scientists at Petronas to engineer the molecular structure of the fuel and ensure that the fuel chemistry would work in harmony with the engine. While the 19th-century technology represented by the internal combustion engine has indeed come a long way, the fundamental principle remains the same. It is an incredibly inefficient means of creating power, particularly when its energy source is finite and the emissions produced by burning it add to the stock of greenhouse gases warming our planet.

Simply put, Formula One's continued use of fossil fuels is unsustainable, and to achieve the sport's 2030 targets, the use of this form of energy has to end. Naturally, thoughts initially turned to the trend towards battery-powered electric vehicles.

Parallel to Formula One's introduction of hybrid engines in 2014, the FIA sanctioned the creation of Formula E – a racing series featuring battery-powered electric vehicles. This captured the attention of many of the world's automotive manufacturers as they geared up for a shift towards battery electric vehicles, primarily driven by the regulations that have resulted from governments signing up to the 1997 Kyoto Protocol on climate change and, subsequently, the 2016 Paris Agreement.

Under the United Nations Framework Convention on Climate Change the specific goal, agreed by over 191 nations in Paris, commits to limiting the increase in global average temperature to below 2 degrees C above pre-industrial levels, with efforts aimed at limiting this to 1.5 degrees C. One of the significant ways to achieve this is through the reduction in greenhouse gases, and the automotive industry has to move away from its reliance on fossil fuels in order to meet government-enforced emissions targets.

Norway was one of the countries to take the lead in this regard, phasing out the sale of fossil-fuelled cars by 2025. By the final quarter of 2020 two-thirds of new car sales in Norway were battery electric vehicles, so while only 9 per cent of the country's 2.8 million vehicles are electric, the change that is taking place is sudden, dramatic and non-negotiable.

The UK, which initially introduced a ban on fossil-fuelled cars by 2035, announced in November 2020 that the ban on petrol- and diesel-powered vehicles would be advanced to 2030, with a stay of execution until 2035 for hybrid vehicles capable of driving 'significant distances' on electric power.[21]

Against this backdrop, the pressure on Formula One to abandon fossil fuels and maintain road relevancy is clear, and yet the battery-electric-vehicle route pursued by Formula E has limitations. Simply put, based on current battery technology, it would be impossible to create an all-electric Formula One car capable of achieving the performance required for a 300-kilometre Grand Prix.

A one-solution-fits-all approach is not going to work. In the same way that Covid-19 was tackled using a variety of vaccines, the transport industry's move away from fossil fuels will require multiple solutions.

While battery-powered cars offer a partial solution, a much bigger challenge is faced by the demand for high-performance or long-distance vehicles, heavy-goods vehicles, shipping and air freight. Added to which there will continue to be many millions of cars, vans and buses powered by internal combustion engines long after the UK, Norway and other nations committed to the Paris Agreement have met their targets of electric vehicle sales.

Faced with this challenge, Formula One's solution has been to look for an alternative approach; one that is based on its strengths for rapid innovation, providing a laboratory that can be used by both the car and energy industries to develop solutions with applications across the entire transport sector. As a result, by 2025 Formula One cars will be powered by renewable energy in the form of e-fuels. One route involves biofuel produced from bio-waste, the other a synthetic fuel created by pulling carbon dioxide out of the atmosphere to create a hydrocarbon, which when burned will not add to the store of greenhouse gases.

Paddy Lowe, former technical director of the Mercedes and Williams Formula One teams, is focusing his efforts on the development of synthetic fuels. He advocates a move away from the linear use of finite resources into a world where technology enables a circular, sustainable ecosystem.

'Every bit of CO_2 that you or I put up in the atmosphere during our lifetimes is still up there', he told me. 'Even the CO_2 that Stevenson's Rocket produced is still there. The shocking thing about CO_2 is that it just accumulates. The thing we have got to do as a human race is to invent a way to have it both ways. Can we produce these materials, energy and hydrocarbon feed stocks in a circular way rather than in a linear way, so that we can go on indefinitely?'

'That is actually all achievable, we just need to get on with it', says Lowe. 'Formula One is a great example of a linear consumer, but that needs to change and set a path into a more circular process.'

He also believes that the visibility of Formula One moving towards sustainable energy systems is just as important an outcome as the technical solution: 'It's not just a technical task, but a communications task.'

Lowe is advocating an industrial approach to what is a large-scale challenge for society, and one that is not going to be solved through the production of those biofuels that place further demand on the use of vegetation, land and the environment.

As a result, carbon-neutral fuels are a focus of Formula One, produced by taking CO_2 out of the environment – whether from the atmosphere or oceans – and combining it with hydrogen produced by the electrolysis of water. The resulting hydrocarbon fuel can be used without adding to the world's atmospheric carbon emission, creating a circular ecosystem that can play a major part in the transition away from fossil fuels during this century.

'Formula One didn't invent the hybrid [engine] but Formula One showed what a hybrid could be', said Formula One's Pat Symonds at the end of 2019. 'It moved people's perceptions of what a hybrid is capable of and I think we can do the same with new fuel technology and hopefully demonstrate that another viable alternative energy source is possible.'

In the winter of 2020, the FIA provided biofuels produced from bio-waste to Formula One's engine manufacturers to commence testing. This is the start of an evaluation process that will include synthetic fuels, and it is generating significant interest from car manufacturers, energy companies and other parts of the transport sector.

Porsche, part of the Volkswagen Audi Group, has announced a major investment in synthetic fuels as it aims to sustain the use of internal combustion engines in parallel with its commitment to electro mobility. It is investing an initial 24 million euros, supported by a further 9 million euros from the German government, in creating a wind-powered synthetic fuel facility in Chile. The aim is to produce 130,000 litres in 2022, rising to 550 million litres in 2026.

Porsche spokesman Peter Gräve explained that synthetic e-fuels would enable 'the almost climate neutral operation of combustion-engined vehicles'. Porsche calculates that cars powered by synthetic fuels would reduce CO_2 emissions by 85 per cent and are cleaner than an electric vehicle when the environmental impact of battery production is taken into account. The company is also conscious that most of the iconic Porsche 911 models it has produced since 1964 continue to be used. Demand to operate some cars powered entirely by internal combustion engines is likely to continue throughout this century. 'In the medium term, e-fuels have the potential to link the future with tradition', said Gräve.[22]

In March 2021 Porsche's Motorsport Vice-President Fritz Enzinger confirmed that Formula One's approach to sustainability could make a perfect match for his own company's view of using synthetic fuels as one mechanism for abandoning fossil fuels: 'Porsche and Volkswagen AG are observing the constantly changing regulations in all relevant racing series around the world. This is also the case with regard to the emerging new engine and drivetrain regulation for Formula One from 2025', he told BBC Sport. 'It would be of great interest if aspects of sustainability – for instance, the implementation of e-fuels – play a role in this.'[23]

Formula One's commitment to its 2030 goal of achieving carbon neutrality is absolute. It is ideally placed to create a case study of how quickly an industry can pivot and create an environmentally sustainable future. Sceptics will watch to see if the sport's initiatives lead to genuine change, or whether they are used as a fig leaf by an automotive and energy sector still wedded to fossil fuels.

By taking fewer people to events, reducing the quantity of freight and helping to develop the synthetic fuels that will power road, sea and air transport, Formula One has a significant opportunity. Not only to lead by example, but to create new opportunities for business development through technology transfer.

It might just be that the sport's reputation for championing the technologies that have caused so much environmental damage can be transformed – helping to develop the solutions that will enable society to deal with the self-inflicted peril of man-made climate change.

Lessons from the climate challenge

AS A GLOBAL SPORT, FORMULA ONE IS A WITNESS TO CHANGE

Formula One's stakeholders are particularly aware of how small our world is, and the effects that man-made climate change, pollution and urbanization are having on our planet's fragile ecosystems. A global presence gives it a worldwide perspective. Every business has a geographic reach, and can influence that environment.

BUSINESSES RELY ON DATA TO MAKE DECISIONS, MEASURING CLIMATE CHANGE IS NO DIFFERENT

The data-driven environment of Formula One means that modelling and simulation techniques are well understood. With predictive analytics helping drive improved outcomes, the same approach can be taken towards combating climate change. We know what the future holds unless decisions are made to avoid the worst-case scenarios.

THE CHANGES AHEAD ARE NON-NEGOTIABLE, BACKED UP BY REGULATION AND COMPLIANCE

As a result of agreements including the Kyoto Protocol and Paris Agreement governments are seeking to reduce or eliminate carbon emissions. Formula One's close relationship with the automotive and energy sectors means that change is inevitable. The choice is to lead by example or risk becoming irrelevant.

THE CURRENT HYBRID ENGINE TECHNOLOGY SHOWS WHAT IS POSSIBLE

The current hybrid engine regulations have reduced fuel consumption by 35 per cent, converted waste energy into electricity and resulted in the development of the most efficient internal combustion engines in history. The lesson is that innovation is driven in part by setting truly ambitious goals and deadlines.

REMOTE WORKING IS HERE TO STAY IN A POST-COVID, ENVIRONMENTALLY SUSTAINABLE WORLD

The need to reduce global freight and travel during the course of the Covid-19 pandemic has led Formula One to accelerate its use of remote working on a permanent basis. Moving data is better than moving people and freight.

CLIMATE CHANGE SOLUTIONS WILL BE MULTIFACETED

Formula One is focusing on a range of technologies and solutions to achieving net zero carbon emissions by 2030. This will include ending its reliance on fossil fuels in its core activities, developing green fuels that have applications far beyond the sport.

Notes

1 Geographical Association (nd) What are the environmental impacts of deforestation in Malaysia?, https://www.geography.org.uk/teaching-resources/singapore-malaysia/What-are-the-environmental-impacts-of-deforestation-in-Malaysia (archived at https://perma.cc/M7BT-A3H4)

2 UN Environment Programme (2019) Deforestation In Borneo is Slowing, But Regulation Remains Key, https://www.unep.org/news-and-stories/story/deforestation-borneo-slowing-regulation-remains-key (archived at https://perma.cc/H8MT-9VZX)

3   Macrotrends (2021) Shanghai, China Metro Area Population 1950–2021, https://www.macrotrends.net/cities/20656/shanghai/population (archived at https://perma.cc/W4RW-UYWD)

4   Hallmann, C A *et al* (2017) More Than 75 Percent Decline Over 27 Years in Total Flying Insect Biomass in Protected Areas, *Plos One*, https://journals.plos.org/plosone/article?id=10.1371/journal.pone.0185809 (archived at https://perma.cc/5Z5X-6LNE)

5   Møller, A (2019) Parallel Declines in Abundance of Insects and Insectivorous Birds in Denmark Over 22 Years, *Ecology and Evolution*, https://onlinelibrary.wiley.com/doi/full/10.1002/ece3.5236 (archived at https://perma.cc/S4B4-MWBE)

6   Formula One (2021) Formula 1 Announces TV and Digital Audience Figures for 2020, https://www.formula1.com/en/latest/article.formula-1-announces-tv-and-digital-audience-figures-for-2020.3sbRmZm4u5Jf8pagvPoPUQ.html (archived at https://perma.cc/C25E-BMVW)

7   Xiaoying, Y (2021) *Carbon Brief*, China's 2060 Climate Pledge is 'Largely Consistent' With 1.5C Goal, Study Finds, https://www.carbonbrief.org/chinas-2060-climate-pledge-is-largely-consistent-with-1-5c-goal-study-finds (archived at https://perma.cc/EZL3-BNGP)

8   Ball, P (2020) The Lightning-Fast Quest for Covid Vaccines – And What It Means for Other Diseases, *Nature.com*, https://www.nature.com/articles/d41586-020-03626-1 (archived at https://perma.cc/4PSJ-3NW2)

9   EPA (nd) Greenhouse Gas Emissions, https://www.epa.gov/ghgemissions/sources-greenhouse-gas-emissions#transportation (archived at https://perma.cc/KK3C-7CAC)

10   Ritchie, H (2020) Cars, Planes, Trains: Where Do CO_2 Emissions From Transport Come From? *Our World in Data*, https://ourworldindata.org/co2-emissions-from-transport (archived at https://perma.cc/BT4G-N5ZZ)

11   Offshore Technology (2020) Top Ten Oil and Gas Companies in 2020, https://www.offshore-technology.com/features/top-ten-oil-and-gas-companies-in-2020/ (archived at https://perma.cc/MW3L-5SYK)

12   Corley, T A B (1983) *A History of the Burmah Oil Company, 1886–1924*, William Heinemann, London

13   Formula 1 (2019) Fuelling Up For Sustainability, https://corp.formula1.com/fuelling-up-for-sustainability/ (archived at https://perma.cc/H4EU-3KNH)

14   Formula 1 (2019) Formula 1 Announces Plan To Be Net Zero Carbon By 2030, *FIA*, https://www.formula1.com/en/latest/article.formula-1-announces-plan-to-be-net-zero-carbon-by-2030.5IaX2AZHyy7jqxl6wra6CZ.html (archived at https://perma.cc/78ZG-NQAW)

15   Duxbury, A (2020) Formula 1 Logistics – How Do Teams Move Equipment Between Races?, *Auto Sport*, https://www.autosport.com/f1/news/formula-1-logistics-how-do-teams-move-equipment-between-races-4980912/4980912/ (archived at https://perma.cc/GR4Q-YT3W)

16   Chase Carey (2020) Formula 1 Sustainability Strategy, *Formula One*, https://corp.formula1.com/wp-content/uploads/2019/11/Environmental-sustainability-Corp-website-vFINAL.pdf (archived at https://perma.cc/6J79-RYF3)

17   Rencken, D (2020) Why F1 Is Talking Wind Tunnel Bans and Driver Salary Caps – But Not an Engine Freeze, *Racing Lines*, https://www.racefans.net/2020/11/04/why-f1-is-talking-wind-tunnel-bans-and-driver-salary-caps-but-not-an-engine-freeze/ (archived at https://perma.cc/38C9-WNJT)

18 Formula One (2021) F1 MTC Tour, *YouTube*, https://www.youtube.com/watch?v=UucBA8MkLRY (archived at https://perma.cc/7S27-X7R6)

19 Mitchell, D (2008) Televised Traffic is Nothing But a Crashing Bore, *The Guardian*, https://www.theguardian.com/sport/2008/jun/14/formulaone.motorsports (archived at https://perma.cc/3U37-GWSA)

20 AMG Petronas (nd) https://www.mercedesamgf1.com/ (archived at https://perma.cc/3S6T-2W3A)

21 Ahuja, K (2021) More Than Half of New Cars Sold In Norway Last Year Were Electric Vehicles, *The Sunday Times Driving*, https://www.driving.co.uk/news/half-new-cars-sold-norway-evs/ (archived at https://perma.cc/73FU-T9TN)

22 Martin, N (2021) Porsche To Produce Fuel 'As Clean' As Electric Vehicles, *DW*, https://www.dw.com/en/top-stories/s-9097 (archived at https://perma.cc/3FG4-LZCS)

23 Benson, A (2021) Formula 1: Porsche & Volkswagen Group Considering Entering F1, *BBC Sport*, https://www.bbc.co.uk/sport/formula1/56272450 (archived at https://perma.cc/M2CV-2C99)

CHAPTER NINE

Esports revolution

Brendon Leigh is a double world champion and part of Ferrari's driver line-up. He won his first world title aged 17, repeated that feat the following season, and firmly established himself as a top talent to the extent that Mercedes snapped him up. Then, in a sensational move, he switched to Ferrari at the start of 2021, opening an exciting new chapter in the career of a driver who, just a few years before, had been a trainee chef in Reading.

'Brendon Leigh has won the title twice and represents a unique combination of youth and experience', said Ferrari's Marco Matassa. 'He brings the right abilities to our team to tackle the upcoming challenges alongside (teammate) David Tonizza. I'm sure that with this impressive line-up, we can once again fight for the Drivers' title and also try to win the team prize for the first time.'[1]

Leigh is relatively unknown to Formula One fans over the age of 40, but highly regarded and borderline famous to many younger fans – particularly millennials, Zoomers and younger – the Generation Z, Y and Alpha age demographics. The reason lies in the fact that Leigh's achievements have been online, in the world of computer gaming, competitive simulation (sim) racing and professional esports, an industry that has been growing fast since millennials started to embrace the connected world of video games. It's a sector that has seen its growth accelerate further during the mandatory lockdowns that marked the Covid-19 pandemic, an ideal outlet for young adults stuck at home, eager to be entertained.

For a company like Ferrari, the move to embrace sim racing and professional esports is the inevitable consequence of the sector's rise in importance. Even for a luxury brand such as Ferrari, the shift towards online gaming has significant relevance to its fans and customers.

No lesser a figure than Mattia Binotto, Scuderia Ferrari Formula One Team Principal, has said: 'We understand the importance of gaming for the new generation, and esports is part of our Ferrari Driver Academy programme. It's not something that is fully separated, it is a part of it.'[2]

Liberty Media's decision to invest heavily in Formula One's computer gaming, sim racing and professional esports offerings is telling. It illustrates the extent to which computer gaming has become an important development for a sport that has struggled to reach younger audiences through traditional media.

While Formula One under Bernie Ecclestone was happy to earn revenue from arms-length licensing agreements, Liberty's executives recognized that creating and owning content would enable them to open up opportunities. Particularly given that online computer gamers are highly engaged, 'sticky' and eager to participate.

Contrary to its reputation among older adults, particularly parents concerned by the amount of time their children are spending online, the computer gaming generation is highly social. The sense of community and ability to build networks is one of its major appeals.

That online gaming includes the opportunity for players to chat, message and interact with others, whether real-world or cyber friends, makes for a rich experience, one that is far removed from the perception of uncommunicative nerds. Even professional Formula One racing drivers have come to recognize that the interaction afforded by online gaming has enabled them to reconnect in a way that is close to impossible in 'real world' racing.

Speaking about his relationship with Formula One rivals including Williams's driver George Russell and Red Bull Racing's Alex Albon, Ferrari's Charles Leclerc had this to say after Formula One's Virtual Grand Prix Series, run during the course of Europe's first pandemic lockdown: 'We probably lost a little bit of contact in terms of speaking to each other over the years with the different categories (of racing) we were doing. Now in a situation like that [the pandemic] it is great to find each other again and to have fun all together racing and doing what we like.'[3]

Every Formula One team now has an esports equivalent competing in the official Formula One Esports Championship. The series requires teams to compete in 12 races over the course of four online events, each race featuring a different circuit taken from Formula One's World Championship calendar. These virtual races run to a fixed distance of 105 kilometres, representing 35 per cent of the 300 kilometres distance used in actual Grands Prix. This makes the races much more compact, intense and appealing to online audiences.

Anyone can attempt to qualify, whether using a PC, PlayStation or Xbox console, and each circuit features real-life scenarios designed to test driver skills. The fastest gamers then go through to a series of knock-out races leading to the Pro Draft. It is here that each Formula One team aims to select at least one gamer to add to their line-up for the Formula One Esports Pro Series Championships.

This 'bedroom to podium' opportunity is open to all. Its popularity is unsurprising. In 2020 a total of 237,000 gamers attempted to qualify, 117 per cent more than in 2019.[4] As the numbers have risen, even the most conservative of companies have come to realize the opportunity.

Ferrari was a latecomer to Formula One's esports evolution, joining the official series in 2019 after recognizing that they can ill afford to ignore millennial gamers who are now up to 40 years of age. The advent of the gamer-to-racer world, in which computer gamers are making the transition into real racing, also creates the gamer-to-customer opportunity. No one can avoid it.

Unlikely as it may seem, Ferrari was in at the beginning, albeit indirectly. It was the prize of winning a Ferrari that brought to prominence the gamer who has the honour of holding the Guinness Book of World Records title as the world's first professional esports player.

Over a five-year period in the mid-1990s, US teenage video gamer Dennis Fong won every tournament in which he competed, coming to international prominence when he won the Red Annihilation Quake Tournament in Atlanta, USA. John Carmack, co-creator of 'first shooter' video game Quake, offered his red Ferrari 328 to the tournament's winner, netting Fong a valuable prize that attracted much media comment.

The development of professional video gaming, initially known as electronic sports and now esports, has mirrored the growth in online gaming. Enabling players to play and compete online was important, but the rise in online gaming and esports has been multiplied by the impact of streaming sites including Twitch, owned by Amazon, and Google's YouTube Gaming.

Enabling fans to watch other gamers, whether amateur or professional, and then to message, chat and stream live content opened up an entirely new opportunity. Tens of thousands of subscribers logged on to watch the experts at work, providing entertainment, an appreciation of world-class skills and the opportunity to learn techniques that they themselves could apply when gaming with their friends.

Launched in 2011, Twitch's focus on live-streaming video games was groundbreaking. Sold to Amazon in 2014 for what seemed a healthy US $970 million, that investment now appears inexpensive. In 2020 Twitch saw 17 billion hours of content viewed on its service, 83 per cent higher than 2019.

In a demonstration of how engaged its users are, a one-off appearance by US politician Alexandria Ocasio-Cortez to join some of the platform's stars in the game Among Us generated 435,000 viewers, Twitch's fifth largest audience of all time.[5] In precisely the same way that previous generations of sports fans could tune in to watch a tennis, golf or football star demonstrate their superior skills, computer gamers have quickly adopted the same approach to enjoying their pastime.

The initial growth in the popularity of esports came from an unexpected place. Not from the United States, its Silicon Valley packed with technology start-ups, nor from Japan, home to Sony, Nintendo or games pioneer Namco. Rather it was South Korea, which rolled out a high-speed broadband network at the turn of the century and saw its government support the growing online gaming industry. The Asian country gained an edge over its rivals thanks to infrastructure development, the inclusion of computer gaming as part of the university curriculum and the passing of legislation in 2006 aimed at protecting both the industry and its players.

This investment meant that South Korea was not only able to lead the world in terms of the development of computer gaming, but create a talent pool of players and coaches who have come to play a pivotal role in the growth of esports.

Back in 2014 the Grand Finals of the League of Legends World Championship were held in Seoul's World Cup Stadium, a capacity crowd of 45,000 fans enjoying a tournament involving 16 teams from around the globe, with games streamed live on Twitch and the final on ESPN3. The prize-money purse was US $2.13 million, and with 288 million cumulative viewings online it set a new record for an individual esports tournament.[6]

While League of Legends has continued to be among the most popular games, multiplayer first-shooter game Counter-Strike and fantasy battle game DOTA 2, sequel to Defense of the Ancients, have remained at the forefront of the competitive gaming and esports landscape. In reality, new titles will emerge as the popularity of games including Fortnite, Overwatch and PlayerUnknown's Battlegrounds (PUBG) has demonstrated.

One of the intriguing aspects of the wider computer games industry, and esports at the professional level, is that while players can acquire and develop skills, the game itself can change, the rules alter, so that the challenge has no limits. This is the case either within a specific game, should the developer continue to evolve it effectively enough to maintain user engagement, or in the release of new games designed to offer players new experiences, challenges and rewards.

Formula One is by no means new to video gaming. Sony PlayStation launched its first fully licensed Formula One game back in 1996, but as long ago as 1982 players were able to enjoy arcade games such as Namco's Pole Position. Early gamers soon had a plethora of titles to enjoy on personal computers, with games including Geoff Crammond's Formula One Grand Prix released in 1991 for Amiga and Atari.

Early games often licensed the names of specific circuits or individual drivers, giving rise to titles including Ayrton Senna's Super Monaco GP II or Nigel Mansell's World Championship Racing, a sure sign that Formula One's monolithic approach to licensing had fragmented the market. It was the rapid development and wider access to the internet that enabled multiplayer online gaming to progress in the early 2000s. The arrival of Microsoft's Xbox Live in 2002 helped motivate Sony to create the PlayStation Network to coincide with the 2006 launch of its fully internet-enabled PlayStation 3 console.

Motorsport has always had a following within the gaming community, if not to anything like the extent of the shooter, battlefield and fantasy games that have predominated. Geoff Crammond's F1GP of 1991 was the second racing game he had designed, following the earlier success of REVS, but once Formula One developed its exclusive licensing agreement with Sony PlayStation the competition soon developed games based on an eclectic range of motorsport.

From rallying to dirt-bike racing, circuit racing through to ovals, a prolific range of arcade, console and PC games soon emerged, racing categories including single seaters, sports cars, touring cars and rally cars. The market for racing was clearly there, but no one games developer was achieving the optimal level of game play, technical sophistication and graphics quality demanded by consumers.

That changed with the arrival of the Gran Turismo video game in 1997, developed exclusively for PlayStation by Polyphony Digital, a games development business within Sony Computer Entertainment. Selling over 80 million units by 2018, generating US $4 billion in sales, the Gran Turismo series was a breakthrough title in several areas, a trailblazer for others to follow – the official Formula 1 game and esports offering included.[7]

Gran Turismo moved the experience away from arcade-style gaming towards a more realistic race-simulation experience. Players could race on accurate representations of a wide variety of real racing circuits and drive a similarly broad range of race and road cars licensed by real-world automotive manufacturers.

The authenticity of the experience was clear from the start, and users flocked to subscribe. Likewise, with the advent of multiplayer gaming, the appeal was very clear: being able to choose the car of your choice and compete against friends and rivals, and honing real-world skills in terms of circuit visualization, car set-up and reaction times.

By the early 2000s Gran Turismo was capturing attention, and not only of racing fans. Diehard computer gamers also appreciated the technical challenge, the realistic nature of the simulated racing environments, and the increasing buy-in of car manufacturers and teams offering users real-world satisfaction.

Its creator Kazunori 'Kaz' Yamauchi, CEO of Polyphony Digital, was passionate about making Gran Turismo the best, most realistic racing game available. The objective was to provide a true-to-life experience, summarized by game's marketing strapline 'The Real Driving Simulator'.

In 2006, with the launch of Sony's PlayStation 3 (PS3) and PlayStation Network, Gran Turismo's developers capitalized on the ability to connect gamers online through the launch of Gran Turismo 5 Prologue. This enabled users to compete with up to 16 gamers on track at the same time. The shift towards online gaming and competitive, multiplayer racing was later completed with the launch, in 2017, of Gran Turismo Sport. This was the first in the series to focus solely on online racing.

It's worth returning to 2006, however. The launch of the PS3 saw Japanese car manufacturer Nissan strike a deal to merge sim racing with real-world racing. Nissan had already built a strong relationship with Gran Turismo through the in-game popularity of its high-performance GT-R models.

This new agreement offered something quite exceptional. Nissan, Sony and Gran Turismo created a gamer-to-racer opportunity that would give computer gamers the chance to build a career as a professional racing driver. The GT Academy would merge online and offline, creating a life-changing experiencing for those sufficiently talented and committed to succeed.

It created compelling content that positioned Nissan's brand together with its high-performance models in an entirely new way. It motivated gamers to become brand loyal, generating sales among a consumer demographic that was no longer using traditional media.

Nissan's innovation was to recognize computer gaming as a route to market, a means of engaging with and inspiring a fan base that would ultimately drive sales and position the GT-R as a product that millennials would aspire to own. The halo effect of the programme, through traditional as well as new media, would reach far beyond the computer gaming market.

Nissan's head of motorsport at the time was Darren Cox, now CEO of motorsport digital media company The Race Media. He recalls the reaction of Sony executives when presented with the opportunity to give Gran Turismo video gamers the opportunity to become an actual racing driver: 'The guy from Sony said "This is either crackpot or genius" because it had never been done before. There was no book to tell you how to do this, to merge real racing with gaming. At a corporate level inside Nissan there were major concerns about the safety risks involved in putting gamers who had won an online competition into the seat of actual race cars. As a result, I think the operations manual ran to something like 280 pages, with a major emphasis on safety.'

As Cox recalls, the experts involved in putting together the gamer-to-racer programme at the GT Academy soon realized the strong correlation that existed between gamers and racers: 'The professional race instructors we worked with were soon telling us that, when compared to the average driver who turns up at a race school, track day or corporate event, these gamers really knew how to drive. I well remember the first test we did in Bedford (Autodrome Test Track). That was an inspirational moment.'

By 2008 Nissan and Gran Turismo were ready to launch the GT Academy, the competition attracting 25,000 PlayStation 3 gamers from a dozen European countries. The winner, Lucas Ordóñez from Spain, was rewarded with a professional racing career in 2009, and he subsequently competed in World Championship sports-car races including the world-famous Le Mans 24 Hours.

The motor-racing community had mixed feelings about drivers entering directly from the world of computer gaming, as Cox recalls: 'When we first brought Lucas Ordóñez into the paddock there was a degree of animosity towards him. People did not like the fact he had come from the world of computer gaming. There was a hint of other drivers feeling "My dad has spent all this money on my career from karting onwards, and all you have done is buy a PlayStation." However, we knew we were on to something. As with all innovation you will have doubters, but we proved them wrong.'

It helped that Cox had the necessary buy-in and support from the senior leadership within Nissan, as well as their counterparts at Sony and Polyphony Digital. Carlos Tavares, now CEO of Stellantis, the world's sixth largest automotive company, created following the merger of Group PSA and Fiat Chrysler Automobiles, was at that time a vice president at Nissan. He secured sign-off for Cox's GT Academy project from none other than Carlos Ghosn, Nissan's CEO.

'Ghosn's view was that if Nissan had to advertise the new GT-R high-performance sports car using traditional means, we had failed', recalls Cox. 'The proposition behind the GT Academy was that millennial gamers would become engaged with both the GT-R and its predecessor, the Nissan 350Z, through combining online content with real-world high-performance driving and motorsport. It was all about the marketing.

'As a result, we used the excitement created by the GT Academy and the launch of the GT-R to undertake a huge pre-sale, pre-delivery activity in Europe, enabling customers to try out the car and place a deposit. The result was better than anyone expected.'

Nissan's success in using computer gaming and competitive esports to drive customer engagement represents a template in how to merge offline and online. It was unprecedented, a neat innovation using the technologies already available at that time, but combining them in a way that had never been tried before.

Today Cox continues to build on the lessons learned through programmes including The World's Fastest Gamer (TWFG), which has been run in conjunction with brands including McLaren, and represents one pillar of his digital media business. In 2017 a 26-year-old Dutch salesman, Rudy van Buren, won TWFG, becoming one of McLaren Formula One's official simulator drivers the following year.

The use of race-driver simulators across the motor-racing spectrum over the last 15 years has helped to accelerate the acceptance of competitive computer gaming as being entirely relevant to real-world racing. Sim racing is therefore popular among gamers and racers alike, accelerating the convergence of virtual and real life through games including iRacing, Project CARS 2 and rFactor 2, in addition to the made-for-console titles such as PlayStation's Gran Turismo or Xbox's Forza Motorsport.

Many racing drivers, including in Formula One, now regard sim racing as supplementary to their real-world careers, a way to stay sharp, keep your brain trained within the world of racing and have some fun. As the games have developed, they have progressed closer to giving users a real-world experience, mirroring the complexities of driving an actual racing car.

Gamers demand an immersive experience, this being the degree to which your brain starts to respond to the onscreen images in precisely the same way as it would in the real world. Everything a gamer sees, feels and hears impacts on their experience.

To keep pace with the fast-developing world of computer gaming software, a hardware industry has evolved to meet that gamers' demand for race-style seating, steering wheels and pedal sets. These offer similar ergonomics, functionality and feel of their real-world counterparts. The physical sensation of the feedback provided by the steering wheel and pedals helps gamers to develop the sensitivity needed to explore the limits of their virtual cars.

One major difference is the cost. The price of entry to computer gaming is tiny when compared to real racing. A sport that has traditionally, and accurately, been regarded as expensive and somewhat elitist has suddenly come within reach.

To start with gamers can play on their mobile phone, before moving to a PC or dedicated games console, usually plugged into a TV monitor at home. With amateur gamers practising for three to four hours per day, and esports competitors two or even three times that, it is usually the case that the family TV is soon replaced with games monitors.

Most gamers start with a single screen, then progress towards triple-screen layouts at which point the visual impact starts to mirror the real world more closely. The ultimate step for some is to use virtual-reality headsets, providing a 360-degree view of the virtual racing cockpit. Many racing drivers and their sim-racing counterparts insist this creates an exceptionally high degree of immersion and real-life accuracy.

Inevitably the increased investment includes sophisticated steering wheels, race seats and pedal sets. Manufacturers including Fanatec, Thrustmaster and peripheral manufacturer Logitech are among the best-known suppliers.

Logitech is a partner of the McLaren Formula One team and the team's commercial relationship with Dell perfectly illustrates how the world of gaming hardware has come to represent an important opportunity. Almost half the world's online gamers use PCs.

Specialist suppliers include games equipment manufacturer Playseat, founded by Dutch businessman Fernando Smit in 1998. He saw the opportunity early, spending almost a decade selling racing-style seats to individual gamers prior to the dramatic rise in multiplayer, online games. A former kart racer, in 1995 he had the idea to mount an actual racing seat and pedal set on a metal frame so that he could enjoy gaming with the correct seating position. By 2003 he had started manufacturing in quantity, and soon secured a licensing deal with Sony. He is ideally placed to comment on the growth in popularity of online racing games and the recent development of esports.

'In the early days we could only compete against the computer. In 2010 we held the first competition with 16 PlayStations linked together over a network hub', recalls Smit. That event would be won by 12-year-old Max Verstappen. 'After that PlayStation and Xbox were connecting online and the online competitions started. At each level you could compete against others anywhere in the world. The networks connected you with similar drivers of the same level, and this is great fun because it always gives you the feeling that you have a chance to win.'

Smit is keen to point out that one of the reasons for the success of racing games is that 'everyone can be a racer and everyone can be a winner'. Racing games broke down the barrier to entry in a sport famed for being expensive and elitist.

In 2021 Playseat's entry-level Challenge product retailed for 199 euros, with a top-end, simulator-style product such as the Red Bull Racing and Ferrari licensed Formula Intelligence unit selling for 2,500 euros.

For a relatively small investment gamers can have the best equipment with which to compete in a sport that, even in karting, demands tens of thousands of dollars just to get started. Computer gaming, sim racing and esports have opened up Formula One and the wider motorsports industry to the estimated 3 billion gamers who will enjoy online entertainment by 2023.

It is little wonder that the sport's owners have moved quickly to adapt to the opportunity. To do so they turned to someone who was better able to understand the opportunity, being right in the middle of the millennial demographic that has represented the core gaming audience.

In his late twenties, Dr Julian Tan is Formula One's head of digital initiatives, joining the company in time to oversee the championship's first move into esports in 2017. With a doctorate in composite engineering Tan could easily have ended up with a technical role in a Formula One team, but following two years at the Boston Consulting Group he took up the opportunity to guide Formula One through the esports minefield.

Tan admits that when Formula One first entered esports the sector was still relatively new in mainstream terms, even if competitive gaming was decades old. He also recognized that the opportunity existed to help define esports at a time of exponential growth, rather than merely adding it as another stream to Formula One's business.

There was also an early understanding that Formula One's entry into esports was not an end in itself, but rather a means by which to support the core business of real-world racing. With a suite of digital tools readily available, the task was to explore the creative possibilities and flexibility of esports to reach larger, younger audiences together with the commercial opportunities that would bring.

'Of our participants and viewers within our esports initiatives 80 per cent are below the age of 35, and when you compare that to traditional F1 it is a much higher ratio', says Tan. 'Esports is definitely helping us to reach a younger audience, and that is important because you only have to look at the hours spent by people below the age of 35 on gaming compared to those over the age of 35 spent watching television to know that there is a generational shift.'

With younger audiences unwilling to use traditional forms of down-the-line broadcast media, whether terrestrial, satellite or cable, the way in which they engage, interact and consume online means Formula One had to respond. Online gaming creates a vital route to market.

'As a sport looking towards building the longevity and health of our fanbase, it is important we play where the opportunities are', says Tan. 'Gaming and esports helps us to create a product to speak to our younger audiences in a language that they understand, providing additional touchpoints for them into the world of F1.'

Combined with Formula One's post-Ecclestone-era approach to investing in social media, gaming and esports forms part of a larger strategy to engage with and grow its global audience, irrespective of age, culture or socio-economic background. Tan and his colleagues also realized that, in terms of accessibility, Formula One had been an unachievable dream thanks to its high cost of entry. Meanwhile sports such as football, basketball or tennis are open to anyone who has a ball or racquet and wishes to try it for themselves. In this respect online gaming, sim racing and esports create the opportunity to break down barriers, making Formula One inherently more accessible.

Starting in 2017, Formula One's esports events met with growing success. Audiences were attracted to the sport's offering combined with its approach to embracing streaming platforms and social media.

Then, in January 2020, word began to spread that China was experiencing the initial stages of what would become the Covid-19 pandemic. This prompted Formula One to consider cancelling the Grand Prix scheduled to take place at the Shanghai International Circuit on 17–19 April. Thoughts turned towards alternative ways of hosting the race, including the creation of an online virtual Grand Prix.

'We saw the opportunity and moved very quickly to use our capabilities within esports to see what we could do in this space because it offers us flexibility and scalability', recalls Tan. 'When that news came out everyone, including all of the teams, mobilized to put together a concept where we would replicate the Chinese Grand Prix, but to run that from here in London.'

Matters escalated when, on Friday 13 March 2020, Formula One was forced to announce the cancellation of that weekend's opening round of the World Championship in Melbourne, Australia. Unable to stage real racing, and with creeping lockdowns around the world curtailing any events for months ahead, the Formula One racing industry was plunged into crisis.

Suddenly Tan found himself faced with an altogether more ambitious task than replacing the Chinese Grand Prix. His department was given the challenge of pivoting the entire World Championship online, creating a virtual replacement for real-world racing, a means to engage with fans and entertain global audiences subject to lockdown restrictions. It would also become a means by which Formula One's commercial sponsors could activate marketing activities.

'We had a plan for the Chinese Grand Prix designed for single weekend use', says Tan. 'So we pulled together the concept of the Virtual Grands Prix. In a matter of five extremely busy days, we moved incredibly fast to create something that was scalable, that we could put on week after week.'

Given the impact of the growing pandemic, not only on Formula One but on the world at large, Tan admits they felt a responsibility to generate content their fans could enjoy during an unprecedented period. Playing to its core competencies the sport approached drivers past and present, as well as up-and-coming talent.

'There was a wider appreciation that our fans wanted to see our drivers race', says Tan, 'and if they cannot see them race in the real world then they would still want to see them racing a different kind of way.'

One of Formula One's greatest assets was to have a pool of drivers already experienced in the world of computer gaming, sim racing and competitive esports. The sport's leaders also realized that, with an online offering, fans could perhaps get to know their heroes a little better. In the world of real racing the drivers are cosseted in their cars, invisible inside their cockpits and helmets.

An example of the degree to which fans were being allowed inside the lives of their heroes occurred in May 2020 when the girlfriend of Ferrari driver Charles Leclerc found herself locked out of their apartment. He was sim racing at the time. She had to resort to subscribing to his Twitch streaming account in order to contact him online and ask him to open the door.

Naturally Leclerc's 620,000 followers on Twitch found this interaction highly amusing, bringing them into the real life of a racing star through his online racing presence. However, it is this level of access that is playing an important part in expanding the appeal of online racing. The racing is important, but it is the level of engagement, entertainment and interaction that builds audiences.

Darren Cox sees this as critical to the sport's continued online growth. 'There has to be a lifestyle element to the online gaming that draws people in. Through TWFG people get to see normal guys and girls experiencing something they aspire to, whether that's going to Las Vegas or LA, driving Porsches or Ferraris. They want to watch not only the best but the funniest, coolest personalities. That has to apply to Formula One's offering too.'

Naturally, Formula One's success in esports has been attractive to sponsors and corporate partners. Heineken's long-term investment in Formula One was announced in June 2016, with traditional sponsorship activation including trackside advertising and naming rights to individual races.

Given the potential for Heineken to be accused of promoting drink driving, an issue that all alcohol beverage manufacturers face in motorsport, the company was careful to follow previous industry sponsors by promoting responsible drinking. Its 2017 launch of Heineken 0.0 (Zero), an alcohol-free beer, was a major commercial success, thanks in part to its use of the platform of a global sport such as Formula 1.

The opportunity for brands to reach younger adults, using the flexibility of online gaming to create a wide range of content and experiences, offered an opportunity. In May 2020, at the height of Europe's first Covid-19 lockdown, Heineken's brand ambassadors David Coulthard and Nico Rosberg headlined one of Formula One's esports challenge series, competing against each other as well as other drivers, sports stars and influencers. Using the hashtag Challenge Heineken Legends, this enabled one of the sport's major sponsors to use its commercial assets online in a new and topical manner, achieving 1.9 million views across digital platforms.[8]

During the four-month delay to the 2020 Formula One World Championship, Julian Tan and his team successfully delivered two esports programmes and witnessed a substantial growth in participants and viewers. The Virtual Grand Prix Series saw Formula One drivers including George Russell, Lando Norris, Alex Albon and Charles Leclerc compete against professional gamers and stars from other sports.

In fact, 11 of Formula One's current 20 race drivers participated in at least one event, and this drew 21.8 million views on digital platforms, including Formula One's owned YouTube, Twitch and Facebook channels. Television viewership was estimated at 5 million, but in a sign of the demographic to which the series appealed, Twitch saw 2.7 million viewings alone.

'There are so many opportunities that we can continue to explore', says Tan, 'whether that is in continuing to develop grass-roots opportunities into Formula One through to driver development, talent searching and contributing to the wider development of the sport. We need to have the courage to take a path that maybe has not necessarily been fully developed.'

One example of the merging of online and offline experiences came when gaming title Fortnite staged a live Travis Scott concert in April 2020, attracting 12.3 million concurrent players, according to developer Epic Games. This is seen as typical of the opportunities presented by online gaming, a future in which the real and virtual merge into one seamless brand experience.

The blurring of lines between gaming, sports, music and wider entertainment offers a very real opportunity. The tools are already there. The creativity arguably needs to catch up with the functionality and integration already available.

Ultimately the takeaway from Formula One's experience of embracing the world of amateur computer gaming, competitive sim racing and professional esports is that the world of virtual racing offers parallel opportunities to the existing real-world business. The growth in gaming and esports accelerated during the course of the global pandemic, advancing Formula One's strategy by three to five years. The prospect for future, further integration of online and offline remains high.

Given that Formula One is a data-driven sport, with teams managing race strategy remotely, the opportunity to see real and virtual events merged, with events running concurrently, is clear. Being able to watch a professional esports racer compete real-time with Lewis Hamilton is not so far removed from where we are today.

The launch of F1 2020, the latest version of its computer game, saw players invited to create their own team. This included selecting a teammate, choosing an engine supplier, designing their own livery and signing sponsors. Success within the game enabled players to invest in better facilities and recruit staff to help improve car development. These features had been deployed in previous racing games by developer Codemasters, the UK firm later subject to a 2021 US $1.2 billion takeover by Californian video gaming giant EA Sports.

The ease with which in-game functionality can be trialled and tested on one product and then easily transferred to another is part of the inherent flexibility offered by video gaming products. Esports offers a mechanism by which Formula One can expand the number of events it holds each year. Owners Liberty Media have the ambition to stage 25 Grands Prix in a season, for the rights fees paid by promoters are a central source of revenue for the World Championship. Inevitably there is a limit to the number of real-world live events that can be staged.

Virtual Grand Prix can be added to this, much more than have been trialled to date. If the pool of Formula One drivers and teams can continue to collaborate, providing entertainment and engagement with the global fan base, the opportunities for continued growth are significant.

A Virtual World Championship running in parallel to the actual World Championship seems a natural step, allowing the industry to grow in ways that traditional audiences could never have imagined, and that new ones will relish.

Lessons from esports

ONLINE IS PROVIDING AN ENTIRELY NEW OPPORTUNITY FOR FORMULA ONE TO DEVELOP

Given the enormous shift away from traditional media among younger audiences, the online gaming community is providing an opportunity to interact very directly through a key pastime.

THE GAMING COMMUNITY IS HIGHLY SOCIAL AND INTERACTIVE

Computer gaming and professional esports is a social network with a purpose, offering an immersive experience whether participating or watching.

THE OPPORTUNITY FOR VIRTUAL AND REAL-WORLD INTEGRATION IS ONLY NOW BEING REALIZED

The popularity and flexibility offered by computer gaming and esports has shifted gear during the global pandemic, Formula One now building on the successes previously enjoyed by pioneers including Nissan's GT Academy.

THE CONNECTED ENVIRONMENT PROMOTES DIVERSITY

The global reach and appeal of computer gaming is enabling and promoting greater ethnic diversity, as anyone, anywhere in the world, can participate if they have internet connectivity.

THE GAMER-TO-RACER CONCEPT IS PROVEN

Starting with Nissan's partnership with Gran Turismo more than a decade ago, the concept of real-world talent being discovered and proven online is widening. Formula One teams harness the capabilities of gamers in their simulators.

DEBATING THE MERITS OF REAL VERSUS VIRTUAL IS REDUNDANT

Motorsport is moving towards an ecosystem in which both real racing and computer gaming will increasingly merge. The technology already exists, but the business models are still immature. The scope for development is very significant.

Notes

1   Ferrari (2021) Brendon Leigh Alongside David Tonizza, https://www.ferrari.com/en-GN/ esports/articles/ferrari-fda-esports-team-new-driver-season-2021-brendon-leigh (archived at https://perma.cc/ZA9X-C6CE)

2   Van Osten, P (2020) Binotto Wants Esports To Help Supply Ferrari Driver Academy, *F1i*, https://f1i.com/news/365991-binotto-wants-esports-to-help-supply-ferrari-driver-academy.html (archived at https://perma.cc/4YGJ-ZEFC)

3   Aggarwal, A (2020) Charles Leclerc Reveals How Esports Changed His Relationship With F1 Rivals, *Essentially Sports*, https://www.essentiallysports.com/f1-news-charles-leclerc-reveals-how-esports-changed-his-relationship-with-f1-rivals/ (archived at https://perma.cc/WK6L-67CV)

4   Formula One (2021) Virtual Grands Prix To Return for 2021 After Record-Breaking Year for F1 Esports Series, https://www.formula1.com/en/latest/article.virtual-grands-prix-to-return-for-2021-after-record-breaking-year-for-f1.7mfMzjdd04QuxooV7aM60.html (archived at https://perma.cc/KDQ4-S5LQ)

5   Bijan, S (2021) Twitch Ended 2020 With Its Biggest Numbers Ever, *The Verge*, https://www.theverge.com/2021/1/11/22220528/twitch-2020-aoc-among-us-facebook-youtube (archived at https://perma.cc/N3F9-N4BR)

6   Esports Marketing Blog (2014) League of Legends Worlds 2014; Riot Games Announces Attendance Figure, http://esports-marketing-blog.com/league-of-legends-worlds-2014-viewership/ (archived at https://perma.cc/5QTZ-NYF8)

7   Fandom (nd) Gran Turismo, https://vgsales.fandom.com/wiki/Gran_Turismo (archived at https://perma.cc/D7KV-8L8M)

8   Formula One (2020) Formula 1 Virtual Grand Prix Series Achieves Record-Breaking Viewership, https://www.formula1.com/en/latest/article.formula-1-virtual-grand-prix-series-achieves-record-breaking-viewership.7bv94UJPCtxW0L5mwTxBHk.html (archived at https://perma.cc/SX83-RBLQ)

CHAPTER TEN

Performance management

Formula One teams are obsessed with performance analysis. They are constantly assessing the performance of the drivers, cars, systems and people. To win a race requires everything to operate in a manner that exceeds the performance of the competition. To win a World Championship requires an extremely high level of sustained performance over time. This is what makes Mercedes' domination of Formula One between 2014 and 2020 so impressive.

Ron Dennis, boss of McLaren for over 30 years, said that sustaining success was the biggest challenge of all. Winning a race is a major achievement, of course, particularly for a team or driver experiencing that level of success for the first time. For the teams focused on winning the World Championship, however, the ability to consistently deliver is critical.

There are 10 teams in Formula One, each one of them designing, manufacturing and developing a pair of Formula One cars with which to compete in the World Championship. Some aim to win races and battle for the title. Others set their sights on a range of goals that might include podium finishes, consistent points finishes or a position in the Constructors' series, which will result in a certain level of prize money.

Several factors determine team ambitions, including budget, technical facilities, team personnel and the quality of the drivers. In 2021, for example, there are two teams with a realistic chance of battling for the World Championship, two who may break through to win a single Grand Prix and two more who have the ambition to do so. This means that 40 per cent of the field are focused on lesser goals, set against their own assessment of team capabilities.

Setting ambitious performance targets may seem like an obvious mindset within Formula One, but the reality is that teams can develop an acceptance of setting lower, more readily achievable goals. This guarantees continued underperformance.

Toto Wolff, Team Principal at Mercedes, has related the story of how the team had a senior management meeting shortly after he joined at the beginning of 2013. Having finished fifth in the previous year's World Championship the discussion focused on what the team's goal should be, including winning the title. It fell to design engineer Aldo Costa to point out that was not a high enough ambition, that as representatives of the Mercedes-Benz company the target should be multiple World Championship titles.

That may have seemed unrealistic at the time, but having worked with Ferrari during Michael Schumacher's five-year dominance of the World Championship, Costa knew that this level of sustained performance was possible. The team needed to first of all set that goal if it was to have the chance of achieving it.

The moment a team sets a target other than winning it creates the acceptance of losing. That decision establishes a compromise that is hard to shake. One of the motivating factors in working with Eddie Jordan was the knowledge that his team had won in Formula 3 and Formula 3000, stepping stones to Formula One. Winning was an established mindset within the team and its leadership. In this way success becomes self-fulfilling. If a team puts enough energy into visualizing success it becomes easier to work out what is needed to achieve that goal.

In setting out on that journey, performance analysis becomes vitally important because of the need to constantly review progress set against the targets. This provides the team with the insights needed to tackle the obstacles that are preventing goals from being achieved.

Working with successful racing drivers illustrates that no matter what their talent, fame or achievements, their constant desire to analyse performance is an intrinsic part of their make-up. The driver wants to see how he or she can improve performance through their own inputs while driving, then work with the engineers to unlock the car's potential. This lies at the heart of all motorsport.

David Coulthard tells the story of how Sebastian Vettel, fresh from winning his first World Championship title at the 2010 Japanese Grand

Prix, went straight into an engineering debrief. In their moment of triumph the team still wanted to discuss what went right, what went wrong, how they as a team could learn and what could be implemented next time out to sustain their success.

In order to monitor the performance of both the car and driver the teams utilize real-time data analysis. Having designed the car in the digital domain, predicting its performance using sophisticated simulation tools, it is then fitted with hundreds of sensors that enable the engineers to analyse real-world performance. They can then compare actual performance with expectations, the competition, or between teammates.

This data-driven environment is one of the reasons why one in six of the commercial sponsors and technical partners in Formula One come from the world of information technology. Data acquisition, storage, security and analytics is supported by hardware, software and cloud-based systems. It is unsurprising that so many companies have come to regard Formula One as the perfect case study of how business performance can be improved through the use of analytics.

When US technology group Cognizant announced its deal to become the title partner of the Aston Martin F1 team in March 2021, CEO Brian Humphries explained why the Formula One environment was a strong fit. 'Technically intensive and engineering dependent', he added that the company would be 'bringing Cognizant's artificial intelligence, internet of things, cloud computing and digital engineering expertise to bear'.[1]

Just a few weeks later Red Bull Racing announced its new partnership with Oracle, specifically in relation to Oracle Cloud Infrastructure, 'with initial projects focused on car performance, machine learning, and analytics'.[2]

Formula One is fuelled by data. Teams recognize the power of performance insights delivered by analytics. With speed being all important, including the quality and speed of analysis, decision making and performance improvement, real-time analytics is where much of the action is to be found.

It has taken a 35-year journey of digital transformation to reach this point. Until the mid-1980s engineers relied on driver feedback combined with their own expertise and gut instinct. To monitor performance, they relied on the stopwatch, combined with basic information provided by simple measurements such as tyre temperature and pressure.

A driver's individual lap times were measured and recorded, a benchmark time then being used to monitor the impact of subsequent changes to the car's set-up. A teammate's performance enabled further comparison, and together their feedback would be used by the engineers to determine the overall direction of car development.

Two closely matched teammates have always been a characteristic of successful teams, as this doubles the amount of useful, comparative information. In contrast, pairings in which one driver was much faster than the other, or where drivers gave inconsistent performances, made things much more difficult for the engineering community.

Pre-data stopwatches could be used to monitor individual corner times, selecting fixed points on the track to time how quickly each driver takes to complete the three phases of each corner – braking, cornering and acceleration – and to monitor the selected racing line or trajectory.

Today's systems allow instantaneous performance management across each millimetre of the racetrack, an approach that Williams Formula One's analytics partner KX describes as the 'microsecond mindset'.

Neil Martin, formerly head of strategy at McLaren, Red Bull Racing and Ferrari, is one of the pioneers of data science in the sport. 'Formula One is a true meritocracy', he explains. 'It is won by those who get the competitive edge by being more efficient in certain areas, to out-develop the competition. The deeper you go into each solution, the more efficient you are and the better the outcome you are likely to achieve.'

Martin explains that early analytics started by modelling a single car and small number of variables over the course of a race. Naturally the complexity increased with the addition of a teammate and nine two-car competitors, together with all the variables of weather, incidents and accidents that can occur during a Grand Prix.

'That's the key point where things changed in terms of modelling race strategy', he says. 'We went from a deterministic world where for a given set of inputs you would always get the same outputs, to embracing risk, embracing the fact that traffic patterns exist, or that the safety car might come out at any time. Traditional engineers would say, 'that's too complicated, it's bad luck', but this is not the case, you are actually making a decision by simply ignoring reality. By embracing risk you can better model traffic patterns, including what to do under a safety car, for example.'

The approach described by Martin means that teams can run tens of millions of simulations, enabling strategists to gain a sense of the shape of the race. This includes knowing the outcome for any given decision, increasing the team's confidence when it comes to running a race and driving results.

Across the season, teams can model each event, determining likely outcomes, going into a Grand Prix weekend armed with accurate performance predictions. This is why real-time performance monitoring is so useful, as the engineers and drivers can see precisely where they stand against expectations.

Teams and drivers have always tackled each event by recognizing the unique characteristics of individual circuits. Tracks can be described as low-, medium- or high-speed, often a mixture, featuring certain topography, types of corners and so on. If you take a circuit like Monte Carlo, for example, it is unique in having the shortest lap of any F1 track, at 3.34 kilometres, and does not feature a single 'straight'. It twists and turns, which means the drivers have to cope with constant, finely balanced changes of direction. It is a low-speed circuit, but one that requires intense focus with little time to relax.

As with every Formula One circuit, Monte Carlo is divided into three sectors for which split times are provided on the official timing system. The first sector takes drivers across the start–finish line down to the right-handed corner at Ste Devote, then up the steep hill, curving left–right–left–right as it goes, before the fast left-hander into Casino Square and then right, downhill towards the Mirabeau hairpin. The timed sector 1 ends just before Mirabeau, which means that an analysis of that sector involves four corners, with the relevant stages of braking, cornering and acceleration.

Comparing teammates over that single sector will show engineers where the opportunities might arise to improve performance; one might be quicker than the other at turn 1, or the roles might be reversed in turn 2. When engineers and data analysts review those performances, drilling into the data of what is happening, they can potentially help both drivers achieve a better performance. Improvements can come from driver performance, a change to the set-up of the car or a combination of the two.

A very different style of track is Monza in Italy, which is 5.793 kilometres in length and high speed in nature: long straights separated by a series of three chicanes and fast-flowing corners. Here is a track where drivers do have time to 'relax' on the straights, and, in the case of Monza, sector 1 features far fewer changes of direction than for Monte Carlo. A long straight leads into the first chicane, a tight right–left taken in second gear, and then a long acceleration around the curving right-hander known as Curva Biassono, ending sector 1 before the entry to the Della Roggia chicane.

As a result of there being 'less to do' in sector 1 of Monza compared to Monte Carlo, with only a single braking and/or downshift in gears as opposed to three, it is easier to see immediately where the difference in performance – or performance delta as it is called – is coming from.

When it comes to planning overall race strategy, teams take all the learnings gathered from practice and qualifying, using simulation tools to determine outcomes. It starts with the goal of completing a 300-kilometre race distance in the shortest possible time. Considering the pit stops are mandatory and that you will therefore make at least one pit stop, factors such as weather, track temperature, tyre degradation, fuel consumption, lap length and pit lane time are just some of the variables taken into account. In the event that two pit stops are chosen, this means that the 300 kilometres are already divided into three parts, namely a first, second and third 'stint'.

Pirelli is the exclusive tyre supplier to Formula One, and they allocate three compounds of race tyre each weekend. It is down to each team to determine which compounds are used, and the tyre data gathered during practice has a significant influence on the length of each stint. In simple terms, softer compound tyres provide more grip, but wear out more quickly than the harder options.

The length of each stint is therefore tyre dependent. On a 5-kilometre track the 300-kilometre race will therefore consist of 60 laps divided into three stints, with the performance over each stint combining to determine the race outcome. Consistency of performance over each lap, and across each stint, is key. Lap times need to be managed effectively by the driver and the team to ensure that, whilst there may be peaks and troughs according to variables such as tyre wear and fuel load, the cumulative effect is to optimize performance over the course of the race.

Starting position is an important variable, of course, since clearly those starting from pole position have a theoretical advantage over the remaining 19 cars and their drivers. With a clear track ahead and no one in front to take into consideration, the driver starting from pole position has a greater range of options than any other competitor. To start from pole position means optimizing car performance over a single lap during qualifying. This requires the driver to have the confidence required to push the car to its absolute limit.

This is where the balance between the technology and the driver comes into play. The driver has to get the most from the car, and the car must allow the driver to achieve their peak performance.

'You really must have confidence in your car if want to drive a perfect qualifying lap', says Mika Häkkinen, two-times world champion with 26 pole positions to his credit. 'Early in my career I experienced having an uncompetitive car, and when you know the car does not have the grip or stability you need, it's impossible to push. When I reached Formula One I spent years learning how to work closely with my engineers, giving them my feedback and looking at the data to see where we could improve. By the time qualifying starts you need to have a car you can believe in, and really push flat out.'

Given that Formula One is such a data-centric environment, the human input remains important. Whilst the driver has to learn how to get the most from their car, there is little point in a car having characteristics that limit driver confidence.

Feedback remains important, therefore. Drivers who can return to the pits and then describe a lap in detail, giving the engineers insight into vehicle performance, are an asset. To aid them, drivers can create markers on the data while driving the car, providing a reference point for post-event analysis.

The ability of top drivers to add to their team's understanding of the car remains vitally important, so too their ability to drive at a consistently high level. This provides the foundation upon which engineers can build future performance. It is for this reason that Mercedes-Benz rates Lewis Hamilton so highly.

'He has been metronomic', says Mercedes Chief Technical Officer James Allison. 'If you think of Lewis Hamilton errors in any given season you are going to struggle to find any more than one a year. He has been at this extraordinary level of perfection for year after year. Lewis is fully integrated into this team and he gives us a weapon so that we know that if we make a car that is reliable and decently quick we absolutely know that he will get the job done for us.'

Hamilton's consistency means that Allison and his colleagues can rely on him, enabling them to focus on issues other than driver input. 'We also know that if our car is not quick enough, it is not because he is having an off day because he doesn't have off days. It is because we have screwed up, and this is an incredibly useful benchmark to measure ourselves against and to keeping pushing us to higher and higher standards.'

For all the technology involved in Formula One, the leading drivers continue to add significant value. In the early days of data analysis, when cars would be plugged into laptops upon returning to the pits, McLaren's Ayrton Senna famously provided feedback to Honda's technicians to the effect that there was something wrong with the engine during a test session. A slight change in tone, something 'different'.

Honda checked everything and came to the conclusion that everything was fine. Shortly afterwards the engine suffered a catastrophic mechanical failure, proving that a sensitive and alert driver could spot problems even the sensors missed. This story added to the mystique surrounding Senna.

At the opposite end of the spectrum was a driver like Jean Alesi, who early in his career could produce a prodigious amount of speed without fully understanding the reasons behind it – apart from his inherent talent, of course. Dropped by Marlboro from its driver academy in Formula 3000, he was snapped up by Eddie Jordan for the 1989 season and would go on to win it in triumphant style, graduating to Formula One the next year.

It was evident to the engineers at Eddie Jordan Racing that Jean could have good days and bad days. During an off day his feedback was that there was something wrong with the car's set-up. This bemused the team's engineers who had more constructive feedback and consistent performance from Alesi's teammate, Martin Donnelly.

On one such occasion the team used the ploy of telling Alesi his recommended changes had been made, except they had left it exactly the same. Armed with the belief that his car had been improved, the newly motivated Alesi promptly set a much-improved lap time.

Imagine one scenario where a driver is producing lap times that are ±0.5 second each lap. That gives the team a one-second variation just because the driver is inconsistent and unable to repeat inputs at the same time and place in successive laps. This makes it extremely difficult for the engineers to determine the result of any set-up changes they may have made, or to drill into any issues. They are working with an unstable and entirely variable baseline.

Then take a driver who is able to replicate performance lap after lap, to within ±0.1 second, giving a spread of 0.2 seconds against a backdrop of the car's performance at the point in time, including fuel load, tyre wear and so on. This is hugely beneficial to the team, as they can effectively forget about the driver as a variable, and know that whatever changes they make to the car will be reflected in lap time, such is the consistency of driver inputs.

At the 2013 Italian Grand Prix, for example, a quick analysis of the performance of four-times world champion Sebastian Vettel shows the extent of his ability in consistency as much as speed. On laps seven and eight of the race he achieved a lap time of 1 minute, 29.119 seconds and 1 minute, 29.101 seconds respectively, a variation of 0.018 seconds, while on laps 10 and 11 he drove the 5.783-kilometre track in 1 minute, 28.985 seconds and 1 minute, 28.980 seconds, a difference of 0.005 seconds.

Five-thousandths of a second over one lap equates to extra distance of 32.5 centimetres, which might be accounted for by a marginally different racing line at one or two corners, but in reality that performance delta will come from a range of minuscule differences in the performance of driver and machine. From an engineering perspective, it is an entirely consistent performance, the variation being 0.0056 per cent.

This is the kind of performance that sets the great drivers apart from the good ones, soon confirmed by an analysis of the lap times delivered by the Vettels and Hamiltons of this world.

Obviously other variables will change, affecting lap time as the race progresses: fuel load for one, as the car starts to lighten as the 100-kilogramme weight of fuel is gradually reduced. Again, looking at the 2013 Italian Grand Prix, Vettel produced his fastest lap on the penultimate lap of the race, as did Ferrari's Fernando Alonso. Meanwhile, Vettel's teammate Mark Webber achieved his personal best on the very last lap, when the fuel load was at its lightest, a perfect performance trajectory.

In some ways telemetry is the ultimate Big Brother system, for we can see in real time how drivers are operating their cars: the precise moment when they brake, steer, accelerate and change gear, the amount of pressure they apply to the brakes, the percentage of throttle being used and, best of all, their ability to deliver sustained performance.

The drivers have the support of trackside performance and data engineers, men and women who are dedicated to examining the real-time data streams, focusing on a specific range of parameters to evaluate performance. The systems are designed to highlight anomalies, so that the analysts are immediately alerted to any problems as they develop.

Most of the information is run-of-the-mill, confirming that everything is working fine. The information that is of interest allows teams either to tackle a problem, mitigate risk, or focus on an area where additional performance can be gained. This is where the advent of data analytics became important because from a Formula One perspective having a lot of data was much less interesting than generating insights.

Real-time data analysis does not lead to localized decision-making trackside, however. Race strategy is run remotely, with teams of software, data and performance engineers viewing all the available information back at base in rooms that resemble NASA's mission-control suites.

Personnel are able to view all the telemetry data in real time together with audio feeds and TV images, far from the heat and emotion of the racetrack. Aside from the data coming from both cars, the strategy team has access to all of the publicly available timing data concerning their rivals, the team's own radio channels and the communications coming from the FIA during the race.

Armed with a helicopter view of the race, and supported by algorithms that generate optimal race strategies, it is strategists such as Neil Martin who can help the team and its drivers to make winning decisions.

One example of this approach came for the McLaren team at the 2005 Monaco Grand Prix when a serious accident on lap 23 effectively blocked the track. While their competitors took the more obvious decision to use the track blockage and safety-car period to carry out a pit stop, Martin, McLaren's chief strategist based at the team's UK headquarters, made the split-second call for driver Kimi Räikkönen not to make a pit stop and remain on track. It turned out to be the winning decision.

In this highly focused world of performance analysis and management there is no room to hide. That suits the Formula One community. The sport is being broadcast live, so the successes and failures are very public.

One of Cosworth's engine technicians related going into his first engineering debrief with the Williams team in 2010 and emerging, ashen-faced, after being confronted by Brazilian driver Rubens Barrichello during the meeting. He had complained bitterly about one aspect of the engine's performance, and the issue could readily be viewed on the telemetry data.

Everyone attending these technical meetings can face detailed analysis of their performance. This could be a driver who made mistakes out on the track, a chassis engineer whose set-up changes failed to have the desired effect, or an engine supplier whose circuit set-up did not provide the right combination of performance, power delivery and fuel economy.

For the drivers it can be an uncomfortable moment, especially if you are being consistently beaten by your teammate. The data from both cars is shared openly, available for all to see. Mercedes CTO James Allison admits that this degree of scrutiny is not easy.

'They are called teammates but actually they are the two drivers for whom the entire world can make a direct comparison of their ability because they have got the same kit', says Allison. 'That introduces a level of psycho-drama that is quite intense because they get put on a stage every couple of weeks and, incredibly visibly, their performances relative to each other are set out for all to see.'

Allison admits that Mercedes approaches this degree of scrutiny with some sympathy for the drivers, recognizing that they have a rather lonely role when compared to the rest of the team. 'Everyone on the engineering side and the logistics side, we are a really close group of colleagues, and we know that we derive our strength from how close we can be with each other', says Allison. 'But the drivers are like gunslingers and they face a different challenge. We have to recognize their job is lonely. Although we want to be close to them, and from a technical point of view we want to support them, they know it is not a friendship (with their teammate) like it is with the rest of the team.'

To ensure that each driver is made to feel as well supported as possible, teams surround them with a support crew who, in Allison's words, would, 'walk over broken glass to support them'. There is nothing that the race engineers, performance engineers and support staff will not do to make the driver's life a little easier, given the level of performance analysis to which they are subjected.

When examining the data the team can show drivers exactly where each gained or lost performance, right down to individual braking points, where they changed gear and how much steering input they were making. Drivers can be shown how they performed not only over a given lap, but over a series of laps, focusing on any inconsistencies.

It is also normal to overlay the data from one driver with that of his teammate. Taking their two best laps, we can then see where the delta in performance arose.

When Sebastian Vettel qualified on pole position for the 2013 United States Grand Prix in Austin, Texas, with a lap time of 1 minute 36.338 seconds and his teammate Mark Webber was second with a time of 1 minute 36.441 seconds, the team's engineers were able to make the necessary analysis in the debrief and see exactly where that 0.103-second delta in performance came from. As the data traces were overlaid there will have been tiny differences in performance visible in terms of vehicle speed, braking and acceleration that together added up to one-tenth of a second over the course of 5.513 kilometres – an incredibly small margin, but sufficient to be the difference between first and second on the starting grid.

Meanwhile, at Williams, at the same event, the margin of difference between drivers Valtteri Bottas and Pastor Maldonado was significant. At 0.53 seconds this was the difference between Bottas making it through to the third period of qualifying – or Q3 – starting the race in ninth, and Maldonado being eliminated after Q1 and starting 18th. Considering they were driving the same-specification car, the focus in the debrief was on this significant difference in performance. The team and drivers will have been able to see where that half a second was gained by Bottas, in this instance around the entire lap. The data led the team to deduce that the Finn had been better able to get his tyres up to working temperature than Maldonado.

This relentless performance monitoring is an accepted part of the Formula One culture. David Coulthard told me that when he retired from racing and became a commentator for the BBC he expected that after each broadcast everyone involved in the production would have a meeting to discuss what went right, what went wrong, and where they could improve next time out. It didn't happen. When David asked why, he was told that such an approach might risk upsetting some people if their mistakes or gaffes were discussed in an open forum.

F1's lesson is that constant performance review is required to drive continuous improvement. It requires certain things to be in place: honesty, openness and transparency for all parties. It also requires that criticism is seen as constructive, that we are all in this together and everyone has to deliver, every time. It cannot succeed where there is a lack of trust or, worse, a blame culture. The purpose of performance management in F1 is to learn how to improve, to learn from mistakes and generate insights that can be used to advance the team towards its goal. Most people will welcome the opportunity to see how they can improve and learn from mistakes. If the process unveils a weak link, whether that be a technical system or person who is underperforming, the team can intervene and set about finding a solution.

The sport's data-driven approach to performance analysis and management helps to drive new levels of performance. The truth of the data is there for all to see, and the deeper the insights are, the faster the team can progress towards achieving its ambitious goals.

Lessons in performance management – key factors to bear in mind

MEASUREMENT IS THE STARTING POINT
One of the reasons Formula One teams are obsessed with data is that it allows them to measure key performance metrics.

AGREE AMBITIOUS TARGETS AND MILESTONES
Successful teams set high targets – and an agreed performance trajectory and timelines to achieving them.

CONSTANTLY REVIEW AND ASSESS PROGRESS

Make the cycle of performance analysis and review part of the daily team operations. Build excitement around analysis.

BREAK THE MAJOR TARGETS INTO INCREMENTAL STEPS

The performance methodology in Formula One is to break each race and lap into a series of measurable goals.

FOCUS ON THE ANOMALIES AND FAILURES

Competitive Formula One teams focus on performance deficiencies, recognizing that every failure is a learning opportunity.

RIGOROUS SCRUTINY DEMANDS EMPATHY

In creating a high-performance culture, Formula One teams 'blame the problem, not the person'. Those facing particular scrutiny require support and empathy from the team.

Notes

1   Hensby, P (2021) Cognizant 'Absolutely Thrilled' To Be Title Sponsor of Aston Martin – CEO Brian Humphries, *The Checkered Flag*, https://www.thecheckeredflag.co.uk/2021/03/cognizant-absolutely-thrilled-to-be-title-sponsor-of-aston-martin-ceo-brian-humphries/ (archived at https://perma.cc/AC2Q-SZUL)
2   Oracle (2021) Red Bull Racing Honda and Oracle Partner to Elevate Data Analytics in Formula 1, https://www.oracle.com/uk/news/announcement/oracle-cloud-red-bull-racing-honda-2021-03-25.html (archived at https://perma.cc/W6Q6-RF2R)

CHAPTER ELEVEN

Innovating to succeed

Victory in Formula One requires many things: a good budget, the best technical resources and, of course, a great team supporting a fast driver. But if there is one aspect of winning teams that stands out time and again it is the ability of top teams to constantly innovate in their quest for competitive advantage.

Innovation fuels success in our sport, driving a culture founded on the understanding that we can never stand still and rest on our laurels. We are only as good as our last race and, even if our last race produced a victory, the need to push onwards and develop even better results remains the same. You can never stop and say, 'This is it; this is as far as we have come and we have no need to develop any further.'

'Our business is all about speed', says Mercedes CEO and Team Principal Toto Wolff. 'Speed of innovation, speed of production, speed of delivery and reliability.'

Developing an innovation culture necessarily means embracing change, taking risks. The two go hand in hand. If you aim to be the best then it is essential to evolve. This includes learning from past mistakes as well as questioning established ways of doing things.

Early Formula One cars, though sophisticated for their time, had not advanced much since the internal combustion engine replaced the horse as the mode of transport. Look at a 1950s F1 car and you see the engine at the front, four rather spindly wheels, and somewhere for the driver to sit at the back.

Attending a fascinating seminar by the US vehicle designer Chris Bangle, at that time head of design for the BMW Group, I recall him sketching the evolution of the car from horse-drawn carriages. He demonstrated how designers took ideas from sleek boat designs and later jet aircraft to develop some of the iconic design features of the interwar and then post-war years. Innovation was coming thick and fast in automobile design, ultimately taking its cue from a multitude of design influences.

In 1950, the inaugural season of the FIA Formula One World Championship was more impressive because of its success in staging an international motor-racing series so soon after the Second World War than for the technical sophistication of its cars. However, innovation was there, fixed in its DNA, from the very start.

Those big, powerful, front-engined Grand Prix cars from Ferrari, Lancia, Maserati and Mercedes-Benz were in for a shock, however, when a British design engineer called John Cooper embarked on a more radical approach. The standard design philosophy tended to promote poor handling characteristics given that the heavy mass of the engine up front was transmitting all its raw power through to the rear wheels and, in so doing, playing havoc with the car's stability. The centre of gravity was simply too high, weight distribution poor.

Cooper's innovation was to move the engine to the middle of the car, initially as the result of using a motorcycle engine that ran a chain drive to the rear axle. In essence he realized that this kind of horsepower could be situated anywhere. Positioning it centrally, in front of the rear wheels, gave the car a lower centre of gravity and more neutral handling style. This would translate into better handling characteristics, together with improved tyre and brake wear. Ultimately the car would be faster.

Cooper's innovation was a resounding success, his designs embarrassing the giants of Formula One. He not only helped to change race-car design forever, but ensured that all 'supercars' of the future would feature predominantly mid-engined design layouts. Cooper was one of the many innovators who appeared in racing during the 1950s and 1960s, including Colin Chapman, founder of Lotus, famed for his lightweight cars and innovative design concepts.

In 1967 Ford Motor Company agreed to sponsor the Cosworth engineering business to develop a new Formula One engine, a 90-degree V8 engine, which would be known as the DFV, standing for double-four-valve. Lighter than its V12 rivals, it offered a good power-to-weight ratio and Cosworth's founders, Keith Duckworth and Mike Costin, developed it to act as a structural part of the car. While the majority of racing engines were held or supported by a metal frame, Cosworth recognized this added weight and complexity, and offered poor torsional strength.

Their solution was to make the engine immensely strong in itself, literally holding together the entire car. The front section of the car, including cockpit, front suspension and wheels, would be bolted to the engine, with the gearbox, rear suspension and wheels attached to its rear.

Fitted to the Lotus 49 of Scotland's Jim Clark, the Cosworth DFV scored a debut win at the 1967 Dutch Grand Prix in Zandvoort. Its performance stunned the opposition, and Clark would go on to win four Grands Prix that season en route to third in the World Championship. Teammate Graham Hill would win the 1968 World Championship outright. The Cosworth DFV became the most significant engine in Formula One history; its design innovation and performance established a new industry benchmark. Ultimately the DFV and derivatives would go on to power 155 Formula One race winners, carrying Jackie Stewart, Emerson Fittipaldi, James Hunt, Mario Andretti, Alan Jones, Keke Rosberg and Nelson Piquet Sr to World Championship titles in its various derivatives up until 1982.

When I took over running Cosworth's F1 business in 2009 I salvaged an old, framed photograph of Keith Duckworth, Colin Chapman and Jim Clark taken in 1967 and put it on the wall of my office. It was there to remind me that the very essence of Cosworth's success lay in a commitment to innovation as well as working with partners who share the vision to succeed.

With mid-engined cars thanks to Cooper, and Cosworth's DFV setting new standards in engine design, the performance of Formula One cars increased dramatically. Sometimes they would literally fly over the crests and brows on the public road courses such as Germany's Nürburgring and Belgium's Spa-Francorchamps.

Design engineers including Chapman began experimenting with aerodynamics. The aim was to generate downforce using wings fitted at the front and rear of the car, Chapman testing these in other categories of racing before joining Brabham and Ferrari in introducing them to Formula One in 1968.

Initially these were mounted high in the airstream, at the tips of improbably tall and flimsy wing mounts, leading to some early failures. However, the point was made. Car-mounted wings could generate 'downforce', harnessing the power of aerodynamics.

These wings operated precisely like the wings on aircraft, the difference being that they were inverted, pushing the cars into the ground as opposed to generating lift. The advent of wings was an innovation that paved the way for the principal area of performance development of the next 50 years. To this day Formula One has embraced the complex principles of aeronautical engineering and found ever more sophisticated ways to harness airflow in order to optimize vehicle performance.

Current Formula One owes more to aerospace than automotive technology, the industry having spent the last half-century flying cars into the ground in order to corner as quickly as possible. Rather like putting the horse behind the driver or turning the engine into a chassis member, flying upside down at 200 mph may seem counterintuitive, but so much innovation has come from questioning standard thinking.

As wings became adopted across Formula One, it was engineers such as Chapman and British colleagues Peter Wright and Tony Rudd who sought to unleash the next step-change in performance. Recognizing that the front and rear wings could generate only a certain amount of downforce, they opted to treat the car as a single aerodynamic platform, essentially a massive wing. The car's upper surfaces could act as the top of a wing; its underbody could be designed in such a way as to accelerate the airflow travelling beneath, effectively sucking the car on to the track. The era of 'ground effect' technology was born.

After being trialled as early as 1976 and introduced the following year, Lotus 79 of 1978 made full use of this innovation. Chapman's solution to the problem of airflow leaking out from underneath the sides of the car was simply to deploy vertical walls, known as skirts. These sealed the gap between the side of the car and the ground, helping to ensure that the airflow under the chassis would accelerate up and out of the rear of the car through a swept diffuser. The car, a 200 mph wing on four wheels, was astonishingly quick. The Lotus 79 swept all before it, winning both the World Championship for Drivers and the World Championship for Constructors.

This was such a sophisticated technological step, a radical innovation, that many teams struggled to understand how to copy and compete. Ferrari, with their powerful but wide Flat 12 engine, had difficulty implementing a design to mirror the Lotus philosophy, but ultimately joined everyone in chasing the benefits to be had from making the most of ground-effect technology.

Unable to replicate the efficiency of Chapman's Lotus design, another innovator came up with an unorthodox yet successful alternative. Gordon Murray, chief designer at Bernie Ecclestone's Brabham team, decided to emulate Chapman's approach to ground-effect aerodynamics by building the world's most powerful vacuum cleaner.

Arriving at the 1978 Swedish Grand Prix in Anderstorp, Brabham drivers Niki Lauda and John Watson found themselves at the wheel of a Brabham BT46B modified with a huge fan driven from the gearbox, channelling the airflow from under the car. It was effective, and in ways beyond those intended by Murray, because not only were the Brabhams sucked on to the track like a 200 mph Dyson, but they fired all the dust and debris out of the back, rendering it impossible for anyone to follow even if they had managed to keep up. The car duly won the race, Lauda triumphant, and the design was promptly withdrawn from competition by team boss Bernie Ecclestone. It wasn't illegal, because no rule maker had ever thought of such a thing, but Ecclestone recognized it was a technical cul-de-sac and politically much too controversial.

Murray's approach to Formula One design remained undiminished. Ahead of the 1978 season, months before the 'fan car' had been conceived, Murray appeared on BBC Television's *Sports Personality of the Year* show and unveiled a Brabham BT46 design featuring a surface cooling system rather than traditional radiators. Providing cooling to the engine and gearbox, radiators have always been regarded as a necessary evil by aerodynamicists, requiring a large surface area to be presented to the airflow. Murray's innovation would undoubtedly have had a profound effect on performance, had it worked. In this case the innovation failed, the heat exchangers incapable of providing sufficient cooling, but it showed how he was thinking. For him performance and innovation were bedfellows.

This insight into the mind of an innovator such as Gordon Murray keeps us on a trail that leads to today's top innovator in Formula One, Adrian Newey, technical director of Red Bull Racing. His cars not only won four World Championship titles for Red Bull between 2010 and 2013, but his previous designs at McLaren and Williams had amassed 12 titles over the past 20 years. As with the innovators such as Murray, Chapman, Duckworth and Cooper before him, Newey's edge comes from looking at every aspect of product performance and questioning defined wisdom.

Consider, for example, that Newey's design teams have taken forward wing design by engineering a degree of flexibility into these previously rigid devices, enabling the wings to bend towards the race track at speed. Welcome to the world of aeroelasticity.

Wings can be made to flex along their length, or breadth, returning to their static shape when the car reduces speed and returns to the pit lane.

In this way, a car's wings may pass all the necessary tests for minimum height above the track surface when measured for compliance. However, once they are on the racetrack they can alter shape into an altogether more aggressive and aerodynamically efficient design configuration.

One of Newey's criticisms of contemporary Formula One has been the stifling of innovation through the creation of rules that leave fewer opportunities for designers to introduce groundbreaking ideas. As the FIA has sought to improve safety, limit costs and prevent teams from incorporating technologies or materials that will prove increasingly difficult to police, so designers are left with a prescribed list of rules and regulations.

Compliance is as important in F1 as with any other regulated business, but for the innovator it is often seen as the enemy. It can prevent exploration, blunt inspiration and resist lateral thinking. But there is evidence that, even in this era of strangled compliance, opportunities for innovation remain. It all comes down to how you read the rule book, not for what it says, but for what it doesn't say.

In 2009, as Red Bull Racing began to exert its position of dominance within Formula One, we became aware of a new innovation. Once again it came from the design office of Adrian Newey, this time in close collaboration with engine supplier Renault Sport, and again it took the form of rethinking established practice.

A Formula One engine's principal purpose has always been to provide the motive power and, since 1967 and development of the Cosworth DFV, act as a fully stressed chassis member. Its efficiency has always been important; an engine that requires less cooling or has lower fuel consumption is seen as beneficial, as is smooth delivery of the power and torque available to the driver.

Engine exhaust gases were first used to enhance aerodynamic efficiency in the early 1990s when exhaust tailpipes were integrated into the diffusers sweeping up from the underbody of the car, the exhaust gases being used to help accelerate the airflow. This was beneficial, but somewhat limited by the fact that the speed of exhaust gas flow was related to the speed of the engine. At lower speeds the exhaust flow would reduce, and with it the aerodynamic benefit diminish.

Newey's design team worked with its engine supplier at Renault to come up with an innovation whereby the engine's role as an 'air pump' would be enhanced such that, even in slow corners, the exhaust flow would be maintained, increasing downforce and enabling the car to corner much more quickly. Initially this was achieved simply by keeping air flowing through the engine even when the driver would come off the throttle as he approached a turn; this would be known as cold blown diffuser technology. Later enhancements would see the engine's ignition timing adjusted so that it would continue to fire without generating torque: 'hot blown' diffusers were born.

Red Bull Racing and Renault's use of this innovation gave them a significant advantage, for even though the Renault F1 engine produced less power than rivals such as Mercedes and Cosworth, its smooth power delivery and lower fuel consumption allied to hot blown diffuser technology delivered an important advantage. Combined with the ever efficient aerodynamics of its Newey-inspired cars, Red Bull dominated Formula One in 2010 and 2011.

Even when blown diffuser technology was banned in 2012 – thanks to compliance again – Red Bull was able to recover some of that performance after a tough start to the season and re-establish its competitive edge in the latter part of the year, thanks to further innovations introduced at the Singapore Grand Prix in September 2012. Developing a configuration that allowed the Red Bull cars to run a much more pronounced front-to-rear rake, harness the remaining exhaust flow and its interaction with the diffuser, and create intricately detailed aerodynamic tweaks at the front of the car helped the team maintain its advantage. The team's domination was reasserted, not only clinching the title for a third time, in 2012, but establishing the edge that carried Red Bull Racing and driver Sebastian Vettel to four successive titles in 2013.

Whilst Newey is right to challenge the restrictive nature of the Formula One regulatory environment, his book *How To Build a Car* illustrates how he has continued to drive innovation by looking for new opportunities. His mindset is to read the rules for what they do say, and then for what they don't say. This curiosity lies at the heart of Formula One's innovation culture,[1] and is one of the reasons why teams have been able to successfully diversify into new markets.

Good examples of this come from a range of Formula One's leading teams. As we have seen in Chapter 7 on managing change, McLaren's Applied division takes innovative technologies and processes, applies them in new fields and creates value for its customers by bringing Formula One's mindset to bear on complex solutions. Williams Advanced Engineering became a successful provider of hybrid powertrain solutions for companies including Porsche and Audi, and today provides technology solutions across aerospace, mobility, transport and energy efficiency. Red Bull Racing's creation of an advanced technologies business has enabled them to develop the

Aston Martin Valkyrie hypercar, while Mercedes is now developing a diversified technologies business offering its world-class innovation capabilities to a range of clients.

Innovation is not just driving these Formula One businesses on track; it is directly helping teams to generate new revenue streams and develop a more robust business model at a time when the traditional sources of funding such as commercial sponsorship have come under threat. With major commercial sponsorship more difficult to secure, owing to the fact that these customers have more choice than ever before and are more rigid in their evaluation of sports sponsorships, the need for Formula One teams to create a range of new revenue opportunities has never been greater. Applying their natural innovation culture to adjacent markets in automotive, aerospace, defence and renewables is opening a new chapter in this sports industry's development.

Understanding the core competences of a Formula One team, and then applying those skills and cultures in new areas of business, is turning out to be a formidable weapon for those teams with the leadership and vision to create a diversified engineering, marketing and business services organization.

McLaren has long held ambitions to outdo Ferrari off the track as well as on it, and their move into becoming a mainstream automotive company began back in 1990 with the creation of the iconic three-seater McLaren F1 road car. Designed by Gordon Murray, it applied an F1-bred approach to vehicle design, including the widespread use of lightweight materials including a carbon fibre composite monocoque. Under the leadership of Ron Dennis and John Barnard, McLaren had been the first team to employ carbon fibre in chassis construction, partnering with the Hercules aerospace company to develop the 1981 McLaren MP4/1.

The innovation of using carbon fibre to construct the driver's cockpit safety cell delivered a multitude of benefits, being not only extremely light and rigid but very strong. In one fell swoop, performance and safety took a step forward, and eight years later it was being employed in a road-going supercar.

McLaren's prowess in applying its Formula One know-how in road-car designs, exemplified by the F1, soon landed them with the opportunity to develop the McLaren Mercedes SLR, including establishing its production facility at the team's new headquarters near Woking. When McLaren's ambitions diverged from those of partner and shareholder Mercedes-Benz, the McLaren Group went its own way, with the development of a new range of McLaren sports cars commencing with the MP4/12C launched in 2011.

McLaren's quest to use its Formula One know-how and innovation mindset led it to create a multitude of businesses within its group, now comprising Racing, Applied and Automotive. In its pre-Covid guise the group enjoyed revenue of £1.486 billion, of which Automotive represented 84 per cent, Applied 4 per cent and Racing 12 per cent.

McLaren is no longer merely a Formula One racing team, but a group of businesses applying a race-bred approach to delivering world-class products and technology solutions.

Developing a culture of innovation requires management to create the environment within which it can flourish. This is often a challenge when the more mundane requirements of producing a product strictly on time, and within a strict set of rules, appear to leave little room for creativity.

As a result, the ongoing development of the product is divided into three clearly identified phases of design innovation and development. The first phase is the design, development and manufacture of the base product, which has to be produced against a rigid timeline so as to make the start of pre-season testing in February each year. Normally this process starts in early summer; at Jordan Grand Prix we would kick off the following year's design in earnest in June, with the new-car designers having used the previous months to look at some overall concepts.

With the base car under way to meet a January build schedule, in the second phase the team starts to look at opportunities to bring further development to the table, some of which may be able to be incorporated within the initial product when it is launched, while others require further analysis prior to being committed. As a result, when the new car is finally launched, there will already be a raft of future developments planned, and these are rolled out during pre-season testing and into the start of the season, optimizing vehicle performance and taking its performance on an upward trajectory.

The third strand is the long-term development of innovations that require more intensive research and development, evaluation and testing to ensure that they meet the requirements of being robust, reliable and safe. This is particularly true when you have a significant innovation that will require a step-change in technology, processes or operations.

A good example of technological innovation came in the form of the 2014 Formula One hybrid powertrain regulations. Originally tasked with producing the same 800bhp power as the 2.4-litre V8 engines they replace, these units feature an extremely small 1.6-litre, single turbocharged internal combustion engine mated to a pair of motor generator units, an electrical energy storage system and control system. The goal was a reduction in fuel consumption of over 35 per cent, and the development of a hybrid power unit, which would ensure that Formula One technology remained road relevant for the automotive companies investing heavily in the sport.

When these regulations were first agreed upon, most of the initial discussion within the industry focused on the electric aspect of the power unit. Specifically this related to the battery, the kinetic and heat energy recovery systems and the way in which this waste energy could be harvested and redeployed.

What few people anticipated back in 2011 was that Mercedes would comprehensively re-engineer the internal combustion engine (ICE). This included revisiting combustion technologies, ultimately achieving over 50 per cent thermal efficiency, a remarkable feat considering that most ICEs operate at around 30 per cent. They also redesigned the turbocharger, splitting the turbine and compressor, allowing for a better packaged and responsive engine.

Although not the only reason why the 2014 Mercedes Formula One car and its successors have been world beating, the innovations within the hybrid powertrain played a significant part in giving the team a competitive advantage. Over the eight years of these relatively static regulations the opportunity to innovate further has diminished, but as Andy Cowell, boss of Mercedes-Benz High Performance Powertrain division, put it, the quest for improvement never stops.

'The hardest thing is having the correct mindset', he said in 2018. 'There is no such thing as perfection, there is always the opportunity to improve and all of us have that mindset. We're always improving every detail – the materials, the hardware and ingredients, but also things like our design tools. The mindset of everyone here is very much that the moment you have completed something and released it to go racing, you know that there are areas to improve. You know there are areas where you can get better. Being self-critical and keeping an open mind is at the core of that mindset. That's the journey we are continuously going through, regardless of whether the regulations change or not.'[2]

The innate curiosity to innovate is a thread that runs through Formula One's history, and is embedded in those who choose to work at the forefront of this sport. They like a challenge, particularly one in which it is unclear whether a solution can be delivered. Add a deadline to it, and it appeals even more.

In the spring of 2020 it was this combination of being faced with a major technical challenge and an urgent deadline that gave Formula One an opportunity to showcase its capabilities.

On Friday 13 March Formula One announced that the opening round of the World Championship, due to commence that very day, was cancelled. The promoter of the Australian Grand Prix in Melbourne had been anxious to satisfy the tens of thousands of spectators who had purchased tickets for that weekend's event, but the fast-moving Covid-19 crisis had intervened.

Following days of uncertainty one of the teams, McLaren, had been forced to withdraw from the event after a team member tested positive for the coronavirus, and from that moment onward the race was never likely to proceed.

Two weeks later all seven UK-based Formula One teams had banded together under 'Project Pitlane' to produce pulmonary ventilator components, breathing aids and medical equipment in response to the government's Ventilator Challenge.

The need to urgently design, test and manufacture healthcare equipment played to Formula One's core strengths. Teams that would normally be competing head to head collaborated in the development and manufacture of urgently needed equipment. Red Bull Racing and archrivals Renault F1 joined forces under Project BlueSky to produce a portable ventilator originally designed by a young NHS doctor.

'At times like this rivalry goes out the window', admitted RBR's Christian Horner, 'so we welcomed with open arms the personnel from Renault F1 into our facility, showing that something like this virus transcends sport.'[3]

In Italy, Ferrari's response was to join forces with the Italian Institute of Technology (IIT) in producing a versatile, easy-to-use and assemble ventilator. From starting out with a clean sheet of paper, Ferrari and the IIT had a fully functioning prototype running and validated in just five weeks, giving rise to the ventilator's name – the FI5.

Ferrari's Innovation Manager Corrado Onorato and Head of Chassis Engineering Simone Resta headed the project, and together with colleagues from the IIT they established the project's scope by working with healthcare professionals from Milan's Niguarda Hospital and the Policlinico San Martino in Genoa.

From a Formula One engineering perspective Ferrari's engineers undertook the CAD design work, defining the pneumatic and mechanical parts as well as running simulation tests. The IIT sourced raw materials, designed the electronics, firmware and control software, with the final FI5 products provided on an open-sourced basis. Once production began the units were being used in Italy and Mexico within a matter of days.

'FI5 is the contribution we made as the Scuderia', said Mattia Binotto, Managing Director and Team Principal at Ferrari, 'fielding the very essence of what makes a Formula One team and, more importantly, all the characteristics that make Ferrari special; its passion, its creativity and its desire to improve.'[4]

At Mercedes-Benz F1 the response was no less impressive, a call from University College London (UCL) leading to the development of a prototype continuous positive airway pressure (CPAP) breathing aid in just 100 hours of engineering. In the early stages of the pandemic clinics in China and Italy had discovered that the use of CPAP devices reduced the number of patients who needed to use ventilators by around 50 per cent.

The UK requirement was to reverse engineer and manufacture 10,000 CPAP devices for the NHS. The Mercedes-AMG High Performance Powertrain division accepted the challenge. The same team tasked with producing world-championship hybrid powertrains for Lewis Hamilton were given an altogether more critical challenge.

The UCL Venture team was soon created, combining expertise from Mercedes-AMG HPP and UCL, as well as critical-care consultants from University College London Hospital. The process of reverse engineering led to improvements to the CPAP device and, as with Ferrari's FI5, it was provided online on an open-sourced basis. By August 2020 over 1,900 organizations in 105 countries had downloaded the designs.

Ultimately the UCL Venture team would receive the Royal Academy of Engineering's President's Special Award for Pandemic Service, and for Mercedes' Andy Cowell it was a project that his team found exceptionally rewarding.

'Delivering difficult technology in extremely ambitious timeframes – that is what F1 is all about', he said. 'Our team is used to working long hours and delivering complex projects to tight deadlines, but this project pushed us to new limits. We're very grateful that we could make a small contribution to the giant task that this pandemic represents.'

The mission-critical nature of Formula One's technical environment attracts talented engineers, eager to contribute to the sport's history of developing innovative technologies, many of which go on to benefit wider society.

'What Project Pitlane demonstrated is the speed at which Formula One can develop things', said Ross Brawn. 'The type of people that get involved in Formula One – their character, their determination, their resourcefulness – they succeed because of those qualities.'[5]

Lessons in innovation – key summary

SUCCESSFUL FORMULA ONE TEAMS STRATEGIZE INNOVATION
They recognize that innovation drives competitive advantage, therefore they put in place the culture and behaviours that support it against a set of agreed priorities.

INNOVATORS ARE CURIOUS AND CREATIVE
This means incubating ideas, enabling creativity and encouraging a flow of ideas that question established practice.

QUESTION THE FUNDAMENTALS
Looking at the approach taken by innovators such as Cooper, Chapman, Murray or Newey, their strongest suit was to question the fundamentals – an approach repeated by Mercedes during the current hybrid engine formulae in Formula One.

SUCCESSFUL INNOVATION GENERATES TANGIBLE OUTCOMES
Formula One's innovators want to innovate and execute, develop an idea and bring it to market. They understand the importance of creating an innovation pipeline.

COMPLIANCE NEED NOT STIFLE INNOVATION
Formula One's innovators examine the rules both for what they do and don't say. There is a constant quest to explore opportunity, to question established ways of operating.

INNOVATION CAN BE TRANSFERABLE AND SCALABLE
The innovation mindset within Formula One has led to the development of technology products and services that have enabled the diversification of its business model.

Notes

1   Newey, A (2017) *How to Build a Car: The autobiography of the world's greatest Formula 1 designer*, HarperCollins, London

2   Silver Arrows (2020) Q&A With Mercedes Engine Boss Andy Cowell, http://www.silverarrows.net/news/qa-with-mercedes-engine-boss-andy-cowell/ (archived at https://perma.cc/3ELW-SDT8)

3   Higgins, C (2020) 'Unthinkable' Seeing Renault Staff Members in Red Bull Factory – Horner, *GP Today*, https://www.gptoday.net/en/news/f1/255311/unthinkable-seeing-renault-staff-members-in-red-bull-factory-horner (archived at https://perma.cc/9ZVY-6ZHE)

4   Smith, L (2020) Motor 1, Ferrari Has Become the Latest Formula 1 Team to Unveil a New Ventilator Designed to Help Covid-19 Patients, https://uk.motor1.com/news/423160/ferrari-ventiliator-coronavirus-patients/ (archived at https://perma.cc/UVT2-9CXR)

5   Daimler (2020) Engineers at Mercedes-AMG HPP Honoured By Royal Academy of Engineering For Help In Fight Against Covid-19, https://media.daimler.com/marsMediaSite/en/instance/ko/Engineers-at-Mercedes-AMG-HPP-honoured-by-Royal-Academy-of-Engineering-for-help-in-fight-against-COVID-19.xhtml?oid=47096486 (archived at https://perma.cc/4WQR-TEN8)

CHAPTER TWELVE

Communication

I have a Ferrari Formula One steering wheel that sits in a case in the corner of my office. It's a replica of the steering wheel from the Ferrari F10 that Fernando Alonso and Felipe Massa raced during the 2010 Formula One World Championship, and I often use it to illustrate a number of points about contemporary Formula One.

The first is the degree of functionality provided to the driver by means of switches, levers and dials on the steering wheel. On the Ferrari F10 wheel there are 29 in total, including dials for the fuel and air mixture going into the engine, one for 'strategy multifunction' and another for the engine torque map. There is even a button to operate a drinks-bottle pump aimed at keeping the driver hydrated.

When you examine the wheel carefully it becomes clear that the engineers have carefully thought through the ergonomics of the unit and agreed with the drivers the best location for each switch or dial. With both hands gripping the wheel only the thumbs remain available. Four buttons are within immediate reach of the thumb, and two sit naturally in range of the thumbs when at rest: the oil pump and the radio.

This tells us a lot about the driver's priorities. The auxiliary oil pump ensures good oil pressure, and thus operation of the engine. The radio button enables the driver to keep in constant contact with the team.

Given that the car is relaying vast amounts of real-time data to the track-side engineers and strategists back at headquarters, the ban on sending data to the car means that the only way for the team to effect changes is to communicate with the driver. He or she has full control over the car's systems, so every strategy call or adjustment has to be communicated.

Efficient and timely communications have been central to some of the greatest successes in Formula One's history. Poor communication has been at the heart of some of the sport's more embarrassing failures. Craig Pollock, former team principal of British American Racing, once said that more races have been lost as a result of communications problems than any other reason.

The teams and drivers who communicate most successfully consistently achieve a competitive edge over their rivals simply by having a more complete picture of what is going on and being able to respond accordingly.

When Daniel Ricciardo arrived for a pit stop while leading the 2015 Monaco Grand Prix, only to find that the team was unprepared and costing him victory, Red Bull Racing admitted that it was due to miscommunication. 'A lot of misunderstanding and not the right communication', was the summary given by Red Bull's head of motorsport, Dr Helmut Marko.[1]

A potential 1–2 finish for Mercedes in the 2020 Bahrain Grand Prix was ruined by a botched radio communication, with race leader George Russell speaking at the same time as the team's sporting director Ron Meadows. The pit crew, only able to hear one voice channel at a time, was unprepared for the subsequent 'double stack' pit stop involving both Russell and team-mate Valtteri Bottas. The resulting chaos cost the team victory, not to mention a degree of public humiliation.

It is noticeable how often the ability of drivers is proportionate to their communication skills. When you examine how the great world champions such as Ayrton Senna, Michael Schumacher and Lewis Hamilton work, their ability to process information and communicate effectively with the team is a core competency.

During the 1998 season the team manager at Jordan Grand Prix commented that one of the revelations of working with Damon Hill was that, whenever he entered the pit lane, he would simply say, 'In the pit lane'. This simple discipline meant that the pit crew knew they had 10 to 15 seconds to ready themselves for a pit stop.

The previous year we had worked with Giancarlo Fisichella and Ralf Schumacher, two relative rookies. Communication was not their strongest suit. In Hill we had a driver who had seven years and 21 Grand Prix victories behind him. Experience of working with the Williams F1 team had taught him a great deal, particularly in terms of ensuring accurate and timely communication.

It is these little moments of discovery that are so important in racing. Something as simple as a driver informing the team when he is in the pit lane may seem obvious, yet can be so easily overlooked.

Viewers watching Formula One racing have become used to hearing radio messages from the drivers as part of the broadcast. These messages are delayed and are a fraction of the radio communications that take place.

For drivers working in the confines of their race car having the right information at the right time is critical. The drivers' view of the world is limited. The steering wheel in their hands provides a menu of information via the digital read-outs. Separate dashboards have long since disappeared. The driver will glance down at these displays, but primarily on the longer straights.

They can see the track in front of them, perhaps for 300 to 500 metres, and are focused on steering the car through the best trajectory on the race-track. The only other information can be gleaned from a quick look at the delicate rear-view mirrors situated on either side of the cockpit. They are not very large, 150 millimetres wide and 50 millimetres high. Drivers can use them to confirm that there is a car behind and, from its colour, which team it belongs to.

The information available to drivers is quite limited, therefore, providing only a small slice of the information necessary for them to respond to what is happening around them. Quite often the most critical factors affecting the drivers' race are happening somewhere else on the circuit, far beyond their vision or understanding. A rival may have pitted unexpectedly, an accident occurred or rain started to fall on another part of the track.

The Formula One drivers' desire for information is so great that it is quite common for them to log the position of the giant spectator screens situated around the track and glance up at them. Watching TV while driving at 320 kph may seem unlikely, but a quick look at a screen may divulge some piece of vital information, particularly given that the broadcast director will be focusing attention on the most interesting developments in the race. Awareness of an accident, or seeing a rival in the pit lane, might just provide a winning edge.

One of Ferrari's senior engineers confided in me at the height of Michael Schumacher's five consecutive World Championship wins that one of the most impressive aspects of his ability was the constant dialogue he maintained with the team throughout each race. He wanted to know how the strategy was evolving and the performance of his immediate rivals. Driving the car flat out came naturally to him, so he was using his intellectual bandwidth to the fullest extent by communicating. Schumacher knew the importance of sending and receiving the right information so that the team could improve the speed and efficiency of decision making.

Jordan Grand Prix won the 1999 French Grand Prix in Magny-Cours because we had a critical piece of information relayed to us by a team member who had been dispatched to monitor the fast-changing weather. Jordan's secret weapon came in the form of Dave, the driver of our hospitality unit, who volunteered to become our human early warning system. He was able to advise us how long the rain was likely to last.

Based on that critical information our engineers were able to switch Heinz-Harald Frentzen from a two-stop strategy to a single stop. Initially maintaining his fifth place, he later was elevated one place at a time when Michael Schumacher, David Coulthard and Mika Hakkinen had peeled off into the pit lane for more fuel. Against the odds, but thanks to a timely piece of vital information, Heinz-Harald moved into the lead and won the race. Standing in our hospitality unit with 450 guests I was delighted to be able to confirm that while Heinz had driven superbly, Dave was the hero of the day.

While effective communication during a race is critical, it is no less important in our day-to-day business activities. During the course of my executive career I found that establishing strong working relationships with both customers and suppliers depended on having strong, open lines of communication.

I had often noticed the effort to which a team would go to secure a corporate sponsor only to fail when servicing them, poor communications being a common problem. Fortunately there are now a number of excellent customer relationship management (CRM) tools and platforms available for businesses to help avoid these kinds of outcomes, but none replace the benefit of human interaction and communication.

At Jordan Grand Prix I often looked to McLaren as the benchmark in CRM, given their decades-long customer relationships with companies like Marlboro, Hugo Boss, Exxon Mobil and TAG Heuer. As a result I implemented a series of initiatives aimed at improving communications and delivering more value to our customers. This included appointing dedicated account managers to maintain regular communications with the customers, hosting an annual customer networking event and launching an intranet that gave customers online access to a range of team assets.

Similarly we initiated a range of tools that enabled us to communicate better with our suppliers. The objective was to change those relationships from being transactional to added-value. Supply chain management is critical within the manufacturing and operations of a Formula One team. This includes every tier-one supplier recognizing the non-negotiable nature of our production deadlines, together with the need for every component and assembly to be in the right place at the right time.

Again we introduced a supplier networking event, and included them in many of the communications that had previously been reserved for customers. One popular example was *J Magazine*, our in-house publication, in which we featured both our commercial sponsors and key suppliers. We were the first F1 team to produce a commercially viable, quarterly publication enjoyed by all the team's core audiences and stakeholders.

While it is correct for suppliers to tender for business in the normal manner, once they have been appointed they are regarded as part of the team ecosystem. For all that we discuss the importance of teamwork between individuals, including both personnel and contractors, collaboration with key suppliers is equally important.

When I was invited to run the Cosworth Formula One engine business I made sure that we avoided having a purely transactional relationship with the teams with which we worked. We worked hard to ensure that Cosworth contributed as fully as possible to their Formula One programmes, and our regular meetings, phone calls and visits played a part in ensuring a high degree of engagement.

Chris Jilbert, a talented engineer who ran factory operations at Cosworth, once said that the most important part of a Formula One engine was the part you don't have. Formula One engines are assembled by hand, the engine builders working from a kit provided for each unit – and not having one small component, seal or grommet can stop the entire operation. A Formula One team customer such as Sir Frank Williams expects his engines to be delivered precisely to schedule, and I recall him asking me to ensure that Cosworth met each deadline.

The culture within the sport requires that it should be possible to call a supplier 24/7. A Friday night telephone call asking for an overnight machining job to be loaded should not be unexpected. It may not be an ideal scenario, but the nature of our industry is such that everyone understands that there are times when we have to do whatever is necessary to ensure operational delivery.

This is one reason why being the last member of staff to fly to a Grand Prix can be an interesting experience. The team's supply chain managers will know that you could potentially bring out any last-minute components required by the team on the other side of the world. For that reason the team's travel schedule is circulated internally days before each event, ensuring that key departments know who is available to help with last-minute requirements. As a result I have at various times had to pack a wiring loom, suspension components or spare steering wheel in my luggage. It can make for an interesting check-in conversation.

I recall standing behind Jackie Oliver, boss of the Arrows team, when he was checking in for a flight. In answer to the question about luggage he had to admit he would need a little excess allowance as he had a Formula One engine weighing 110 kilogrammes in a freight container. It wasn't a cheap flight.

Being in close communication across our business and with key suppliers is vital in our delivery-focused environment. A combination of formal and informal communications ensures that unexpected surprises are avoided, maintaining a high degree of collaboration.

Staff engagement is another area where effective communication has a significant role to play. Given that up to 90 per cent of the staff in a Formula One team never travel to events, maintaining their motivation and commitment is just as important as for the mechanics geared up for a two-second pit stop.

Consider the position in which a factory-based member of a Formula One team finds themselves. Working in R&D, a design office, production or in an administrative role, there is a risk they can feel far-removed from the Grand Prix events attended by the race team. Left unchecked this can easily become a problem. The race team travels the world, working in different, interesting places. The work may be intense, but it can appear to be a glamorous lifestyle, quite different from their colleagues working in the headquarters factory facilities.

It becomes critically important to ensure that the team does not start to develop a split, everyone recognizing that each colleague and every department contributes to the company's performance. We have to ensure that the factory-based staff are recognized as being as valuable to the team as any mechanic, engineer or manager gracing the pit lane. Part of the way in which this is achieved is through ensuring consistent communications across the business, the leadership driving home the one-team message in what they do and say.

In the early stages of Jordan Grand Prix's history Eddie Jordan, team manager Trevor Foster and technical director Gary Anderson knew every single member of staff. There were around 35 of us in January 1991. This close-knit team had good morale and excellent communications. Eddie could stop while walking through the workshop and ask a mechanic how his girlfriend was, or debate a football result. The relationships were personal and very typical of a start-up business.

Later, as the team grew, Eddie stated that he didn't like not knowing all the staff any more. He didn't even know the names of some of the people he was meeting in the corridors or canteen. He even said that if the team employed more than 100 people he would sell up and do something else!

As the team grew and staff levels approached 300, we dealt with the issue of staff engagement by communicating in a number of ways and providing activities that could bind the workforce together. This included post-race debriefs for the factory staff and ensuring communications cascaded through the organization. At least twice a year we held events for the families of personnel, typically at the British Grand Prix, during an open day or at the end-of-year celebrations.

The post-race debriefs were held on the Tuesday or Wednesday following each Grand Prix, and these are now commonplace across the industry. At Jordan they were held in the race shop, which had the largest available floor area. We had a second facility, the wind tunnel centre in Brackley, and the debrief would often be repeated since their workload meant that a trip to headquarters at Silverstone was not always possible. Prior to the age of live streaming and video conferencing, face-to-face debriefs were the order of the day.

Attendance was seldom 100 per cent, which came to be an interesting topic in itself. The very people who failed to attend were usually those who complained about the company.

The debriefs were hosted by Eddie Jordan as CEO or, if he was unavailable, the managing director or technical director. There would be a review of the past race weekend, an update on developments from both a technical and a commercial viewpoint, and then a Q&A. Individual members of staff might be recognized for their particular achievement, or some issue affecting the company discussed. The whole point was that the communications channel was open and two-way.

Today's debriefs drill somewhat more deeply into the race weekends, and in the case of Mercedes-Benz they now share a video with the media in which a senior member of staff talks through the issues and challenges they faced. Team boss Toto Wolff has pointed out that their post-race debriefs can start to sound like a catalogue of failure, so focused is the team on learning from any mistakes, irrespective of whether they have won the race or not. The focus on continuous improvement is driven company-wide, and town-hall meetings have become a means for underlining that approach.

Mercedes has also run lunchtime sessions during which external speakers can share insights and experiences with staff. For example, Formula One engineer and author Calum Douglas was invited to give a lecture on the battle between Allied and Axis engineers to achieve air supremacy during the Second World War, as detailed in his book *The Secret Horsepower Race*. As CTO James Allison explained, Mercedes' engineers found the lecture truly inspirational, reflecting many of the same challenges they face in F1's sporting battles of today.[2]

Using internal communications initiatives in this way can help drive positive outcomes, including promoting innovation. At Jordan staff communications included the implementation of an ideas box into which personnel could post ideas to be considered by the management board. These were split into a number of categories including 'making the car go faster', 'improving efficiency' and 'saving money'. These ideas were reviewed each month and evaluated based on criteria including cost and practicality.

As described in Chapter 2 on leadership, the importance of top-down communication was shown in Dietrich Mateschitz's inaugural address to the workforce at Red Bull Racing. In spite of being head of a multibillion-euro business he came to Milton Keynes to address the staff personally, sharing his vision of what he wanted to achieve with the team and the foundation for its development. It was personal, heartfelt and credible. No one who was present can look back today and say he wasn't a man of his word. He outlined the path ahead, and asked everyone to join him on the journey.

Two other stakeholder audiences that are an important focus for communications strategies in Formula One are the media and fans. Owing to the popularity of Formula One we enjoy an enormous fan base, and at Jordan Grand Prix we built a formidable following that placed us among the top five most popular teams in the sport. This was partly due to the 'brand' we built as an Irish team led by a maverick entrepreneur. Our positioning was slightly anti-establishment, avoiding the corporate tones of McLaren or the elitism of Ferrari, promoting Jordan as a challenger brand eager to disrupt the status quo.

We also liked to have fun; Jordan became known for being a team that knew how to enjoy itself whether it won or lost, and since we did more of the latter than the former it came in quite useful. Eddie's decision to host an after-race barbecue at the British Grand Prix, to wait for the traffic queues to subside, developed into the Jordan rock concert, which became a great favourite for fans, media and even our rivals. The team communicated its sense of enjoyment, and a passion for what it did. These were appealing brand attributes.

Building a relationship with fans was made possible through the creation of Club Jordan, initiated in 1997 and managed by the father–son combination of Paul and Russell Banks. Although we charged a subscription, the revenue was reinvested to create a range of benefits that fans could enjoy. This included regular communications, discounted merchandise and a factory open day.

Club Jordan arranged an official trip to the Belgian Grand Prix each year, commencing with a tour of our factory followed by a coach trip to Spa-Francorchamps for the weekend. On the Saturday evening we would host our annual Club Jordan dinner, which Eddie Jordan and the drivers usually attended. It was a hugely popular event and generated very positive feedback.

At its peak, when Damon Hill and Ralf Schumacher were driving for our team in 1998, we had over 10,000 fans on our database, 50 per cent of whom were full subscribers.

These are small numbers, but they had a disproportionate impact on the impression of our team. We only needed 20 or 30 in a grandstand opposite the pits to create a noise such that other teams were left wondering why Jordan was attracting such attention. The activities we arranged at Silverstone and Spa were so successful that the international media commented on the support we had. Jordan's core fans amplified the team's position within the sport.

Those diehard fans had an enthusiasm that was infectious and their support helped to create further momentum behind the team. Jordan's corporate sponsors recognized this and began to leverage the support we had generated.

Club Jordan was an inexpensive means of driving fan engagement, but the halo effect of that initiative influenced our corporate clients, the media and helped with our positioning in the sport. It was entirely self-funding, and yet its impact was far reaching, contributing to Jordan's reputation as one of the most popular teams in contemporary Formula One.

Reaching out to the media was until recently the primary means of communication with the world, but the advent of social media and proliferation of digital platforms have radically altered the communications landscape. The world of digital media is driving rapid change, offering a rich opportunity to engage with audiences using a variety of means.

Within Formula One there is a travelling media corps of several hundred journalists, broadcasters, film crews and photographers servicing the demands of the world's media across a multitude of traditional and digital platforms. Individual journalists may be writing or broadcasting for trade media, national press and international outlets. Most have a wide spectrum of media and platforms to service.

As with any industry there are the key opinion formers: the media who have covered our sector for many years and/or report for the most prestigious outlets. They know the key industry figures on a personal basis and are regarded as having the gravitas and credibility to influence world media opinion. That does not necessarily mean that the key opinion formers are the elder statesmen and women of the press office, or that they report on the sport for a multitude of outlets. It might just as easily include a young journalist who reports for a particularly important trade or business magazine that has a disproportionate influence.

During my Formula One apprenticeship in the 1980s I learned that media communications should always be consistent, credible and informative. As the range of digital communications tools has expanded there are more ways than ever to communicate with the media, and the leading Formula One teams have invested heavily in creating multiple touchpoints.

Team websites, so long the main portal for sharing information, are increasingly a repository for media assets such as copyright-free film, photography and official statements. To push messages to media, and the public, teams have embraced major social media platforms, particularly Twitter, Facebook and Instagram, while LinkedIn now sees extensive information about Formula One's business environment and corporate partnerships.

On Twitter the 10 teams had 17.6 million followers in 2021, but with an individual driver such as Lewis Hamilton sporting 6.3 million on the same platform and 22 million on Instagram, the sport stars themselves can directly communicate without necessarily going through the team. It is potentially a minefield, but teams have developed social media guidelines for all their personnel – drivers included – recognizing that everyone who works for them now has the potential to influence the media and global audience.

Meanwhile, on WhatsApp, teams create media groups, using it as a distribution tool for audio and video files, press statements and personalized, real-time updates during races. In the time is takes a member of the communications team to write a short text, they can WhatsApp broadcast commentators with live updates. Post-race debriefs from senior personnel can be shared by uploading the files on WhatsApp, and through the teams' official YouTube channels, with video content now playing a central role in how teams communicate with stakeholder audiences.

At Jordan we maintained a strong relationship with the media and aimed to be highly responsive to requests. Our policy was to try to accommodate media requests as much as possible, recognizing we had to work harder than the well-established teams to generate exposure.

We also liked to share our sense of fun with the media, and the regular media receptions, lunches and dinners that we hosted with our sponsors ensured that we had good personal relationships. This was important when we wanted to communicate the positive things we were doing, but perhaps even more vital when times were more difficult and we had issues to address.

I recall Ron Dennis, team principal of McLaren, complaining that the Jordan team was getting too much media coverage relative to its results. It was a compliment indeed, for it was precisely because we couldn't be sure of winning the race on Sunday that we put so much effort into working with the media Monday to Friday.

One of the basic ways in which we cultivated a strong relationship with the key opinion formers was to host a breakfast on Friday mornings in the Jordan motorhome. This was a very informal affair, and it achieved a number of things. First, it helped us to set the media agenda for the weekend, because invariably the journalists who turned up would ask us for our thoughts on whatever the current big topic was within the sport. Second, it gave us the opportunity to deliver key messages about our own team direct to the key media in an informal way. Members of the management team would host individual tables of media.

It was also popular with the media because, wherever we were in the world, we served a full breakfast, which went down very well with the UK-centric media corps. When a travel-weary journalist staying at an inexpensive hotel in Japan or Brazil turned up on a Friday morning, you could see the delight at being presented with some home-comfort food.

The communications landscape has changed dramatically in recent years, the development of digital media creating a whole new set of challenges and opportunities for communicating with stakeholder audiences. Television companies now broadcast on TV and online, with services giving viewers the opportunity to watch our sport at the time and place of their choosing and also the ability to self-edit the coverage they watch. All media have moved online, with industry publications such as *Autosport* and *Motorsport Magazine* augmenting their weekly or monthly magazine publication with rolling news 24/7. Meanwhile, subscription-based services including Formula One's own F1TV and independent outlets such as motorsport.tv offer a deep-dive into the business.

During the course of the global pandemic the popularity of podcasts grew significantly. Formula One's official offerings, Beyond The Grid and F1 Nation, have enabled listeners to enjoy in-depth interviews with industry figures, together with drivers past and present. This facilitates a more detailed conversation, which traditional media outlets cannot cater for.

With the number of podcasts globally edging towards 1 million, and the majority of listeners doing so using a mobile device, this means reaching audiences is set to grow further. In a cluttered marketplace it can be easy to get lost, but the successful Formula One podcasts have identified niche areas, creating unique conversations with their audiences.

Since 2017 Formula One has witnessed rapid growth in social media, thanks to Liberty Media's approach to permitting teams and drivers to post content from events, with clips of racing being shared with fans to enjoy. The previous leadership of Formula One under Bernie Ecclestone would not allow footage to be broadcast on social media, reserving that solely for broadcasters who had paid rights fees. The footage that has been shown has helped to build interest in the sport and grown the audience, particularly among younger fans. Video content shared across F1's website, the official app and social media channels reached 4.9 billion views in 2020, a rise of 46 per cent on 2019, and driven in part by lockdowns during the global pandemic.[3] Year on year the sport has enjoyed the greatest social media engagement of any major sports league, from NFL to European football, PGA Golf to WWE.

This significant growth has been further bolstered by the success of Formula One's *Drive to Survive* series, broadcast on Netflix each season since 2019. The behind-the-scenes nature of these 10-part series has allowed new audiences to learn about the sport and get to know the personalities, including team bosses, drivers and technical directors. The human interest has been explained in a way that appeals to a wider audience, and the accessibility provided by the teams has appealed to the core fans.

Nielsen Sports data has forecast that by April 2022 Formula One will have a global fan base of 1 billion, with a 16–35 age demographic seeing the largest surge in numbers, thanks to a combination of the sports profile across social media, esports and digital content, including *Drive to Survive*.[4]

For Formula One and its constituent teams, this audience growth is very positive. While the proliferation of digital media can appear complex, the reality is that shrewd investment in content can generate a significant return when packaged and distributed across key channels and platforms.

Ultimately it has never been easier to reach audiences, internal or external, suppliers or customers, and to influence stakeholders with well-curated content. For a sport that was built during the television age, the new media landscape offers significant rewards for businesses eager to share their message.

Insights in communication

EFFECTIVE COMMUNICATION IS VITAL
Formula One teams know that the speed and quality of decision making depends on accurate, timely communications.

STRONG INTERNAL COMMUNICATIONS ARE PIVOTAL IN DRIVING TEAM COHESION AND ALIGNMENT
In a fast-paced environment in which teams are often geographically dispersed, creating the time and place for regular, consistent communication is essential.

CROSS-FUNCTIONAL COMMUNICATIONS FUEL OPERATIONAL EXCELLENCE
A silo mentality can quickly develop inside a busy organization whose functions are focused on their own urgent tasks and targets.

BY DRIVING A COMMUNICATIONS CULTURE, WE ENCOURAGE PROBLEM SOLVING AND INNOVATION
Mercedes uses its race debrief to discuss problems openly, while at Jordan staff were encouraged to feed ideas through to the senior leadership.

THE MEDIA APPRECIATES A RESPONSIVE ORGANIZATION WITH WHICH IT CAN BUILD A RELATIONSHIP

Jordan was able to generate a disproportionate amount of coverage because it was highly responsive and media friendly.

OPEN CHANNELS TO BOTH CUSTOMERS AND SUPPLIERS

When developing communications initiatives aimed at building loyalty among customers, consider applying these to the supply chain in order to move away from a purely transactional relationship.

MAKE THE MOST OF TODAY'S DIGITAL MEDIA PLATFORMS

There has never been a richer opportunity to communicate with stakeholder audiences. Utilizing video, audio and messaging across social media platforms, teams can deliver strong, consistent messages to global audiences.

Notes

1 Planet F1 (2016) Marko Apologises For 'Misunderstanding', https://www.planetf1.com/uncategorized/marko-apologises-for-misunderstanding/ (archived at https://perma.cc/3LEV-YSQ7)

2 Douglas, C (2020) *The Secret Horsepower Race: Western fighter engine development*, Morton Books, Horncastle

3 Formula One (2021) Formula 1 Announces TV and Digital Audience Figures for 2020, https://www.formula1.com/en/latest/article.formula-1-announces-tv-and-digital-audience-figures-for-2020.3sbRmZm4u5Jf8pagvPoPUQ.html (archived at https://perma.cc/C25E-BMVW)

4 Kalinauckas, A (2021) Research Says F1 Could Reach One Billion Fans In 2022, *Autosport*, https://www.autosport.com/f1/news/research-says-f1-could-reach-1bn-fans-in-2022/5900701/ (archived at https://perma.cc/G48J-UQXJ)

Index

rar   Arts